John Michael Talbot

COME TO THE

THE PRINCIPLES

OF CHRISTIAN

MEDITATION

JEREMY P. TARCHER/PUTNAM

a member of Penguin Putnam Inc.

New York

Most Tarcher/Putnam books are available at special quantity discounts for bulk purchase for sales promotions, premiums, fund-raising, and educational needs. Special books or book excerpts also can be created to fit specific needs. For details, write Putnam Special Markets, 375 Hudson Street, New York, NY 10014.

Jeremy P. Tarcher/Putnam
a member of
Penguin Putnam Inc.
375 Hudson Street
New York, NY 10014
www.penguinputnam.com

Library of Congress Cataloging-in-Publication Data

Talbot, John Michael, date.
    Come to the quiet : the principles of Christian
    meditation / John Michael Talbot.
        p.   cm.
    ISBN 1-58542-144-8
        1. Meditation—Christianity.   I. Title.
    BV4813 .T33   2002
    242—dc21   2001054197

Printed in the United States of America
10   9   8   7   6   5   4   3   2   1

Book design by Ralph Fowler

I would like to lovingly dedicate this book to the memory of Yvonne Perkins, who respected all faiths of the world, and to the memory of John Pratka, Sr., who gave so much to our family and community.

ACKNOWLEDGMENTS

I would like to thank my father and mother, Dick and Jamie Talbot, for instilling a great love for world religions within me during my formative years; Jim Cosgrove for his many hours of encouragement and service in putting this manuscript together; the Brothers and Sisters of Charity for supporting me in this teaching throughout the last five years; and Fr. Martin Wolter, OFM, for teaching me the way of balance in approaching spirituality.

CONTENTS

PART THREE

THE FAR EAST

Come to the Quiet

Introduction

MEDITATION HAS BECOME A HOT TOPIC today. For the first time since the 1960s, books on meditation are big sellers in the secular media. The Dalai Lama is a media hit, though he considers himself only a simple monk exiled from his home country of Tibet. Monks, nuns, and lay leaders from the various ancient faith traditions of the world are on the lecture circuit and are writing books and articles that the public seems to consume as quickly as they consume any other product.

There is a hunger within us. It is a hunger that the materialistic things of this world cannot satisfy. It is a hunger of the spirit and soul. It is an innate human hunger for the divine. We call it different things in different religions and philosophies, but the hunger is the same. It is because of this hunger that we search through book after book, and shelf after shelf, for guidance in prayer and meditation.

Whether from a religious or secular perspective, meditation has been advocated as a healthy exercise by health professionals, monks, and religious clergy. Medical doctors tell us it is good for the body. Psychologists tell us it is good for the emotions and the mind. Ministers and monks tell us it is good for the spirit and the soul. As our world becomes more and more immediate and fast paced, we who must live in it find the need for quality times of solitude and silence more and more necessary.

Recent studies have indicated the healthy role of prayer and meditation in the healing process after serious surgery or illness. It is now a commonly accepted fact that those who engage in some form of prayer or meditation heal more rapidly and completely. Those who do so with the support of a community of prayer and meditation are even more apt to find a more complete healing. And those who do so in a religious environment with a belief in a personal God are even more likely to find full healing. Ironically, those conducting the studies do not necessarily believe in or practice these things themselves, but they cannot help but acknowledge the effects of such things when the results are so overwhelmingly clear.

Meditation is also prescribed as a common method for healing in counseling and therapy. Sessions with one's therapist often include a secular version of meditation in order to calm body, emotions, and thought, and so help the patient get in touch with their deeper human realities. Meditation periods at break time are even popular in some businesses. It is not uncommon to see meditation periods at lunch breaks advertised outside of churches in the thriving and hectic metropolises of American cities. I know an executive secretary of a high-powered law firm in New York City who leads contending clients through a voluntary meditation at the lawyer's request. It almost always leads to agreement and the avoidance of painful and time-consuming litigation. The secular lawyer has become a believer because it works!

I write from the perspective of a Catholic, Christian, Franciscan, and monastic heritage. I began my vocation as a simple Franciscan hermit in the woods of a Franciscan retreat center and went on to found The Brothers and Sisters of Charity at Little Portion Hermitage, an integrated, monastic-based community, including a celibate brotherhood, sisterhood, and family monastic expression as well as a domestic expression of those who live in their own homes. I am part of the family monastic expression and the General Minister and spiritual father of the community. I have now had twenty-three years to live this call, to make ample mistakes and, by God's goodness, to have lived it right a few times. Through the years I have seen just about everything. Nothing much surprises me anymore when it comes to human sin and weakness. I am continually surprised by the goodness of God's people in our midst. It is prayer and meditation that have proven to be my greatest strength as I have faced the many challenges of remaining faithful to a call when so many other seemingly good people do not persevere, and to lead when I know deep down that I am not worthy except by the grace of God. It is my daily discipline of prayer and meditation that has proven to be the God-given tool to actualize any of the wonderful characteristics of Jesus in my own life.

Meditation most likely began as the simple human need to be still and quiet in the midst of confusing or conflicting ideas and situations. Meditation is mentioned by the Greek philosophers, and became an important part of the premonastic philosophical schools. Meditation is seen in India in what today we call Hinduism. It is a central practice of Buddhism, and is seen as an important development of Taoism. The Middle Eastern religions of Judaism and Islam also include forms of meditation.

It comes as no surprise, then, that meditation is also a most important part of Christianity. This is especially true in the more ancient expressions of the Orthodox and Roman Catholic churches. Rich and developed traditions of meditation exist in the monastic and contemplative heritage, which is so important to both of these venerable expressions of Christianity. This heritage includes the approaches unique to the Eastern and the Western expressions of the Church.

The East gifts us with an understanding of the human person as body, soul, and spirit, with a journey through each of these human realities in our relationship with God. Concepts such as hesychia, or stillness, penthos, or compunction from the deepest place of our human being for sin, the journey through the eight vices and corresponding virtues, the use of the breath with the Jesus Prayer, and a deep understanding of a contemplative state beyond all images, forms, words, or ideas, are aspects of Eastern Christian meditation. This was practiced by the Desert Fathers, and is seen in the writings of the monastic mystics in the venerable compilation of books called the *Philokalia,* or "the study of the beautiful."

The West embraces a similar understanding of the human person as body, lower soul, and higher soul (spirit), and a journey with the divine through sacred reading, vocal prayer, meditation, and contemplation. This is the vision of writers such as William of St. Thierry. Later, the concepts of the purgative, illuminative, and unitive stages of prayer developed with bride-bridegroom mysticism, which were used by mystics such as St. Bernard and St. Bonaventure, and reached a culmination in the Spanish mystics St. John of the Cross and St. Teresa of Avila.

Catholic spirituality has also included an integration of the meditative tradition from other major world religions in a way that retains the integrity of its own beliefs, and those of all. It is believed that a very real dialogue occurred between the mystics of the Moslem faith, called the Sufis, and the monks and friars of the Middle Ages, as well as with the mystical schools of the Jewish faith that sojourned amidst the world of Christendom. Thomas Merton, the Cistercian monk of the twentieth century, paved the way for the monastic dialogues between the Benedictine and Buddhist monks of the recent past. Since Vatican II, the Church has engaged in appropriate Christian interfaith dialogue with other major world religions. Meditation has certainly been an area for common experience and mutual sharing in this process.

But what does meditation mean? How does it actually work in the mystical experience and as a tool to that end? The word "meditation" means somewhat different things to different traditions, but the experience is much the same everywhere. In the Christian tradition, it means to visualize and conceptualize certain concepts or images, such as the image of Christ and his life, or concepts of faith and morality, as a pathway to wordless and imageless contemplation and our intuitive union with God. In the Far Eastern traditions, it means total absorption in reality beyond all concepts, images, or words. They call it "samadhi," and it fits at the very end of their own journey through images, concepts, and words dealing with the steps and stages of their own faith and morality. So what we call meditation is not really what a Hindu or Buddhist means by the same word in English. By "meditation," they mean what we would really call, "contemplation," though meditation would be an integral intermediary step toward contemplation for us.

The same is true of the word "contemplation." The Greek philosophers used this word to describe what modern Christian spirituality means by "meditation." So they would speak of "contemplating" certain ideas and concepts of religion and philosophy. Philosophers were, by nature of their profession, contemplatives who lived the contemplative life. But this is not what we mean by the same terms. Eastern religion tends to do the same. For them, contemplation is a step toward meditation, whereas for Christians, it is the exact opposite, though we really are describing the same process. So there is a complete reversal of definitions of the words "meditation" and "contemplation."

This all has a very personal meaning for me. Originally, my whole religious experience was mystical, and involved a natural understanding and experience of meditation and contemplation in prayer. I searched through the sacred traditions of most of the major world religions. I found good things in them all. I was especially drawn to the mystical traditions of each faith. But the *reality* I read about was still just an idea for me. It had yet to become my own experience, awakening, or rebirth. I prayed, "God, are you a he, a she, or an it?" I didn't care what the answer was. I just wanted to know.

One night in 1971, in a hotel room on the road with the band I was part of, Mason Proffit, I looked up out of this now-familiar prayer and saw a Christ figure standing over me. He didn't give me any great commission, or anything like that! He simply *was* the answer to my prayer. I also knew that I was loved in a divine love. All that I had read about in all of the faiths of the world had become personal for me through Christ. From then on, I began calling myself a Christian again, though I didn't understand Christian theology. I only knew that God had revealed himself to me in the person of Jesus Christ.

Some people say that this vision was psychological. It could be. God created me with a psychology, so if he wants to use it to reach me, that is fine with me! All I know is that it changed my life for the better. I went from being a typical lost and self-centered young man to someone with a sense of positive purpose, and a growing sense of God's love for all people. That seemed all right to me.

At first, the Christian change in my life was well received by my family and friends because it made me a better person. I was more friendly, compassionate, and human. Soon I was attracted to other Christians who seemed genuinely excited about their faith. Unfortunately, this group was also very fundamentalist in its approach. The fundamentalist theology that absorbed me was very skeptical of any other religion, so I dropped all of my interfaith studies.

After a few years, that kind of fundamentalism and superficiality of faith began to fail. I became a pretty terrible person to be around. If anyone had a question or a problem, we had a scripture. I became the proverbial "Bible thumper." My friends left me. My family worried about me. Finally, the wife of my childhood marriage at age seventeen left me. I had hit bottom, but I was so arrogant that I thought I was still above everyone else!

About this time, my road manager gave me a book about St. Francis of Assisi called *The Journey and the Dream,* written by Fr. Murry Bodo, OFM. In it, I rediscovered the simplicity of faith that had so filled me at the beginning of my Christian conversion. Francis was a radical, a mystic, and a contemplative, but with a gentleness and humility that I had altogether lost along the way.

I also discovered the writings of Thomas Merton, a Cistercian monk of the Strict Observance, who went through his own journey to Christ and the Church through the contemplative tradition, and who helped to popularize an interfaith dialogue with mystics and monks of Eastern religions, which appropriately retained the integrity of each religion's beliefs and practices, and in no way compromised his own belief in Jesus, the Church, or his own monastic tradition. Through him, I discovered a whole world of contemplatives within the ancient expressions of Christianity. I started with *The Imitation of Christ* by Thomas à Kempis, and continued right on through to St. John of the Cross, and the anonymously authored *Cloud of Unknowing*. I felt as if I had come home!

But there was one *huge* problem. They were all Catholic! This led me on a journey of study through the early Church Fathers, who gave us the scriptures, and the wider contemplative and monastic traditions of the Church, which culminated in my becoming a Catholic in 1978. The Lord said, "She is my first Church, and I love her most dearly. But she has been sick and nearly died, but I am going to heal her and raise her to new life, and I want you to be a part of her." At that point all I could do was say, "Amen," or so be it.

What I found in the Church was a rich and wonderful contemplative and meditative tradition that is still developing today. It can integrate the Christian East and the West, the Protestant love for scripture with the Catholic love for liturgy and sacrament, and the meditation of the Judeo-Christian heritage with the yoga, Zen, and Tai Chi of the Far East, without jeopardizing our unquestioned focus on Jesus as the humble fulfillment of all, or the integrity of another's own faith decision.

After I became a Catholic, I began to live as a Franciscan hermit in the woods at Alverna Retreat Center in Indianapolis, Indiana. A community was formed around me made up of celibate men, celibate women, and families. Eventually, we outgrew the facilities the Franciscans had so graciously given us, and the Franciscan organizational structure, which could not accommodate such integrations in consecrated community, though they supported it. We moved to the diocese of Little Rock, Arkansas, and founded the Little Portion Hermitage in 1982. In 1990, The Brothers and Sisters of Charity were established as the first integrated monastic community in the United States with canonical approval, after almost ten years in Arkansas.

The pastoral care of this community was not easy. As most all of the founders and foundresses of past communities in the Church attest, the founding of community is a crucible, a living crucifixion that defies comparison in any other vocation in life. This is especially true in today's environment of rampant individualism, sexual promiscuity, and materialism, and the resulting disintegration of the very society in which we live. It can be a most frustrating experience, especially if all you do is hold on to the countercultural teaching of the Church all the tighter as the world you live in systematically rejects them. This rejection demanded that I either let go of those teachings, or find a new way of living them. After years of leadership as the spiritual father of the community, I found myself burning out, despite living in a hermitage and using all of the positive means of devotion and prayer that the Church afforded me. Soon my health began to give out, and I began suffering from violent migraine headaches that left me disabled 80 percent of the time. I really felt that I was close to death, or at least I wished I were!

It was at this point that I rediscovered the very things that helped draw me to the Church in the first place. I began practicing meditation, specifically breath prayer, once again. I integrated the use of Tai Chi and yoga into my morning workout. Slowly, I began to mend. My frustration level dropped, even though the world continues to reject the traditional teachings of not only Jesus Christ and the Catholic Church but of any traditional faith. I refound the peace of St. Francis, the early Desert Fathers and Mothers, and all of the saints. I found the enlightenment of the Buddha and the Bodhisattva, the way of the Taoist and Confucian sage, and the freedom of the Hindu sannyasin, or holy man, through this full integration in Christ.

It is this tradition that I want to share with you in this book. It is something incredibly relevant to the issues of chaotic modern life. It is an approach to spirituality that is built on solid tradition, yet something altogether unique and new. It is something that is unquestionably Christian in the fullest sense of orthodoxy yet able to share with and learn from the best traditions of the major religions of the world.

Part One

THE
CHRISTIAN
WEST

Triads and Threes

M Y EXPERIENCE OF CHRISTIAN MEDI-
tation is very simple but is built on the rich experience of the Christian East and the West, integrating both with the
addition of the meditation of the Far Eastern religions in a way appropriate to Catholic Christianity. Essentially, it takes the series of
triads and threes found in all of these and puts them together in creative and almost spontaneous integration. The triads include the anthropology of the human makeup and the stages of mystical and
contemplative life.

The earlier monastic triads of the Christian West are *sacred reading, meditation,* and *contemplation.* I would also include the *purgative, illuminative,* and *unitive* stages of later Western mysticism. In
the Christian East, we would find the former mirrored in the three
powers of the soul, namely, the *incensive,* the *rational,* and the *intellection.* In both, we would find a human anthropology of *body, soul,*
and *spirit.* In the West, this would be expressed in terms of body,
lower soul, and higher soul, or what we call spirit. In the Far Eastern
religions of Hinduism and Buddhism, we often hear of *body, mind,*
and *spirit.* In this understanding, the mind would be used similarly

13

to our definition of soul. This further corresponds to Taoist *vitality,* or jing; *energy,* or chi; and *essence,* or shen.

The definitions of these words reveal their similarity. With body, soul, and spirit, body would include the senses and the passions, or emotions. Soul would include the cognitive powers of awareness, or mind. Spirit would be the pure intuition of our deepest essence beyond sense, emotion, or thought. With incensive, rational, and intellective, the incensive would include the passions and emotions. The rational would include the cognitive powers of awareness and mind. Intellection would be the pure spiritual intuition beyond emotion or thought, concept or form.

The Christian East would say that all beings are made of both *energy* and *essence.* Energies are that which is knowable through objective sense, emotion, or mind. Essence is our deepest self and can only be known through spiritual intuition. Body and soul, or incensivity and rationality, would constitute our energies, or that which can be known through concepts and words. Spirit, or Intellection, would constitute our essence.

In the West, sacred reading would direct and stir the thoughts and the emotions through positive input about God, or godly things. This would lead to meditation, where these things deepen in the very soul. Then we pass over almost effortlessly into contemplation, beyond all sense, emotion, or thought, but building on them all. Later in the West, the purgative would deal with bodily and mental asceticism. The illuminative would deal with the illumination of the soul, or mind, and the initial breakthrough to the spirit. And the unitive would deal with the dwelling in the spirit and the union of all else around it.

It is also good to recall another triad in later Western anthropology. That is of memory, intellect, and will. St. Bonaventure would say that each of these human faculties leads us to God. The memory leads us to God's eternity beyond time. Intellect leads us to God's truth and reality. The will leads us to God's love, for the will is the seat of love.

This also highlights that the will is most important in our spiritual life. We must choose to follow God in response to his choice to create and redeem us. We must decide whether or not we will follow Jesus and become a disciple. As the Buddhists say, you need great determination, as well as great faith, to persevere. In Christianity, we have often heard it said that love is a decision. Faith has an object. It is a matter of choice. It is a matter of the will.

Any of these threefold anthropologies helps explain the human makeup, but they can also degenerate into a fractured understanding of the human being if misunderstood. As with the Blessed Trinity of God's makeup, you cannot really have one part without the other. You cannot dissect the human being like a cadaver on a medical table. The full human being is whole and integrated. The three parts work in harmony with each other to make up and serve the whole. This cannot be overlooked.

The following chart might help in visualizing these triads.

West/East	Far East	East	Early West	Later West
Body	Body/Vitality	Incensive	Reading	Purgative
Soul	Mind/Energy	Rational	Meditation	Illuminative
Spirit	Spirit/Essence	Intellection	Contemplation	Unitive

Essentially, what all of this means is that we begin our spiritual life from where and who we are. We do not try to deny our senses, our emotions, or our thoughts. As a human being, we are a body, a soul, and a spirit. Our spirituality includes *all* of who and what we are as human beings. We use these definitions to help understand that which we know through intuition anyway. Unfortunately, we have often been so fragmented and cut off from our very selves as whole beings that we are often unable to awaken our intuition properly. So we use definitions like these to help awaken us to that which is our most basic reality in the first place, a reality we have often covered up or lost.

I believe that God conceived each of us in our mother's womb with a beautiful and wonderful purpose. He willed us to be holy and loving and true. We are his children. This is what the Buddhist might call "the face we were born with." It was what the Taoists describe as becoming like a newborn baby again. It is what Christians mean when we talk of being born again.

What is this face? It is love, joy, peace, patience, kindness, generosity, mildness, chastity, and faith. It is a humble and gentle spirit, more ready to forgive than judge, to be just than seek revenge, to be selfless for others instead of self-centered in response to others. This is the face we were born with. This is the real you, the real me. This is what we all desire for ourselves, and our world, at the deepest part of our being, in our spirit and soul.

But the world has reversed the priorities of the three aspects of the human being. This happens through what we of the Judeo-Christian tradition call "the fall." Different faiths and philosophies call it by various names, but we all believe that not only is there much good and right with our world but that something has also gone wrong. Originally we are spirit, soul, and body. The spirit is the deepest essence of who we are, so it leads the whole being. The soul, or cognitive thoughts and ideas, facilitates the things of spirit. The body, or the passions and senses, serve to house and empower the soul and the spirit. Unfortunately, through what each religion calls by a different name, the fall has reversed this priority. Now the senses and passions of the body lead the way. We usually do what we desire, or at least lust after with compulsive love. When we do not get what we want, we get angry, and so on. These disordered desires and passions control the mind, leaving it filled with negativity, clouded and confused, like a muddy pond. The spirit is almost totally forgotten except as some vague, lingering intuition in the darkest recesses of our being. This is the condition of fallen humanity and is the reason for our suffering.

This suffering gets passed on to each child born into this disordered world. Almost as soon as we are conceived, we begin to assimilate that which surrounds us. In the womb we are picking up the disordered ways of the world into which we will soon be born. We can sense the mood of our mother and of the environment in which she lives, including the family, and her friends and co-workers. Once we are birthed, we begin the transformation in earnest, if for no other reason than to simply survive as best we can in a sometimes hostile and aggressive environment. By the time we go to school, we really begin to learn this way fast. By the time we are adolescents, we have almost totally covered over that original child God created us to be. And by the time we are adults, we have usually forgotten that the child is even there. Thus, through the normal course of life, we put on a self-identity that is illusory and false. The self-image we carry around with us is usually not the real self that is waiting at the center of our being, a self covered over by an almost totally false self we have put on in the image of a disordered world. This is why Jesus says that we must be born again and become like little children to enter the kingdom of God. This is why the Buddhist says to seek the face we were born with. This is why the Taoist says we must become like newborn babes again.

These triads and sets of three are the classical ways that Christian monks, mystics, and contemplatives have realized the way of Jesus for two thousand years. They are also the way that the mystics from other faiths have realized their own version of rebirth and awakening. Reading, meditation, and contemplation, purgation, illumination, and union, using the incensive, rational, and intellective powers of the human being, as well as the classical ascetical tools in a way that correctly corresponds to each, are the ways they realized the rebirth of Jesus as a tangible reality in their lives, rather than just remaining an unreachable ideal.

In this book, we will take a journey through each way. I invite you to join me as I retell the principles and stories that have helped me on my journey. Perhaps they will help you too. I tell this from my own Catholic Christian monastic experience, but I hope you will find something for yourself no matter where you are from, where you live, or what you believe.

In this book I will share with you what I myself have found and lived. I will share from the perspective of over twenty years of monastic experience within a new, yet ancient, expression of monasticism within the Church, which includes celibate monks and nuns, and married couples and families as well. I will share from the perspective of integrating all of the great traditions of meditation and prayer, yet without claiming to know it all. We will begin with the traditions of the Christian West. Then we will move to the Christian East. Finally, I will share my own experience of integrating the meditative and contemplative traditions of the Eastern religions with my own orthodox Christian faith.

The
Christian
West

I WRITE FROM A UNIQUELY WESTERN perspective. I was born in the midwestern United States in Oklahoma City, Oklahoma, and grew up in Arkansas and Indiana. I was raised in the Methodist tradition that shaped much of Middle America. My adult conversion to Christianity came through the Jesus movement in the 1960s, which was a predominantly American phenomenon before its spread to Europe and other parts of the world. Though I became a Roman Catholic because of its international dimensions and universality, I'm still part of an American expression of Roman Catholicism. So, despite my theological and historical leanings toward things universal and timeless, I remain a man of my own time and culture.

Because of this, it is appropriate to begin our treatment of the mystical and contemplative tradition of the Church from a Western perspective. Though, from a Roman Catholic perspective, the Western tradition grew out of the Middle East, I will begin with the West due to my own cultural and sociological experience.

Environment: A Time and a Place

It is important to set the right environment for prayer and meditation. This environment is constituted by a proper prayer place and prayer time. This is already given to us by the example of the Church through liturgical prayer and sacramental celebration. Quite simply, such celebrations take place at a specific place—the church building or chapel—at a specific time, like 10:30 Sunday morning. But we cannot go to church every time we want to enter into meditation and prayer. Consequently, the mystical and contemplative tradition of the Church has recommended additional places and times to be set apart as sacred for the use of meditation and prayer within one's private life.

The Christian East and non-Christian Far East are very clear about setting aside time and space to provide the environment for meditation and prayer. The Christian West is less explicit in its ancient documents and teachings, though it has been very prevalent in recent years. However, it is implied clearly in the most ancient and developing monastic tradition.

SPACE AND TIME

If you do not make an "appointment" for meditation, just like you do with an important business meeting or personal date, you will never do it consistently. This means setting aside a special place and time for this "appointment." I recommend the following:

1. Set aside a special place in your house or apartment just for prayer and meditation. It should be very simple and clean. It should include nothing except what is needed for the purpose of prayer and meditation.
2. If you sit on the floor, use a meditation cushion and mat, or zafu and zabuton. You can also use a meditation bench for

long-term kneeling. These are available at any good meditation supply store locally, or outlet on the web. If you do not want to sit or kneel on the floor, find a simple straight-back chair that is comfortable, but not so comfortable that you will go to sleep in it. You can also use a traditional kneeler as found in Catholic churches and institutions.

3. You may want to include a few sacred images and candles. A cross or crucifix (including the corpus of Jesus), or an icon (a window to heaven) of the divine might be helpful for a Christian. One or two icons or sacred pictures of saints are a nice reminder that we can achieve our goal if we stick with it. A small table or altar may be helpful, if there is room, to set the candles on, plus any extra images or rosaries, etc.

4. Set aside a specific time for meditation and prayer. I recommend twenty or thirty minutes in the morning *before* any other activities have taken place. This may mean rising a little earlier. But I promise, it is time that is better spent than any other time in your life. It will change your life, and every other activity in it. You may also do the same in the evening before retiring to bed, but many working people find themselves too tired by that time to stay consistent with the practice.

5. Stay *consistent*. Do the practice of meditation and prayer *every day*. If you do, you will see positive effects within a few months. If you do not, you will see very few effects. If you slack off after a time, you will see the positive effects you have gained slip away. If you make excuses, you will not stay consistent. If you miss the morning time, at least meditate at another time in the day, but this will prove too inconsistent if this becomes the norm.

The Monastic Cell: Heaven on Earth

Specifically, environment is seen in the importance placed upon the monastic cell. The importance of remaining stable in the monastic cell, and not leaving during times of boredom and wandering thoughts, are attested to throughout the monastic history of the Christian West. It was clearly a teaching of the early Desert Fathers, from which all monastic and consecrated life sprang forth. It can be seen in the Benedictine tradition, especially in the more eremitical reforms of the eleventh century. In particular, St. Romuald, the founder of the Camaldolese hermits, emphasizes the importance of the hermit monk sitting "in his cell like a chick, and destroying himself completely." The Franciscan heritage also emphasizes the importance of the cell. The classical work, *The Imitation of Christ,* is very clear about the importance of staying put in the cell.

Of course, many are familiar with the often-quoted famous saying of the Desert Father Moses, "Go, sit in your cell, and your cell will teach you everything." We also remember the quote of St. Romuald, "If you are unworthy of your cell, it will vomit you forth." The classic *Imitation of Christ* says, "Seek the quiet of your cell and shut out the noise of the world. . . . There you will find the grace that you may easily lose outside. The cell you live in becomes dear to you, while if you are seldom in it, you grow tired of it. If in the beginning of your conversion you're often in it, afterward you will find it to be a dear friend and a real comfort."

The word "cell" makes us think of "celestial," or "cello." All of these imply "heaven." So the monastic cell is the place where heaven comes to earth. The monastic cell is not merely one's room, as one would have in a college dormitory, or private apartment, or house. It is a sacred space set aside for prayer and meditation, a place where God may dwell with humanity and humanity may be transformed in God. It is to retain a certain decorum of holy simplicity. It is to be kept neat and clean, not untidy or ill kept. Visually, it is to help bring a silence and peace to the soul through the eye.

This does not mean that the cell is not practical. It is the private space of the monk. It is called to be both aesthetically simple and pleasing, and functionally practical. One must actually live within monastic cell. This means that there will be a bed and bedding, a closet and a dirty clothes hamper, a desk and workplace, a bathroom and toiletries, and a hobby and recreation area. All of this is found within the confines of a small cell, usually in small increments and areas. In some monasteries, some of the above are found in common areas, leaving the cell free for prayer and just the most basic needs of existence. Only in the more eremitical (places that integrate more strict solitude with community activities such as prayer, meals, and work), and socio-eremitical communities, do we find larger and more self-contained monastic cells. This is due to the greater amount time the hermit spends within the cell.

For myself, I live within a hermitage in a secluded, wooded valley of the Ozark Mountains in northwest Arkansas, in the monastic expression of The Brothers and Sisters of Charity at Little Portion Hermitage. The entire environment of this community is geared toward meditation and prayer, overflowing into apostolic ministry and work. The community is simplicity itself: we grow most of our own food and live as close to the environmental balance of God as possible in today's modern world. The monastic structure guarantees times of silence for the entire community, and solitude from the distractions of the world, both communally and individually. Both private and public prayers are built into the daily schedule, as are our times for group and private reflective study on scripture and the Fathers and Mothers of the contemplative and mystical tradition of the faith.

POSTURE

In order to maintain quiet meditation and prayer for twenty minutes straight, it is best to find a stable posture so you won't be distracted by bodily discomfort and the changing of positions during the meditation. I recommend the following:

1. Sit comfortably in either a straight-back chair, or in the traditional cross-legged position on the floor. If you sit on a chair, rest your feet flat on the ground, legs not too close together or far apart, and the small of your back tight against the back of the chair. If you use the cross-legged position, you may use the "Indian style" most Westerners learned as kids, or the half or full-lotus position from the Far East (see the Far East section for details). If you sit cross-legged, do not force your legs to the point of pulling muscles and ligaments. The point is a stable posture, not physical calisthenics. I also recommend a meditation cushion and mat for appropriate comfort. A folded firm pillow can also work if no cushion or mat is available.

2. Sway your back to the left and the right a few times to "get the kinks out" and to find a comfortable center.

3. Sit straight, lining up your nose with your navel and your ears to your shoulders if possible. This latter alignment may be impossible for those whose spines and necks have already seriously curved due to age or injury. But do the best you can. The straighter you can sit, the less you will experience blocked blood vessels and cramped muscles after ten minutes of stillness. You are also free to shift if you must, but the less you have to shift, the more focused your mediation will be.

4. Rest your hands on your lap so that you will not be fidgeting during meditation. You may place the palms down as a symbol of rest, or palms up as a symbol of openness. There are other traditional hand positions that serve this same purpose.

5. Rest your tongue against the back of your upper front teeth and your palate. This keeps us from worrying about swallowing and smacking dry lips and mouths during meditation.

6. Eyes are neither fully closed nor open. We gaze at an invisible line of "infinity" during the meditations that do not require a

formal visualization. This keeps us from falling asleep with eyes closed (and believe me, a lot of people fall asleep during their first meditation), or becoming visually distracted by what we see during prayer. If we use an internal image, like something from the life of Christ, it is best to close one's eyes. If we use an external image, like an icon or sacred picture, it is best to keep them open.

7. Coming out of meditation is just as important as entering. It is a gentle reentry into the activity of the world. It is neither too abrupt nor too sluggish. Slowly move your body in a way that is not jerky or forced. The traditional teaching emphasizes that if you sit cross-legged, extend the legs in front of you and move the knees and feet gently on the floor. You may also move the spine, neck, and hands in a similarly gentle and nonobtrusive way.

Simplicity for the Average Person

While most people cannot live in a monastery or hermitage, the existence of the eremitical monastic life still has much to say to the average seeker and believer in today's modern world. All of us must seek to simplify our life in the general sense, so that our whole life becomes a better environment for meditation and prayer. Clearing away clutter and distractions helps us to remain focused on the truly important reality of life.

One of the greatest axioms that we have used with our lay followers is, "Is it a want, or need?" It is by habitually indulging in our wants that we kill the needy of the world, and enslave ourselves to addiction to wants, and to the delusion of thinking them to be needs, not to mention the distraction it causes from pure meditation and prayer. This habitual indulgence of wants brings tragedy to ourselves and to everyone we touch in this world. Asking ourselves this simple question about wants and needs can bring the axe to the root of the trees, uprooting from our soul this entire disorder. This brings liberation to ourselves and to everyone we touch. It also clears our life of clutter and distraction, paving the way to successful meditation and prayer.

Most every major religion of the world agrees that the radical simplification of life is necessary before attempting the greater mystical ascent through meditation and prayer. Things clutter the mind and stir the emotions in a negative way, making the perception of spiritual reality difficult, if not impossible. As I have said in other books, it is like the stilling of an agitated pond. As long as the pond is agitated, it remains unclear. Only through stillness does the water begin to clarify so that you can actually see what is in the pond, and so that the waters of the pond are able to reflect an image. Our spiritual life is like a pond. Anxiousness about worldly things and possessions stirs the waters of our soul, making it impossible for us to see the reality of what we are actually made of on the spiritual level, or to really reflect the Divine Image as we were created to do. It is only through the renunciation of unnecessary possessions that we can begin the process of clarifying the waters of our soul. We must still our environment, with its many possessions and cares, before we can really be reborn to a whole new way of life.

Jesus

Jesus is no exception to teaching this venerable and time-tested tradition. Jesus calls all of his followers to complete renunciation of everything they own before they can truly be one of his followers. This teaching is given repeatedly, and in no uncertain terms. It had to be pastorally applied to the various states of life of his followers, such as single or married, but its radical interior and exterior aspect remain to this day. The first community in Acts 2 and 4 held all things in common, as contrasted to the strict mendicant life of Jesus and his most immediate disciples. Later, St. Paul, in Second Corinthians 8, would allow for private possessions, but always with a more basic understanding of the common aspect of all creation, and the equality that is to be voluntarily achieved between the rich and the poor through the sharing of love. This is the teaching of the Catholic Church today for the average layperson. But she has always made accommodation for those who discern the call to a more strict and literal interpretation of the teaching and imitation of Christ for their own life.

So simplifying one's life is a necessary beginning to meditation and prayer. I suggest starting simply. Start from where you are. Do one thing at a time. Give things away as you find people or organizations that can really use them. I guarantee that it won't take long to radically, and naturally, change your lifestyle! It is a unique person who is called to give up everything on the spot. It happened with some of the first disciples. It happened with saints like Francis of Assisi. It could also happen to you! But, more likely, you will be called to a more gradual divestiture of your possessions in a way that will bring life and health to you, your family, and those with whom you share your life.

It is like the difference between trying to broad-jump or walk into simple living. Many, who try to jump too far, too fast, end up falling backwards and going only a short distance. Those who walk a step at a time, day after day, find that after many days they have traveled a great distance. So start where you are, and do what you can. Don't get ahead of yourself and don't lag behind. Follow this call naturally in the spirit, and you will find you will be able to persevere.

BREATH EXERCISE 1: DEEP BREATHING

Focusing on the breath is an important part of many meditation methods in the major mystical traditions of the world. It is also included in Christianity. For us, it represents the Spirit, or Ruah Breath, of God, and a way to refocus on our own human spirit. It is a simple tool to unite prayer with every breath we take in order to, as St. Paul says, "pray without ceasing." It is also a reminder of gospel poverty, by learning to be completely happy just doing the bare minimum of what we need to stay alive: breathe. If we are happy with this, then we can be satisfied anywhere!

Deep breathing is the most natural way to breathe. Deep breathing is from the belly, so that the belly expands with each inhale, and collapses with each exhale. It is the way a baby breathes, and the way we breathe when in deep sleep. We Westerners breathe in the exact opposite way, with the chest expanding with each inhale, and the belly collapsing with each exhale. This means that we breathe with the top portion of our lungs, and only get about one third the oxygen into the bloodstream we are designed by God for. Learning to breath from the diaphragm, or the navel, is a way to relearn how to breathe naturally once again. After the initial discomfort of relearning, this becomes most natural for us all of the time, and keeps us healthier.

Slowing the breathing is a way to slow down and unclutter the whole body and mind, which opens the way to reawakening the spirit in the Spirit of God. It is a method to help really let go of the frenetic activity and mental clutter of our modern world. It unclutters and cleanses the body and the mind. This makes us more open to the things of the spirit. Medically, it has proven to be effective on the physical and emotional levels. It is also effective on the spiritual level.

1. After settling into your meditation posture, rest your left hand on your navel, with your right hand over it. Breathe in deeply, but gently and not forced, through your nose. Visualize, and actually sense, the breath descending from your nose through your throat and into your lungs. As the breath reaches your lungs, expand your belly out, and allow the breath to descend into the depths of your lungs. Feel your belly expand with your hands resting on your navel as you inhale. If this is not occurring, then you are not yet breathing deeply. Count to a slow, but comfortable, ten as you inhale. Be careful not to force this. Let it be natural and comfortable. If you cannot breathe in for

that long at first, just do what you can. You will deepen your breathing the longer you do this exercise.

2. Exhale through your nose. Allow your lungs to totally empty. Count to about eight as you exhale. As with the inhale, do not force this by holding your breath beyond what is comfortable for you. This is not a contest but an aid to deeper breathing. But do make sure that you empty your lungs with this cleansing breath.

3. Repeat steps 1 and 2. Make sure that you are cleansing your lungs and breathing deeper than what is usual for you in daily life.

4. Now place your hands back into a rested position. Allow your breathing to become more natural but with this new pattern of expanding the belly with each inhale and flattening it with the exhale.

5. After about ten natural breaths, do another more intentional deep breath, but without placing your hands over the navel. Then do ten more natural.

6. Repeat this as many times as is comfortable, starting with one pattern, then two, and up to ten, as you learn this way of deep breathing. Eventually, you will discover that you are breathing more naturally all of the time, and it is quite natural and comfortable to do so during prayer and meditation.

Personal Experience

Even though I live within a monastic hermit's cell, I still need specific times and places for more intense prayer and meditation. I set aside space within my small hermitage specifically for various kinds of meditation prayer. I also set aside the earliest hours of the morning before the monastic schedule has begun for more intensive times of prayer and meditation so that they can lead me on into undistracted contemplation.

Generally, I rise about four A.M. Communal monastic prayer does not begin in the chapel until 6:45 A.M., so I have plenty of time. After cleaning up and dressing, I spend about twenty minutes in prayerful stretching exercises consisting of Christianized, or baptized, Tai Chi and Hatha yoga. We will discuss the theology and spirituality of this in greater detail in later chapters. Similarly, I spend anywhere from thirty minutes to an hour in seated meditation. I will also explain this in greater detail in later chapters. I do both of these exercises in a space that is uncluttered and clean and used for little else. From here, I go to my most comfortable chair to ponder the liturgical readings of the day, beginning with the readings for the Mass, and continuing to the Psalms, scripture readings, and Patristic writings from the liturgical Office of Readings.

Please keep in mind that I'm part of the family monastic expression, so I share this small hermitage space with my devoted companion and spouse. Two of us live within two rooms with alcoves for sleeping, and various work areas, as well as two small lofts for prayer. It is not a large space. This means I must also respect my wife's need for rest and privacy as well. In this, I understand well the challenge of setting aside space and time within a family setting.

BREATH EXERCISE 2: THE SPIRIT OF GOD

1. Sit comfortably and do the deep breathing preparation of the last exercise a few times.
2. Be aware that each time you breathe in, you allow the Spirit, or Breath of God, to flow into your whole being—body, soul, and spirit. Some find it helpful to actually visualize the Spirit as water flowing from heaven into our being. (Scripture also calls God's Spirit "living water.") Others visualize it as a beam of light of varying colors. It is important to use visualization at first, but later you will simply intuit this reality.

3. Visualize, or simply intuit, that the Spirit of God is flowing through the top of your head to the tip of your toes and filling your whole being from the top down and the bottom up.

4. Meditate on the fruits of the Spirit, from St. Paul's Letter to the Galatians, filling your life: love, joy, peace, patience, kindness, generosity, chastity, mildness, and faith.

5. With each exhale, visualize the negative aspects of your being, such as anger or attachment, or any other sin, being released from your whole life as dark, negative energy. Some see it as dirty water or just darkness in general. Again, these specifics are not important here. What is important is learning to let go of the negative and destructive forces in our lives that we call "sin."

6. When you see, or intuit, that you are completely filled, allow the water or light to spill or expand out to the rest of the world, beginning with those you know who are in need of God's love and mercy at this time.

7. Conclude as in the previous exercise.

Intentional Space and Time

The time for this extra prayer and meditation must be intentionally set aside, or it will never happen. It takes work and discipline to do it. I must set my alarm and make myself get out of bed every morning. Only on rare occasions do I jump out of bed ready to go. This is especially true the older I get! Yet, the more years I embrace this discipline, the easier it gets on the deeper level, for I can clearly see positive results in my life.

As I said earlier, I generally recommend about twenty to thirty minutes for meditation each morning and evening if possible. If you have to choose between the two, I prefer the morning when I am still fresh and the day has not yet started in full swing. You may have to get up a little earlier to do this, but it is well worth it. If you have to make an appointment to meet with someone important during secular business, how much more should we be willing to set aside an "appointment" with God for quality meditation that can change our whole life.

The twenty- or thirty-minute time period is also significant. Out of twenty or thirty minutes, we will usually only get about two or three minutes of actual contemplative prayer! But that two or three minutes is usually enough to get us through the business of our normal day. It usually takes the whole rest of the time to settle down, still the senses, emotions, and thoughts, and finally break through to the pure intuitive union with the Ultimate Reality we call God in pure contemplation. So that minimum period of time ought to be kept inviolate. If you can get more, wonderful, but that may not be possible for active people. At first, the twenty minutes will go quickly due to the novelty of the experience. Then reality will set in, and you will face the usual boredom with that much seemingly inactive time. At this point, you will be tempted to stop short of the full twenty or thirty minutes. This is a normal but terrible pitfall for those beginning in meditation. Once you really break through to contemplation, the length of time will become secondary, except on the level of practicality and function.

The space also has to be created and maintained. It does not just automatically happen. It takes discipline and work to intentionally set aside special places in one's home or dwelling. First, it means setting aside a reasonable amount of space. This space might have to be used for something else during the day, so you have to figure out how to switch it from one use to the other with relative ease. This is true especially for stretching exercises and seated meditation. The space for sacred reading is easier but not as simple as just using your favorite easy chair for *lectio,* or sacred reading. For meditation, a straight chair is best for most Westerners, though a classical cross-legged position on the floor is also good. We do not get too comfortable in order to avoid drowsiness and sleep. Nor are we so rigid that we become anxious or tired. We slow the breathing down and breathe from the belly, not from the chest, in order to slow down the body, calm the emotions, and unclutter the mind. Likewise, the space around the chair needs to be free of clutter and distraction. This might simply be a matter of cleaning up the space before you go to bed the night before.

While maintaining discipline in establishing the time and space for meditation prayer is necessary, scrupulosity can drive both you, and those with whom you live, crazy. "Scruples" comes from the Latin word which means "pebble." The word is often used in a negative sense to describe trying to walk or run with a pebble in one's shoes or sandals. In other words, a small pebble can keep one from the greater task of walking or running, and reaching the ultimate destination. Scrupulosity can be a curse, and one of the devil's favorite tools, in the spiritual life in general. Setting aside your time and space for prayer and meditation is no exception.

For myself I might set my alarm for four A.M., but if I have had a difficult day or night, I might allow myself as many as fifteen to thirty extra minutes. On some days, I will omit the exercise, and seated meditation altogether and do it after our monastic communal prayers. Likewise, sometimes my own *lectio* space gets more cluttered than I'm personally comfortable with. This is no one's fault but my own. I can either let it upset me, which would, in turn, disturb my wife, or I can simply clean up the space peacefully at an appropriate time. In other words, establish and maintain an appropriate discipline regarding time and space for prayer and meditation, but do not make a god out of that discipline. The discipline is a tool from God, not a god.

So if you want to experience good meditation and prayer, take the time to create a good environment for the experience. Simplify your life. Get rid of the clutter. Then set aside the specific time and space to follow this call in a more intentional manner. Create a prayer time and place in your home. Then use it!

Monastic
Community

A NOTHER NECESSARY ASPECT OF THE
environment for prayer and meditation is community. Within all of the great religions of the world, one must submit oneself to a teacher in order to learn the way of prayer and meditation. Since a good teacher usually has more than one student, community becomes a natural experience for the students and the teacher. Along with this experience of community, the ideals of renunciation and humility, as found in a lifestyle of poverty and obedience, are also implied.

This was the way it unfolded with Jesus and the apostles. It was the way of the prophets and the schools of prophets in the Old Testament. It could be seen with the philosophers and philosophical schools that grew up around each great teacher. We see a similar pattern in other religions, such as Buddhism, Hinduism, Taoism, and Confucianism. In each case, there was a great teacher who attracted students, or disciples. Quite naturally, communities grew around great teachers.

Classical Renunciation

In this classical mode, the prospective disciple was required to give up everything in order to follow the master. In every major religion of the world, there is a direct correlation between the enslavement of thoughts and the passions to illusion and delusion, and attachment to one's worldly possessions. Renunciation of one's illusory needs to possess things, people, or even ideas, is fundamental to the rebirth and openness of attitude needed within the prospective disciple of the masters of the world religions. Jesus is no exception. He requires a complete and absolute renunciation of possessions, old concepts, and relationships in order to become his disciple. Only then can the rebirth he promises become a fact of freedom in the disciple's life.

Only when the disciple fully submits to the leadership of the spiritual master can they fully receive the teachings that lead to liberation and rebirth. Once training is complete, the disciple actually receives the spirit of the teacher. It is called different things in different religions and understood in particularly distinct terms, but the reality remains the same. In Hinduism, the disciple receives the spirit of the guru they study under. Tibetan Buddhism would be very similar. In Zen Buddhism, this is called receiving the dharma transmission, though it is the spirit of the dharma that is received, not of the roshi. In Christianity, this happened in the most profound and distinct way. After the crucifixion, resurrection, and ascension of Jesus, the Holy Spirit is poured out upon the whole Church at the Jewish feast of Pentecost. This is not just the spirit of the human teacher, though it includes this aspect. This is the Spirit of God poured out upon humanity for the ministry of the incarnate Word of God.

BREATH EXERCISE 3: JESUS

1. Prepare as before by sitting and deep breathing.

2. Allow Jesus to enter into your being with each inhale. Visualize him as he *is*, not only as popular preachers preach him. You may want to see a particular scene of the gospels unfold in your mind. Allow your emotions and senses to be moved, yet without getting attached to these movements.

3. From this, you move into simply intuiting with your thoughts and emotions of the soul and the pure spiritual intuitions of the spirit of all that he is in the gospels, especially in the Beatitudes or the Sermon on the Mount.

4. Allow the real Jesus to fill you with his being, humanity, and divinity.

5. With each exhale, allow all within you that is not like Jesus to be released. Simply let it go, relax, and breathe it out of your life. As with oil and water, the water of Jesus simply displaces the oil of all that is not like Christ in our lives. It happens almost naturally, and in a way that brings great peace.

6. As you are transformed into Jesus, and are filled with him, as with the meditation on the Spirit, allow Jesus to naturally and peacefully flow out from you to all the world, beginning with those you know who are in most in need of his love and mercy.

7. If granted the grace of contemplation in this session, allow the faculties of your being to simply pass over beyond the mind, emotions, and senses to simple union with Jesus, which is Spirit to spirit, and Being to being. Allow yourself to stay in this sacred place unhurried and uninterrupted for as long as possible.

8. Add a specific thanksgiving to God for any grace received from this meditation, and give him all of the glory for any spiritual accomplishment or development.

9. Conclude as before.

Community

Though this is a very personal experience for each disciple, it is also communal. At Pentecost, the disciples were gathered together in one place as community. As soon as they heard the personal call to follow Jesus, they found themselves with other disciples in community. This is where the teaching of Jesus is tested most intensely, for the teaching of the love of God and neighbor is only as good as how well we love God in and through our neighbor in community.

Today this classical pattern flies in the face of Western individualism. Individualism is individuation gone bad. Individualism places the individual over the community in which the individual lives. Certainly community must protect the uniqueness of each human person, but when community becomes subservient to the desires of each individual, then community will eventually disintegrate and collapse. Individuation recognizes the legitimate needs of the individual and the duty of the good community to protect those needs and rights, but always places the individual within the broader context of community.

Nature itself teaches us this balance. Within nature there are many wonders in the individual expression of the various species. There are many species within nature itself, sentient and nonsentient, human and animal, but there are also common elements to all at each level. Nature is a beautiful symphony of the diversity of individual expression and the unity of the common good.

Jesus says that if it rains, it rains on all, the good and bad. The same is true of sunshine, and all the various expressions of something as simple as the weather. This simple, and self-evident, reality teaches us this basic lesson of the individual and community with clarity and great profundity. It is as simple as life itself.

We live in the computer age where individuals have instant access to great knowledge without ever having to deal with the real experience of other human beings. The experience of others that we have through the computer is always sifted through the impersonal aspect of the technology. Such technology can be a great gift to humanity as long as it does not replace the real experience of human relationship as found in the nitty-gritty experiences of community.

The Monastic Three-Tiered Tradition

The monastic tradition of community has developed into a threefold expression of all of the cenobitical, semieremitical, and eremitical models. The cenobitical comes from the word "cenobite," which develops from the Greek word "koinonia," which simply means "fellowship." The eremitical comes from the word "eremite," which simply means "hermit." Semi-eremitical is, as you might imagine, part hermit and part community.

The development of this three-tiered expression happened quite naturally. At first, those who renounced all to follow Jesus went into the desert to seek the solitary aspect of Christ as depicted in scripture. Soon, others followed, and they sought the direction of those more experienced in this monastic way. What resulted were loose-knit colonies of hermits. This amounted to solitary hermit cells loosely arranged at about one day's walking distance from the common chapel and community building. The hermits would meet once a week on Saturday night for the "synaxis," or gathering prayers, and to celebrate a Mass, or Eucharist liturgy, on Sunday morning followed by a common meal, or agape. After this, they would return to spend a week in solitude, fasting and praying all of the liturgical offices of the Church on their own. At the most, one or two monks would share the cell of an elder in order to learn the way of solitude directly from him, much as did the apostles from Christ. This constituted the initial eremitical and semi-eremitical ways. This way is symbolized by St. Anthony of the desert, the father of Christian monasticism. Shortly thereafter, St. Pachomius, a retired military commander, set up a monastic life more intentionally in common, to be lived by a great many people at one time. This constituted the foundation of the cenobitical expression of monasticism. With this, the three-tiered system was naturally established and secured in place.

Today, it is lived out in the opposite order in order to better help the young monk ascend the way of monastics in contemplative prayer. Today, the young monk will begin in the cenobitical way in the cenobium or monastery, to learn how to live the way of love in the context of the responsibility of relationships in Christ. After you spend ten years or so learning the cenobitical monastic way, one may petition to retire into the semi-eremitical way, in what is called the "skete," or "kellion." The skete is a gathering of isolated cells around a small chapel under the direction of the spiritual father. The kellion is a small monastic cottage with a chapel, also under the direction of a father. The skete may be independent of or under a monastery. The kellion is dependent upon a larger abbey, or a cenobitical monastery under the direction of an abbot, or abba, meaning a spiritual father recognized by the Church. After ten or so years in semi-eremitism, one may petition to withdraw into total seclusion, or strict eremitism. There is actually a fourth step after this sometimes recognized in both the Christian East and West, as well as within the Hindu structure. This would be the state of the itinerant wanderer, pilgrim, or mendicant. Those such as St. Romuald, the founder of the eleventh-century semi-eremitical Benedictine reform called the Camaldolese, or St. Francis of Assisi, the thirteenth-century founder of the Franciscan family, entered into this latter state of life in combination with the others.

Many Ways to Community Meditation

The significance of this threefold monastic expression for the average practitioner of prayer and meditation today is that there are many ways to live in community. Some are called to more intense expressions of community, such as can be found in monastic and consecrated life for celibates, or in the more contemporary covenant communities that include families. Others are called to less intense community, which might meet in monthly, bimonthly, or weekly cell groups. These patterns can be found in ancient monasticism and applied in a creative way to our contemporary experience.

BREATH EXERCISE 4: COMMUNITY

1. Instead of sitting alone in your meditation space, go to a prayer or meditation group, and practice as a community in Christ. The Zen Buddhists say that trees grown close together in the forest grow higher and straighter as they stretch upwards toward the light than those that grow alone in a field.
2. Sit together in a Christian meditation group and breathe deeply.
3. Do the meditation exercises described in this section, especially those that take you through body, soul, and spirit. Find a communion, or common union, with the others in your group in attempting to let go of the senses and emotions of the body, the thoughts of the mind, and breaking through to the pure spiritual intuition of the spirit. Especially find communion with the others in the spirit in God's Spirit. Here, despite external differences of age, sex, culture, or personal opinions, we can find a deep communion in the things of Spirit that breaks down all of these other barriers. Even if the others are not finding this breakthrough yet, take personal responsibility for your own breakthrough. Even if others are not yet acting very Christlike toward you, see Jesus in them in the spirit in God's Spirit, and act Christlike toward them through this interior change.
4. By letting go of your ego and self, let go of the insistence of getting your own way, and of always being right. Now you can really listen to others, communicate on the level of the spirit, and really hear what they are trying to say.
5. Find the good points in others, and find the good things even behind the things that we do not like about them, or disagree with them about.

6. Let go of the times others have offended others or us. So often our claims for seeking "justice" are really just attempts to get even through revenge or self-justification. Only when we are free of this pattern can we really accomplish God's justice, which has mercy at its heart.

7. Now forgive those who are offensive to us or to others. Though we may not condone the actions of those who have wronged us, we must always have an attitude that offers forgiveness whenever they are ready to approach us. Plus, we must never use the excuse of not condoning wrong actions as a disguise for an attitude of judgment, rather than forgiveness, of others.

8. Feel happiness and joy in this communion with the other members of the community in the Spirit.

9. Thank God for this communion.

10. Conclude together as in an individual meditation session.

Integration

The Brothers and Sisters of Charity at Little Portion Hermitage integrate all of these expressions within one general community. Our integrated monastic expression includes a celibate brotherhood, celibate sisterhood, and family monastic expression. This would include the more intense cenobitical and semi-eremitical expressions of monasticism. Our domestic expression is made up of those who live in their own homes, in less externally intense houses of prayer, and neighborhood clusters who come together on a monthly, bimonthly, and weekly level in cell groups, or in less intense daily gatherings for prayer than what would be found at the monastic Motherhouse of the Little Portion Hermitage.

You may choose to join our community to find support in creating this environment of lifestyle for prayer and meditation, or you may do it within another expression of community within the Church. One thing is certain: In order to enter into prayer and meditation in a way that is consistent with classical expressions of the major world religions, one must enter into some form of training under a teacher, which places one into some form of community with brothers and sisters under the same teacher, in which the lessons of the teacher are lived out and authenticated in daily life. This is especially true within the Christian tradition and its monastic expression, which has produced the highest of its contemplative and mystical achievements.

Conclusions

So where do we fit? Are we afraid of real community? Do we want the blessings of traditional mysticism but do not want to pay the price through real commitment? You cannot have it both ways. There are appropriately different ways to enter into training under a teacher within the Church, or the communities and ministries of the Church, but ultimately we must make a choice and make a commitment to the way best suited for us. If the way of the masters is correct, that way will involve sacrifice of self through situations and circumstances we cannot even begin to second-guess. Our first temptation is to turn the other way and run, but that is not the way to real spiritual growth. It may seem like it at the time, or even for a period of years after we turn away, but ultimately we will have to turn back around, face our own demons and weaknesses, and go forward.

I encourage you to seek out a good spiritual community and teacher. Do not give up only a few years into it when the honeymoon is over, and things get really tough. Stick it out for the distance, and you will receive a reward that this lopsided world of ours simply cannot give, despite its many benefits and blessings.

Lectio Divina

THE MONASTIC WRITERS OF THE WEST list *lectio divina*, or sacred reading, as the first of the steps toward contemplation. It is not the same as study, and it certainly is not the same as the speed-reading of modern educational techniques. If anything, it is the opposite, but it is far from being without use.

Lectio is the slow reading of a short text that leads to meditation. It allows one to ponder the meaning through the creative use of imagination. As Mary "pondered these things within her heart," so do we, as the new Mary of the Church, ponder the things that we read so as to give birth to Jesus, as the words on the page become reality in our lives through meditation that leads to contemplation.

The Texts: Scripture and the Fathers

The texts used in *lectio* are usually the scriptures, especially the words and life of Jesus from the four gospels. The monastic East would recommend starting with the Fathers, especially the monastics and mystics, so as to avoid the misinterpretation of the more subtle and difficult passages. The West tends to emphasize the use of scripture

43

at the beginning, with care to reference the more difficult passages to the Fathers. With today's interfaith dialogue, it would also be permitted to use the scriptures of the various world religions, taking care to keep the centrality of Jesus and orthodoxy in faith and morality.

It is important to understand the use of scripture in this highly personalized context so that one is not led to harmful misinterpretation before diving headlong into the very personal approach. Otherwise you may end up in some very dangerous interpretations of "what God is saying," pretty quickly.

For the Catholic Church, and the early Church, it is important to remember how we actually got the scriptures. In the Old Testament, God wrote humanity a letter through his revelation to the Jewish people. It is said that he wrote the initial Ten Commandments with his own finger. Nobody really knows exactly what that means, but we do know it meant that it was a very direct revelation and communication of God to the Jewish people and to all of humanity. Unfortunately, it didn't work out that well for either. Both continued to stray from God in rather big ways. So in the New Testament God paid all of humanity a personal visit through Jesus Christ. He is the Word incarnate, or "made flesh."

When Jesus revealed the new Word to the world, he did not write a letter or a book. He simply lived it. He *is* the Word. He *is* Word when he speaks and when he is silent, when he is active and when he is still. This is experienced especially in the clarity and the mystery of the paradox of the cross and the resurrection. It is morality, faith, and mysticism all proclaimed as ultimate Word in one silent act. This is the way of complete revelation and mystery all at once. It is clearer and more mystical than a merely written word.

When he spread that special Word, he did so through people, from Master to disciple, from Person to person. He gathered disciples, or those who followed his way of life and embraced his discipline. During his ministry he chose the twelve apostles who would lead. Of these, he was especially close to three, and on one, Peter, he bestowed a special primary role of leadership among the twelve. After his ascension he sent the Holy Spirit upon the Church, and upon those leaders in a special way. This Spirit was to empower them all with supernatural love and faith, and was to guide them to all truth necessary for the salvation of all humankind for all time.

As these apostles went forth and established churches, or gatherings, or *"ecclesiae,"* they established successors to their leadership and prayed for the gift of that same Spirit upon each community and leader. Those same leaders would often go out and repeat the process as the Church began to spread throughout the known world. Thus, a certain apostolic succession was established. As the apostles died, the churches that were established especially by them carried a greater authority, or authorship, out of reverence for the twelve original apostles. This was especially true of the bishop of Rome, who was the direct successor to St. Peter.

When debates inevitably arose concerning the true nature of Jesus and the Church, these special successors to the apostles were sought after to clear up the disagreement with apostolic authority. This was especially true regarding an appeal to, or an intervention by, the bishop of Rome.

As the apostles wrote letters, and gospel accounts of the life of Christ and the Church, there were also questions and disputes as to how to interpret them. The establishment of a simple principle, given to the Church by the Spirit, decided this: The scriptures came forth from the authority of God in the Church, so if there is a confusing passage of scripture today (and there are a few!), then it makes good sense to go back to the Church from which the scriptures came in order to see if there is a substantial agreement in the early Church as to what it means, and then we can apply it to our situation today in a developed way. If we ignore the authority of the Church, then we destroy the authority of scripture.

How does this effect sacred reading? We need grounding in the basic understanding of scripture regarding faith and morality as taught by the magisterium, or teaching authority, of the Catholic Church before we try to apply it too creatively to our daily meditations. I have seen a great many people get way off track spiritually before they even knew there was a track laid down by God for the train of his people, the Church. Once a basic understanding of the Catholic faith is substantially in place, then the use of scripture in *lectio divina* can become a wonderful experience of the existential journey of the Spirit in our lives through scripture.

This is why the later Eastern Christian Fathers recommend starting *lectio* with the ancient Fathers on meditation and prayer, rather than going directly to scripture. This is a little hard for those of us who were formed as young Christians in Protestant theology. We also remember that the Eastern Fathers do not agree with the notion of the Roman Pope. But it is a very understandable premise when viewed from the perspective of the many souls who have gone astray through erroneous personal interpretations of scripture. Nontheless, the Western tradition values the more immediate use of scripture for *lectio,* as long as it is done under the direction of the teaching of the Church regarding faith and morality.

Spiritual Direction

So we are free to use scripture and the Fathers for sacred reading. It is also good to have a spiritual director, after the fashion of Jesus and the apostles, or the first monks in the desert. Even with the teaching of the Church, it is easy to get sidetracked. The angel of darkness often comes as an angel of light, and the young disciple usually needs the loving yet strong guidance of one more experienced in this way of mediation and prayer. Only occasionally does a soul make it without the help of a spiritual father or mother, as in the case of St. Francis of Assisi, or the Buddha. Yet even they had help at the beginning of their vocations.

Today this is especially problematic as it becomes more and more difficult to find a truly qualified spiritual director. Yes, there are more and more books being written, and more and more workshops being given, but there are fewer and fewer who truly live the life of a spiritual master anymore. Most who are called get bogged down in the worldliness of fame and success. Only a few really live the life anymore.

The Eastern Fathers, the Buddha, and the Taoists have some practical advice about their situation: "Better no spiritual director than a bad one!" It is not ideal, but it will have to do when no one qualified presents himself or herself to a genuine seeker. Of course, this does not relieve the serious obligation to follow a spiritual father or mother when they are available, keeping in mind that no spiritual director will ever be perfect! The classics are filled with admonitions to humbly and joyfully follow the obedience of the master even when we disagree, as long as the teaching of the master is not against the teaching of the Church on faith or morality, or against the rule and constitution of the community of disciples we are a part of. So we might need to go the way by ourselves, but it is always better to place oneself under the teaching of a spiritual father or mother as elder.

Here it is good to remember the classical teaching that we are to see Jesus in the spiritual father or mother, no matter how fallible and human they may be. Again, this is no excuse for sloppy leadership, and there are ample checks and balances in the Church for this. I am reminded of a teaching in the Tibetan Buddhist *Lam Rim*. It says that even if the teacher is only one eighth correct in their teaching and lifestyle, it is still better to place yourself under the direction of such a teacher, and in this case see the Buddha in them, than to try to navigate the tricky waters of spiritual life on one's own. This is similar to the Western teaching of learning to see Jesus in the spiritual leader, even if that leader is less than perfect.

The Practice of Lectio

The actual practice of *lectio divina* involves just sitting with the sacred text and choosing a few lines of a passage. These are read slowly. Time is taken to fully digest the words not only on the objective level but also on the subjective level of what they say to you in the here-and-now. This personal interpretation is set against the backdrop of a proper understanding of scripture as interpreted by the Church, so some preparation through study is required. But the point is not objective study but what the Spirit is saying to you through the text on a very deep level. This deeper level helps to lead us on to personal contemplation on the intuitive level of the spirit beyond all ideas and words. The words of the sacred text are really just a vehicle to transport us to that deeper place.

For myself, once a certain familiarity with the scriptures is established over the course of many years, I will often just sit with an open Bible on my lap as I meditate. The simple act of being aware of its contents on an intuitive level is sufficient to take me to the place of real meditation and contemplation. I would not recommend this for those not strongly grounded in scripture and its proper interpretation through the Fathers and magisterium of the Church.

St. Bonaventure tells us that we are to use our imagination when we meditate on scripture or other sacred texts. We are to visualize what we read "with vivid imagination." But there is more to it than what is often normally understood by "imagination." For me, it means to find eternity in the words and ideas of God's action in space and time. This means finding eternity beyond image and form in the very color and feel of the images brought to mind. Likewise, it means going beyond the words on the page to the space between the ink in the letters that make up the words. This is an intuitive knowing of reality in the real things of God found in classical meditation.

This is not unlike the music I compose and play. It is meditative music and requires a certain understanding of reality to compose, perform, and listen to. In meditative music, we listen not only to the notes but also to the space between the notes. Behind every note there must be the ability to play a hundred, or the simplicity becomes a cop-out for lack of skill. But we do not play every note we are able to play just because we can. No. We play the right note at the right time. This one note is worth more than a thousand played at the whim of the musician. The one note breaks through to eternity if played from the place of eternity, and will lead others there as well.

It is like that in meditation, too. We meditate on the images and forms brought to mind from the texts of sacred reading. These images are positive and have a tangible history or ideology in time and space. They have form and real content. But in meditation we move through and beyond these realities into a Reality beyond image and form. Here, through the things of image and form, we find God's Image and Form, which is beyond all image and form. This breaks through to eternity through the things of space and time, in a way beyond the concepts of either. This is incarnation and transcendence in one event. It is enlightenment and rebirth.

Jesus

Of course, Jesus *is* the great Reality. He *is* God's image and form that takes us beyond image and form through image and form. He *is* eternity in space and time beyond all space and time. He is the fulfillment of all logic and philosophy in a mystical Event that breaks through to paradox. In this, *he* is the ultimate sacred reading and divine text. He is the ultimate meditation. He *is* the fulfillment of all for philosophers and mystics of all faiths.

We open a passage of scripture or another sacred text. We do not read as we read a newspaper or book for recreation or study. We read slowly. We allow ourselves to visualize fully the scene in the text. We see the colors. We smell the scents and odors. We feel the texture of the sand and wind of the Mideast or ancient setting. We allow ourselves to fall into the text fully as if we were really there, transcending the limitations of space and time.

Creation

Ironically, *lectio divina* isn't the only source that supplies objective guidance to lead us on into meditation and contemplation. Creation itself can be a great source for meditation. *The Imitation of Christ* says that for those who are holy within, all of creation becomes a holy book of sacred doctrine. St. Francis is said to have found all of creation becoming a ladder through which to climb to the throne of God. His *Canticle of the Creatures,* or *Brother Sun, Sister Moon,* is an anthem to the Christian appreciation of nature that is universally recognized around the world. St. Bonaventure, the great Seraphic Doctor from the Franciscan heritage, put all of this into theological language in the tradition of St. Augustine when he said that all of creation bears God's traces, humanity bears God's image, (though, as a mirror obscured by the dirt of sin), and the Church is the very Body of Christ.

This means we must develop more than a mere ideological appreciation of creation. We must get out into it in order to enter into this mystical aspect of creation's part in God's plan in our life. There are many simple ways to begin. Take a walk on a beautiful, or not so beautiful, day. Work in a garden. Sit outside instead of staying pent up in the constant artificiality of an air-conditioned environment. Or, if you are physically handicapped, sit by a window and watch the birds and squirrels at a feeder. For myself, I do walking meditation, where I slowly walk the grounds of our monastic hermitage and intuitively take in all the sights and sounds of the people and the place where I live.

All of the same principles of *lectio* apply to enjoying creation as a way to meditation. St. Bonaventure tells us that everything in creation leads the truly awakened observer back to the contemplation of the mystery of God. The creation always leads to the Creator. The interdependence of all things leads us back to dependence on God, "through whom we live, and move, and have our being," as says sacred scripture.

Humanity

Bonaventure would say that this is especially true with humanity. Our faculty of memory, as understood by the scholastic neo-Greek philosophers of his time, leads us to appreciate God's timelessness, for time is a limited reality of eternity. The intellect leads us to appreciate God's truth, for the ability to grasp truth leads us to Universal Truth. Our will leads us to appreciate God's love, for the reality of love, which we all need and acknowledge as an important aspect of the human condition, resides in the human will. These examples from the accepted philosophy of Bonaventure's time can certainly be applied to the anthropology and philosophy of our own time.

Liturgy

Liturgy can also be a great source of inspiration for *lectio*. Certainly the liturgies of the Church are chock full of scripture and patristic writings. A prayerful state of listening during liturgies can become a wellspring of inspiration during our private meditation and prayer times. For me, this simply means bringing the words of the liturgy into my prayer time. As I have said before, my early morning routine includes a time for meditation on the readings of the day for our Eucharistic Liturgy, or Mass, and a slow and meditative read of the Office of Readings, which includes both the Psalms and so many wonderful patristic and Church writings. A leisurely read of these sources never ceases to direct me into meditation and prayer.

Devotions

The devotions of the Church are also excellent sources for meditation and prayer and can serve the same purpose of sacred reading in the process toward deep contemplation. These devotions include the Marian and Jesus Prayer rosaries, the stations of the cross, and the many other novenas and such as advocated by the Church. All of these provide objective guidance and input for the mind regarding the life of Jesus, and our participation in it, and can help lead us on toward meditation and contemplation. This is especially true of devotions because of their childlike quality. They were developed for the laity in a time when they could not read, so all had to be committed to memory through repetition. In a time when we pride ourselves on our education and sophistication (though recent studies show the United States one of the more illiterate nations in the developed world), the intentional use of such simple and childlike devotions are actually good for our humility and can, therefore, better lead us to our desired goal.

I would like to share a way that I pray the rosary and the Jesus Prayer. I combine the two classical prayers by using the original part of the Marian rosary with the Jesus Prayer. The prayer then goes like this: "Hail Mary, full of grace, the Lord is with you. Blessed are you among woman, and blessed is the fruit of your womb, Jesus. Jesus Christ, Son of God, have mercy on me, a sinner." I unite this prayer with my in-and-out breathing. This slows the pace of the prayer to a natural rhythm and helps to interiorize it to the level of an intuitive rather than a strictly discursive meditation.

LECTIO DIVINA: SACRED READING EXERCISE

1. Sit comfortably in your meditation space. Breathe deeply and allow your body to slow down and relax. Let go of any preconceived opinions or agendas. Then do the same with your emotions and your mind. Be as quiet and calm as the waters of a still and clear pond. Soon you are ready to hear the Word of God clearly.

2. Open your sacred text to an appropriate place. You may choose this place by selecting a favorite passage, going through the text in order or thematically, or at random. Some liturgical biblical texts, such as the missal or Divine Office, are already arranged.

3. Read the text slowly, but not so slowly as to be artificial. Get to the deeper meaning of the text. Allow the actual reality of the words to soak into your soul and permeate outward to your body and inward to your deepest spirit. This is not the same as

getting the intellectual meaning of the words, though this is good for prior preparation for this sacred reading meditation.

4. Allow the text to direct your emotions in a positive and healthy way. Allow it to direct your mind similarly. Even allow it to stir your senses through imagination in a good way. CAUTION: do not allow these stirrings of the faculties of the soul and body to rekindle negative sensual, emotional, or intellectual patterns. However, if they do surface, it may indicate that they are still hiding in the inner recesses of your being and need to be dealt with through further letting go and detachment.

5. Deal with any negative emotions, thoughts, or senses. Allow the positive to again displace the negative through a good use of the thoughts and emotions, and even the senses through this meditation.

6. Allow this positive to fill your being and flow out from you to anyone in need of the aspect of God's love and mercy indicated in the sacred text.

7. If God grants it, allow the reality of the sacred text to pass over to a pure spiritual intuition in his Spirit, so that you simply *become* what you have read in a way appropriate to your own situation and experience today. This is contemplation and may not occur at the beginning stages of, or at every, meditation.

8. If God has given you this grace of contemplation during this meditation, spend some undisturbed and unhurried time in this sacred state. If not, proceed to the next step.

9. Give thanks and glory to God for any illumination you received through this encounter.

10. Slowly come out of the meditation as described in previous sessions.

Conclusions

So sacred reading can include an appreciation of creation, humanity, the Church and her liturgies and devotions, as well as the more commonly understood use of sacred text in private meditation and prayer. No matter what we use as our source, the *most* important thing is to prayerfully digest it in mediation and prayer. This is *not* done as research, or as a study of the Bible, or any other sacred subject. This is done as, what the classics call, "a holy leisure." It will not be graded, published, or preached except under the most extraordinary circumstances. Most of my *lectio* mediations are most private and are for God and me alone. This practice is between you and God *alone*. It is not for recognition, public affirmation, or fame. It is done within the secret silence of the Holy of Holies for the New Testament believer. When kept in this sacred reality, great things can truly happen through this practice. If done as if in public, or to impress anyone, it becomes an exercise of egocentricity and pride, and is a spiritual waste of time. Use your time well. Enter into the true practice of sacred reading.

Meditation

After *LECTIO DIVINA* comes medita-tion, or *meditatio*. This is the simple use of the imagination to actually visualize the scenes or ideas we read about in a leisurely and creative way. Since this is the goal of sacred reading, it might be added that we can also use devotions such as the rosary as our resource to lead us into meditation.

Vocal Prayer

While vocal prayer is not always considered meditation, it can be seen as a stage between *lectio* and meditation. This was true in the early Church, and is again the case in *The Catechism of the Catholic Church*.

The Jewish concept of meditation actually included vocal prayer. For them, to meditate was to speak out loud in a deliberate fashion. We see it again today with The Navigators, a group that uses a scripture memorization method including vocal recitation. Speaking out loud helps concretize the verses into the memory. Vocal prayer is still a vital part of Catholic prayer of a liturgical nature. Even when said in private, the Divine Office, or the formal prayer of the Church at various times throughout the day, is really to be recited vocally. This usually means forming the words with the lips without making any noticeable sound.

I am reminded of the past Visitor (a representative of the Church who visits a community or a church regularly) to our community, Fr. Alan McCoy, OFM. When we traveled to Nicaragua with him to set up our Monastic Mission on the island of Ometepe in the Diocese of Granada, he would often say the Divine Office while on a plane or bus. I noticed that he moved his lips while reading the Psalter. I knew that he was not having trouble reading, since he is a very well-read and educated man, so I asked him why he did so. He responded that he was trained to pray liturgical prayers out loud, or by moving his lips, even when praying them in private. He said that it caused him to deliberately pray each word and be less inclined to skip over them in a speed-reading fashion. So here was this "giant" of spirituality and social justice from the Franciscan tradition praying his Office like a little child who was still learning to read! I was amazed and thoroughly impressed at his training and simplicity. The "young bucks" of spirituality would probably consider this habit beneath them, yet here was a leader of us all still obediently following the training of his religious youth. I must say that I am now inclined to follow his lead.

One day sometime later, I observed my wife doing the same thing! For exactly the same reasons, she said her Office out loud when praying privately. She did the same with her scripture meditations. Of course, she was trained in monastic discipline. I soon followed her lead as well. Now I tend to move my lips when praying the Office to insure that I really take the time to meditate on each passage and word.

Why is vocal prayer sometimes helpful in meditation? It slows us down so that we must really pray and meditate on each concept and word. When we say each word out loud, at least to ourselves, we have to really read each word and concept. We cannot skip over anything, as we might in speed-reading and the like. We come from a society that values knowledge. We expect to obtain information in seconds through the computer, the internet, and the countless magazines and newspapers in circulation. But with all of this knowledge available to us, how mush wiser are we really becoming? The apocalyptic scriptures say that in the last days "knowledge will increase while iniquity abounds." St. Paul says that "knowledge puffs up, but love builds up." Today we are indeed puffed up with arrogance and pride, while real wisdom and love seem hard to find.

VOCAL PRAYER EXERCISE

1. Sit in your meditation space, or go to a monastic church or chapel for the Divine Office, and breathe deeply for a few minutes of preparation. Allow your body and mind to slow down as you let go of them. Allow your inner spirit to emerge.
2. Take up the Divine Office, or the four-week Psalter of the official Roman Catholic prayer book. Other Psalters will do nicely as well, such as the *Book of Common Prayer* from the Anglican tradition, the Psalter from the Eastern and Orthodox churches, or simply the Psalms from the Bible.
3. Begin to pray the Psalms out loud in a whispered or subdued voice. Take the pace slowly.
4. Allow the words to soak into your whole being. What do your senses feel like while saying the Psalms? What is happening to your emotions and thoughts? NOTE: The more violent Psalms are applied symbolically toward any evil in our own life, not toward other people or institutions. Let your whole being participate.
5. If you find doing this alone too difficult, go to a monastery or religious house nearby as often as possible and participate in the Divine Office, or common praying of the Psalms. Benedictine monasteries usually have the most consistently prayerful and beautiful services of this type. Others often have beautiful services as well.

6. If you are leading, or are alone, make sure that you allow silence between each Psalm and reading for meditative and
   contemplative reflection.
7. Conclude as written, and then spend a few minutes absorbing
   what the Lord has given during this Hour of the Office.

Thoughts, Words, Emotions, and Actions

There is also a connection between thoughts and emotions. In the
fallen pattern we spoke of earlier, thoughts are conditioned by unruly
emotions, which are stirred up through disordered passions and
senses. When the senses are quieted through ascetical disciplines,
such as fasting, vigils, and manual labor, then the emotions become
less unruly. They also become quiet. Then we can redirect them with
positive thoughts and meditations on godly and beautiful things,
rather than on negative and destructive things. Thoughts redirect
emotions. Then emotions can be used by the mind to empower the
positive use of the soul in leading to the full rebirth of the spirit in
contemplation. Because of this, the scriptures are filled with admonitions to use the mind properly in our spiritual life. It has been said
in modern times that the battle for the soul is in the mind. Scripture
would fully agree.

The Book of Proverbs says clearly that "we become what we
think." This is remarkably like the first chapter of the primary Buddhist scripture, *The Dhammapada,* which says, "We are what we
think." In the New Testament, we are told repeatedly that "your
thoughts should be wholly directed to all that is true, all that deserves
respect, all that is honest, pure, admirable, decent, virtuous, or worthy of praise." Paul to the Romans says, "Do not conform yourselves
to this age, but be transformed by the spiritual renewal of your mind,
so that you may judge what is God's will, what is good, pleasing, and
perfect." All of this is the New Testament version of the Old Testa-

ment admonition of the first Psalm to "meditate on the law of the Lord day and night."

Of course, the greatest of all New Testament scriptures about the use of the mind is found in St. Paul's Letter to the Philippians, where we are told to have the very mind of Christ. But what does this mean? Does it mean filling our heads with correct theology and doctrine, of conforming our opinions to that of the teaching of the Church in faith and morality? Certainly these are good things in their proper place and time. But at the time of this ultimate meditation, we are called to something else, something deeper and purer.

Furthermore, there is a connection between what we think and what we say. This connection leads clearly to what we do. The scriptures say that what we think, we will become, and what we say materializes ideas into reality, for better or for worse. If we say it, we have to really think it! If we say it, we are far more apt to actually do it. This connection is most powerful. Therefore, to say the sacred text out loud helps us to really bring its fullness into our thoughts in meditation. From this, we will be far more apt to act upon it in our lives. We will also be more apt to cross over into passive contemplation beyond all words, images, or forms.

Scripture says that the power of "life and death are in the tongue," and that "confession on the lips leads to salvation." It is replete with warnings against the hasty use of speech, and cautions us to remain silent until we really have something constructive to say. Speech can destroy friendships more easily and deeply than the sword, and once words are spoken, they are more difficult to undo than even the most violent and destructive of actions. This is also why gossiping, or saying a true thing to an uninvolved, or inappropriately involved, person is as destructive as warfare. St. Francis, and the entire monastic tradition of the Church, sees this as the most destructive force in building community, and the famous Lutheran theologian and martyr, Dietrich Bonnhoffer, likens the gossiper to a murderer on the spiritual level.

Charismatic Praise and Thanks

The scriptures say that we "enter his courts with thanksgiving and praise." St. Paul tells us that we are to "thank God always, and for everything in the name of our Lord Jesus Christ." Praise and thanks speaks positive things into reality, rather than giving into our negative thoughts and emotions, which bring destructive energy to relationships and our own spiritual life. We do this by faith, "which is the object of things hoped for, and unseen," for surely we do not always feel like thanking God when a seemingly bad thing has happened in our life. So we often praise and thank God precisely when things are not going well. But we do this by faith, not because we feel like it. This is not intended to make us into uncaring robots, or to keep us from experiencing appropriate grief, as did Jesus when his friend Lazarus died, but to keep us from falling headlong into negativity, depression, and despair when the inevitable bad things of life eventually do come our way.

Connected to this is the often-misunderstood charismatic gift of tongues. This gift is clearly part of the experience of the early Church, as depicted in the Acts of the Apostles and the writings of St. Paul. It was seen in the early Church Fathers such as St. John Chrysostom and even St. Augustine in their description of *jubilatio*. This is where the congregation sings a vowel sound, or a simple alleluia, without there being any words or written melodies. This is what today's charismatics call "singing in tongues." It is a truly beautiful experience when authentically done in the Spirit. My own mother was helped enormously in her conversion to the Catholic Church when she experienced this as a beautiful and angelic experience with the Catholic Charismatics in Indianapolis, Indiana, at St. Monica's parish.

But what is going on with tongues? My experience of it is this: Thoughts direct emotions. Words concretize thoughts. Thoughts and emotions eventually overflow into action. This can be either positive or negative. The positive is life-giving and godly. The negative is destructive and brings death. When we are so overwhelmed with negative thoughts and emotions that we cannot even bring ourselves to objective positive speech or praise and thanks to God in order to redirect the thoughts and emotions anymore, then we begin praying out loud to ourselves in tongues. This is the prayer of the Spirit, which is, as St. Paul says, "groanings that cannot be expressed in speech." In other words, we speak the unspeakable by speaking vowel sounds and consonants that do not fall into the category of known human language. This stirs up the nonobjective praise and thanks of God that comes from the Spirit. Once the Spirit is stirred up, then the Spirit can reach down and cleanse our minds of the overwhelming negativity that imprisons our emotions. When this happens we can then begin to think objectively positive and godly thoughts once more, and our emotions can be redirected to good and positive things.

For me, charismatic praise and thanks is like a powerful upward motion of Spirit that cleanses out all of the gross impurities of our life. It is like a "wave offering" to God. Everything is thrown up into the wind, which scatters it far from our life. The problem is that some of it still falls back down into the container of our life.

PRAISE AND THANKS EXERCISE

1. Sit in your meditation space and breathe deeply.
2. Begin to call to mind the good things that have happened to you today or lately.
3. Remember the good things that have happened to you from long past.
4. Think of the bad things that *could* have happened that did not!
5. Thank God even for all of the seemingly bad things that still help teach us the lessons of God. No matter how bad the situation seems, God is still in control.
6. Give thanks to God for all these things. First use your mind and will so that praise and thanks is a matter of choice, not of what

happens to us. Next, allow your emotions to get involved so that they are turned from the destructive spiral of negative emotions to the positive emotions that give life. Allow your body to get involved as you sing with your lips and mouth, and raise your hands, kneel, lie prostrate, or dance with your body. Let this praise transform your whole being.

7. If you are so graced by God, allow yourself to pass over into contemplation beyond words, ideas, or senses, but including and fulfilling them all.

8. Conclude by quietly thanking God for this wonderful gift.

Contemplation, and specifically breath prayer, are like two stoppers on the very bottom of our feet that are opened up, allowing everything to flow and drain out of our life. By simply being still, the sheer natural power of gravity allows all the impurities that have fallen back into our life to finally drain out. It is far less spectacular than charismatic praise, but it is ultimately more effective in getting the last vestiges of the false self out of our life.

As I have explained in my book *The Fire of God,* the kindling needed is simple praise and thanks, even in the face of a bad situation. The roaring fire that follows is charismatic praise. As much fun as the roaring fire may be, it is the quiet but steady, hot burning coals of breath prayer and contemplation that best heat the house. Indeed, if the roaring fire burns too long in that way, it actually draws heat up the chimney and out of the house! It spiritually burns you out.

CHARISMATIC PRAISE AND THANKS EXERCISE

1. Sit in your meditation space, go to a prayer group, or go to a Charismatic Mass.

2. Begin to sing the songs of praise and thanksgiving that are customary.

3. Allow your mind to see the things spoken in the songs.
4. Allow your emotions to be stirred up in a positive way about the things of God spoken of, or suggested, in the lyrics.
5. As you sing and stir up these things, you may feel constrained by the lyric or the formal melody. Allow yourself to simply sing or speak vowel sounds without there being a formal melody or lyric. It may sound like gibberish, and at first you will feel a little self-conscious about it, but do it anyway, trusting in the Lord's presence in this stirring up of charismatic praise. This is called "singing in the Spirit," or "speaking in tongues."
6. You may also find times when no matter how hard you try to praise God objectively, you cannot. At this time, temporarily bypass the mind and go straight to the heart and spirit. Sing or speak in tongues by faith, knowing that praising by faith in this way stirs up the Spirit. Once the Spirit is stirred up in this manner, God will effectively change your emotional and mental patterns in a way beyond our normal ability.
7. You may also experience the peace of God so strongly that you can no longer stand or sit up straight. You will simply fall over and rest in peace for a period of time. This is called being "slain in," or "resting in the Spirit." It is best entered into at the time of the meeting when there are others there to help those who succumb. If you are in your prayer space, simply rest in the arms of the Lord until the experience passes.

The Basics of Meditation

Before we go much further, let's investigate some more of the real "stuff" of meditation. What, and how do we think during Christian meditation? St. Bonaventure tells us to not be afraid to creatively use the imagination during this kind of meditation. When reading a sacred source, he says to recall the scenes depicted by the text with "vivid imagination." What does this really mean for us today?

Imagination

For me, it means allowing myself to fall through my imagination into the sensual reality of the scene. What do the Judean desert sun, wind, and sand feel like as they get into one's hair and clothing? What does the Mideastern dirt feel like between the toes of the feet in your sandals? These are perhaps not the specific examples that would work for you, but the point is to get specific enough to really enter fully into the reality of the holy scene as best you can. When we allow the imagination to stir up the senses, then the emotions follow in a positive way, and the whole of our being can get involved in a way that will lead us into contemplation. All of this applies to the imagination in union with the sacred text of scripture or the Fathers in either private prayer or liturgy.

This use of the senses and emotions through imagination can also involve the use of devotions, such as the rosary, or the stations of the cross. Here, we again stir up the thoughts, emotions, and even the senses through the similar use of the imagination. If anything, devotions are better suited for this kind of meditation because we need not worry about a heavy book for reading, or the translation from words to images. Devotions rely only on words simple enough to be easily committed to memory and, at most, require a set of beads or knotted string.

This also applies to the use of creation. We use our objective minds in meditating on creation, but we must not be too afraid to creatively use our imaginations and emotions as well. How does being in the midst of creation make us feel? Do our emotions make us feel happy, joyful, peaceful and calm, or afraid and unsure? All of these emotions can help lead us to God in the midst of creation. Do the objective realities of creation lead us on to the use of the imagination, or do we stay stuck in empirical scientific deduction? The latter is good, but it is *not* what we mean by the use of creation in meditation and prayer!

Of course, this kind of use of imagination also has dangers. It would be easy to get stuck in the sensuality, emotions, and images of these visualizations. We overcome the negative use of these faculties by a positive use of them, after having initially settled them down through the asceticism of silence and stillness. But as Evagrius Ponticus, a fourth-century monk of the East, said, we must be careful not to "turn the remedy to passion into a passion." This would be to exchange one devil for another.

The proper use of imagination uses the human faculties in a positive way in order to build on them and surpass them in pure contemplation. Once this stage is reached, it transforms all we do with body or soul into a union with our spirit in God's Spirit.

The Self-Emptying of Christ

Paul says, "Your attitude must be that of Christ: Though he was in the form of God, he did not deem equality with God something to be grasped at. Rather, he emptied himself and took the form of a slave, being born in the likeness of men. He was known to be of human estate, and it was thus that he humbled himself, obediently accepting even death, death on a cross! Because of this, God highly exalted him and bestowed upon him the name above every other name, so that at Jesus' name, every knee must bend in the heavens, on the earth, and every tongue proclaim to the glory of God the Father: Jesus Christ is Lord!"

This scripture shows the primary aspect of the mind of Christ as an attitude of "kenosis," or self-emptying. This is a way beyond the stages of meditation spoken of above. The initial stages are good and even necessary. But these further stages of the full way of Jesus are what make out meditation uniquely Christian, or like Christ.

The self-emptying of Christ is seen in the incarnation of the divine among humanity, but it is seen in a most special way in the paradox of the death and resurrection, the paschal mystery, of Christ. Here, Jesus does not just complement and affirm the other mystics of the various religions of the world, though he assuredly does that, too.

Here he actually *is* the mystery that moves beyond the objective to the actual experience of union beyond all duality. He does not just live and teach the mystery, he *is* the mystery in its fullest manifestation to humanity and creation. No other founder, mystic, or holy person has ever done this: to die and rise, stating the paradox unquestionably for all the world to see. Therefore, the greatest Christian meditation is to simply empty oneself of self after the example of Christ. The greatest meditation would be to have no discursive meditation but to simply *be* through, with, and in he who *is*. Here meditation has reached its end and is ready to move on to the next stage: contemplation.

BREATH EXERCISE 5: THE CROSS

The centrality of the Christian faith is the cross and resurrection of Jesus Christ, the paschal mystery. For us, it is more than the paradox of the mystics of the other great faiths. For us, it is not a teaching or even an experience to be gained by meditation practitioners, though it includes this as well. For us it *exists* beyond teaching in the person of Jesus, the Way, the Truth, and the Life. Genuine Christian meditation must, then, lead us to the actual experience of this mystery if it is to be truly Christian.

1. Begin as in the other meditations: Sit in your meditation space. Breathe deeply to settle and still your senses of your body, emotions, and thoughts of the soul, and be aware of your spirit in the Spirit of God.

2. After breathing deeply, be aware of your body and the senses. Thank God for them as gifts from God. Be aware of the awesome wonder of their interconnectedness with the rest of creation, starting with your parents and family, and reaching out to the earth and all life that springs from it. Then be aware that, despite the wonder of the body, it is only our temporary

home during this lifetime. It will grow old, degenerate, and die. After that, it will decompose in the grave. It will be resurrected, but in a whole new and more wonderful form. Also, beware that, in this fallen world, the disordered sensual self is sometimes a cause of great trouble and pain to the soul. So we bring the body, and all that it is, to the cross of Christ, and let it go. By doing this, all that is dysfunctional and out of order in our body more naturally finds its place in the will of God, and we know peace. We know the first fruits of resurrection and new life in this temporary home of the body.

3. Next, move to the emotions of the body and soul. Go through the same steps as with the senses of the body. Be aware of the gift they are from God, and thank God for them. Know that they are interdependent and conditioned by the other things of this phenomenal world. If we experience pleasure, we are peaceful and happy. If things do not go as we want, we are agitated and unhappy. Know that they are also temporary and impermanent. As conditions change, so do our emotions. They come and go, rise and fall, with the changing of conditions in our life. They are part of us, but they are not the deepest being of who we really are. So, we can relax and peacefully bring them to the cross of Jesus. This brings greater peace as we now experience the emotions as they were originally intended to function—as mobilizers of the things of God, and good in our life.

4. Next, we come to our thoughts. As with the senses and emotions, we first acknowledge our thoughts of today. Are they negative or positive, clear or unclear, confused or focused? We thank God for the gift of thoughts and for the cognition of our spiritual mind. Then we realize that thoughts come and go. They are positive today, negative tomorrow, depending upon what conditions of the phenomenal world affect them. We have thoughts, but we are not our thoughts. Our deepest self is much deeper. So, we bring our thoughts to the cross of Christ and let them go. As we do this, we can sense them draining

away from us, along with the tension and stress they often
cause. We are reborn in the resurrection of Christ through this
process.

5. Lastly, having let go of the senses, emotions, and thoughts that
   so often agitate us, we become intuitively aware of our spirit in
   God's Spirit, essence to Essence, breath to Breath. Simply
   breathe in this wonderful union with the deepest essence of
   God beyond all thoughts, emotions, or sensual perceptions, yet
   building and empowering them all. Take some quality and
   unhurried time to simply *be* here. Breathe the awakening of
   your spirit in the Spirit of God.

6. After some quality time in the place of spirit, conclude as in the
   other meditations, having first thanked God for any graces
   received.

Western
Contemplation

A FTER THE EXPERIENCE OF SACRED reading, vocal prayer, and meditation, we move almost effortlessly into contemplation. For most of us, this is a natural progression and happens whether we understand it or not. However, it is helpful to understand the process so that we can enter into it more fully and intentionally. As the classic Christian theology would say, "Faith leads to understanding" and "understanding leads to faith." But we must be careful to avoid contrivance once we enter into an intellectual understanding of the process. In order for contemplation to be pure, it must build on senses, emotions, and thoughts but surpass them all. Too much reliance upon understanding makes the contemplative experience a contrived and empty imitation of the real thing.

Contemplation builds on inclusion of the senses, emotions, and thoughts, a proper environment, sacred reading, and meditation, but must surpass them all by moving into pure spiritual intuition. Environment, sacred reading, and meditation use the senses, emotions, and thoughts of the body and the soul. Contemplation builds on, yet surpasses the senses, emotions, and thoughts by passing over into the intuition that can only be experienced in the reawakening of the spirit.

Energy and Essence

Contemplation can also be explained through the classical teaching on energies and essence. The body and the soul constitute the energies of the human being. The spirit is the pure essence of our being. Energies constitute the things that can be known and discerned objectively in creation, humanity, and God. Essence constitutes the deepest part of creation, humanity, and God, who can only be known by pure spiritual intuition beyond the objective or subjective knowing of the senses, emotions, or thoughts. In this, there are certain things about creation, humanity, and God that are appropriately knowable. The deeper things of contemplation, however, can only be known through what the mystics call "unknowing." It is the brightest light, so bright that it blinds the normal human capacity for sight, and must be called, with human language, "divine darkness."

For me, a cartoon I once saw of two Franciscans looking at a sunset or sunrise best describes this reality. One says to the other: "Notice his use of color here!" The Franciscans are making use of creation in a way indicative of the whole Franciscan mystical school. What is not clear in the cartoon is whether they are experiencing creation on the level of the senses, the emotions, and thoughts, or whether they have passed over into a contemplative appreciation of the sunrise or sunset to pure spiritual intuition.

It is appropriate to use the senses in perceiving the rays of the sun on the skin, or appreciating the rich and subtle colors to the eyes, as well as the very smells and tastes of the atmosphere at the time of sunrise or sunset. It is appropriate to use the mind and thoughts in appreciation of these things in themselves as part of creation, and in a way that leads through creation to the things of divinity. As Franciscans say, for those who look with faith, all creation becomes "a ladder leading to God." Through this appropriate use of the senses and of the mind and the body and the soul, the emotions and the mind can now be included and appropriately directed in a wholesome way to the things of God.

But the highest way to appreciate the sunrise or sunset is through pure spiritual intuition, or contemplation. In this way, eternity is intuited through the things of space and time. The infinite is intuited through the finite things of creation. This means using the senses, emotions, and thoughts of the body and the soul through the more primary initiation of the awakened spirit. When this happens in a substantial way, this contemplation of creation, humanity, and God occurs constantly on the intuitive level of our human being. Before this substantial contemplative awakening and rebirth occurs, however, it can happen in snatches at particular times and places.

Breakthrough

For me, this has occurred as breakthrough moments when listening to a particular piece of music, or gazing upon nature. It can also happen for me at moments in conversation with other people, when real intimacy of communication in spirit is realized in a way beyond the actual words. I remember these times vividly on an intuitive level of my being. Certain pieces of sacred and classical music have taken me to a Place where the only music that can be heard on earth is silence. Certain moments with nature in my childhood spoke to me of the reality I can only now call God. Conversations about eternal realities with believers and non-believers alike have broken through to a place of pure spirit beyond belief and doubt, where truth simply *is*. Suddenly we know that we have broken through to eternity in an instant. Nothing has changed externally, but within ourselves our spirit has been touched and awakened, and we have become present to eternity and infinity. In that instant, we become present to all time, though our body and our soul are still dwelling in a particular space in time. In that moment, we become present everywhere, though our body and soul still dwell very concretely in a particular place.

This may sound outrageous and pretentious to those who have not experienced such a breakthrough moment. But it is very much part of the mystical theology of the Christian tradition. This is true especially of the Eastern Christian tradition. The Eastern Fathers tell us that, while the body and soul are limited by space and time, the nature of the spirit is infinite. This is especially true when the spirit has been reborn and awakened to the special grace of God's Spirit. Once reborn and awakened, the spirit takes the lead in the human trinity of body, soul, and spirit, and our existence and space and time is transformed by the reality in Christ of simultaneously existing beyond space and time.

Though many people would not state it in such theological terms, the reality of this breakthrough has occurred with most human beings from all around the world. Most all of us have had these moments with nature, with art, or in human relationships. We just don't know what to call them. But there are names for the experience. The common religious experience of the mystics of the world religions call it rebirth, awakening, or liberation, just to name a few. In the Christian tradition, we often call it being "born again." Once you've had the experience, there is really no word or term that can even come close. It simply *is*.

BREATH EXERCISE 6: CONTEMPLATION

After having mastered the preceding meditations, the following is possible. Though I recommend the use of a meditation place, this meditation can be done anywhere, or at any time. I especially suggest it during times of stress in the world.

1. Sit in your meditation place and posture. Breathe deeply.
2. Allow yourself to simply be aware of the breath. Your breath and God's breath merge as one, without losing the beauty of

either. Breath means "spirit," our spirit and God's Spirit. Simply breathe and be aware of this union.

3. If during formal meditation, simply *be* in this place of pure contemplative union with God for the remainder of the period. Do not rush. Do not hurry. This is the spiritual gold you have been digging and preparing for in the previous meditations.

4. This can also be done briefly out in the world during times of stress or tension, to bring us back to peace and centering in God. In this case, I recommend three to ten deep breaths, then going on about our business. If you have time for a short break, take it, and simply breathe. While a place of solitude and silence is optimum, it can also be done in the midst of the crowd.

5. Conclude as before.

St. Bonaventure

Bonaventure says, "If you wish to know how such things come about, consult grace, not doctrine; desire, not understanding; prayerful groaning, not studious reading; the spouse, not the teacher; God, not man; darkness, not clarity. Consult not light but the fire that completely inflames the mind and carries it over to God and transports a fervor and blaze of love. This fire is God. . . . Christ starts the flame with the fire and heat of his intense suffering. . . . Whoever loves this death may see God, for this is beyond doubt true: 'No man sees me and still lives' [Exodus 33:20]. Let us die, then, and pass over into the darkness."

He then continues to describe the logic of divine darkness when he says, "When we face the very light of highest being, not realizing that the supreme darkness is actually the light of our mind, we think we are not seeing anything. The same thing happens when our eyes gaze upon pure light: We think that we are not seeing anything."

Bonaventure says that such mystery is found in the actual being of God: "It is the very first and the very last, it is the origin and final

73

end of all things. Because it is eternal and all-present, surrounding and penetrating all duration, it is, as it were, both their center and their circumference. Because it is utterly simple and utterly great, it is wholly interior to all things and wholly exterior to them. It is an intelligible sphere, the center of which is everywhere, and the circumference nowhere." Because it is supremely actual and immutable, "while remaining unmoved, it imparts motion to all. Because it is wholly perfect and wholly immeasurable, it is interior to all things, yet not enclosed; exterior to all things, and yet not excluded above all things. Above all things, yet not aloof; below all things, yet not their servant . . . even though all things are many and pure beings but one, it is 'all in all'" (1 Cor. 15:28).

And yet, Bonaventure does not limit this language only to the pure being of God in transcendence. He also includes the mysteries and the paradoxes of the incarnation as bringing us to that same great mystical height. He says, "In him the first principal is united with the last to be created: God is united with man, formed on the sixth day; eternity is united with time-bound humanity, with a man born of a Virgin in the fullness of ages; utter simplicity is united with the most composite, pure action with supreme passion and death, absolute perfection and immensity with lowliness, the supremely One and all-inclusive with an individual composite man, distinct from every other; the man Jesus Christ. . . . This consideration brings about perfect enlightening of the mind, when the mind beholds man made, as on the sixth day, in the image of God. Since, therefore, an image is an expressed likeness, when our mind contemplates, in Christ the son of God, our own humanity so wonderful exalted and so ineffably present in him; and when we thus behold in one and the same being both the first and the last, the highest and the lowest, the circumference and the center, the alpha and the omega, the caused and the cause, the creator and the creature . . . then our mind reaches a perfect object. Here, as on the sixth day, it reaches with God the perfection of enlightenment."

This sublime apophatic language (stating a positive reality through negative language due to the inability to state the positive through words) reaches a summit in the West, with some of the great mystics such as the author of *The Cloud of Unknowing,* or in the language of opposites and unknowing in St. John of the Cross, or in the language of complete poverty and emptiness in Meister Eckert's Sermon 52. Let us take a look at some excerpts from these marvelous sources.

St. John of the Cross

In *The Ascent of Mount Carmel,* St. John of the Cross says, "The first endeavor is to be inclined always not to the easiest, but to the most difficult; not to the most delightful, but to the harshest; not to the most gratifying, but to the less than pleasant; not to what means rest for you, but to hard work; not to the consoling, but to the unconsoling; not to the most, but to the least; not to the highest and most precious, but to the lowest and most despised; not to wanting something, but to wanting nothing; do not go about looking for the best of temporal things, but for the worst, and desire to enter for Christ into complete nudity, emptiness, and poverty, in everything in the world. . . . To reach satisfaction in all, desire possession in nothing, to come to possess all, desire the possession of nothing, to arrive at being all, desire to be nothing, to come to the knowledge of all, desire the knowledge of nothing, to come to the pleasure you have not, you must go by a way in which you enjoy not, to come to the knowledge you have not, you must go by a way in which you know not, to come to the possession you have not, you must go by a way in which you possess not, to come to be what you are not, you must go by a way in which you are not, when you turn toward something you cease to cast yourself upon the all, for to go from all to the All, you must deny yourself of all, in all, and when you come to the possession of the All, you must possess it without wanting anything, because if you desire to have something in all, your treasure in God is not purely in all. In this nakedness the spirit finds its quietude in rest, for in coveting nothing, nothing raises it up, and nothing weighs it down. Because it is in the center of its humility."

Meister Eckert

Meister Eckert says in his famous Sermon 52, in language that is not entirely precise, and perhaps overly intense, but nonetheless recognized as speaking a deep and mystical truth in apophatic theological reality, that "a poor man wants nothing, and knows nothing, and has nothing. . . . If you do not understand, do not burden yourself with it, for the truth I want to expound is such that there will be a few good people to understand it."

Wanting Nothing

"First, let us discuss a poor man as one who wants nothing. . . . Some people . . . do not understand this well; they are those that are attached to their own penances and external exercises. . . . Such people present an outward picture that gives them the name of saints, but inside they are donkeys, for they cannot distinguish divine truth. These people say that a man is poor who wants nothing; but they interpret in this way: that a man ought to live so that he never fulfills his own will in anything, but that he ought to comport himself so that he may fulfill God's merest will. Such people are in the right, for their intention is good . . . but I speak in the divine truth when I say that they are not poor men. . . . So long as a man has this as his will, that he wants to fulfill God's dearest will, he is not the poverty about which we want to talk. . . . He ought to be as free of his own created will as he was when he did not exist. . . . In my first cause, I then had no 'God' . . . I wanted nothing, I longed for nothing, for I was empty being, and the only truth in which I rejoiced was the knowledge of myself. . . . What I wanted, I was, and what I was, I wanted; so I stood, empty of God and of everything. . . . Before there were any creatures, God was not 'God,' but he was what he was. . . . Therefore, let us pray to God that we might be free of 'God' . . . rejoice in that everlasting truth in which the highest angel and the fly and the soul are equal. I wanted what I was and I was what I wanted, so I say: If a man is to come poor in his will, he must want and desire as little as he wanted and desired when he did not exist. And in this way a man is poor who wants nothing."

Knowing Nothing

"Next, a man is poor who knows nothing . . . lives as if he does not even know that he is not in any way living for himself, or for the truth or for God. Rather, he should be so free of all knowing that he does not know, experience, or grasp that God lives in him, for when man was established in God's everlasting being, there was no different life in him. . . . Now the actions proper to a man are loving and knowing. The question is: In which of these does blessedness most consist? Some authorities have said . . . in knowing; others say that it consists in loving; others that it consists in knowing and loving, and what they say is better, for they say that it does not consist in either knowing or loving, but that there is in the soul that from which knowing and loving flow; that something does not know or love as do the powers of the soul . . . that something has neither before or after, and it is not waiting for anything that is to come, for it can neither gain nor lose. So it is deprived of the knowledge that God is acting in it, but it is itself the very thing that rejoices in itself as God does himself. . . . Man ought to be established, free, and empty, not knowing or perceiving that God is acting in him; and so a man may posses poverty. The authorities say that God is a being, and a rational one, and that he knows all things. I say that God is neither being nor rational, and that he knows that he does not know this or that (particular things). Therefore God is free of all things and therefore he is all things. Whoever would be poor in spirit, he must be poor of all his own knowledge, so that he knows nothing, not God or created things or himself. Therefore, it is necessary for a man to long not to be able to long nor to perceive God's works. In this way, a man can be poor of his own knowledge."

Having Nothing

"Third, a man is poor who has nothing. Many people have said that it is perfection when one possesses no material earthly things, and in one sense this is indeed true, if a man does this voluntarily, but this is not the sense in which I mean it. I have just now said that a man is poor who does not want to fulfill God's will but who lives so that he may be free both of his own will and of God's will as he was when he was not about this poverty. I say that it is highest poverty. Second, I said that a man is poor who knows nothing of God's words in him . . . and this is the purest poverty. But a third form is the most intimate poverty . . . this is when a man has nothing.

"Great authorities say that a man should be so free of all things and of all works, both interior and exterior, that he might become a place only for God, in which God could work. I say otherwise . . . I say that so long as he is a man, he is not poor with the most intimate poverty, for it is not God's intention in his works that man should have in himself a place for God to work. . . . If God wishes to work in a soul, he himself is the place in which he wants to work. . . . God is his own worker in himself. Thus in this poverty man pursues that everlasting being which he was and which he is now, and which he will evermore remain."

God Beyond God

"When a man clings to place, he clings to distinction, therefore, I pray to God that he may make me free of 'God,' when my real being is above God, if we take 'God' to be the beginning of created things. . . . God is above being and above distinction. . . . What I am in the order of having been born, that will die and perish, for it is mortal.

"A great authority says that his breaking through is no blur, and that his flowing out . . . when I flowed out from God, all things said: 'God is' . . . but in the breaking through, when I come to be free of will of myself and of God's will and of all his works and of God himself, then I am above all created things, and I am neither God nor creature, but I am what I was and what I shall remain, now and eternally. . . . I received an impulse that would bring me up above all the angels. . . . I received such riches that God, as he is 'God,' . . . cannot suffice me; for in this breaking through I perceive that God and I are one, then I am what I was, and then I neither diminish nor increase, for I am then an immovable cause that moves all things . . . man? . . . what he has been eternally. . . . Here God is one with the spirit, and that is the most intimate poverty one can find.

"Whoever does not understand what I have said, let him not burden his heart with it; for as long as a man is not equal to this truth, he will not understand these words, for this is a truth beyond speculation that has come immediately from the heart of God. May God help us to live that we might find it eternally. Amen."

Most commentators feel that Eckert uses an imprecise language in his sermon that, in fact, goes beyond his intent. However, in its intuitive sense, it speaks a great apophatic and contemplative reality in and through the person of Jesus Christ, which is knowable and unknowable, personal and impersonal, in the very being of God. This is the closest thing in Christian Western language to even closely resemble the Buddhist language of, "If you see the Buddha, kill him." Needless to say, neither Christian nor Buddhist language implies that the historical Siddhartha Gautama, the Buddha, or the person of Jesus Christ is not important. It simply means that at a certain point of knowing, that intellectual speculation becomes actually counterproductive, and a hindrance to the great breaking through of spirit-to-Spirit: intuition. This is especially true from our Christian worldview of God, in which the personal is not just a temporary anthropomorphic device so that we can better relate to the divine, but is, in fact, an eternal reality concerning the person of God, but in a way that also accommodates that which is beyond language of personhood or knowability, that within the being of God that is entirely transcendent.

The Cloud of Unknowing

Perhaps the most balanced and yet developed expression of this apophatic way is found in the anonymous work *The Cloud of Unknowing,* from approximately the fourteenth century in the West. It was produced within the school of the English mystics, and there is much speculation as to exactly who may actually have authored it. More than likely, the writer was a monk, and a director of souls. The work represents an apophatic (or negative) mystical theology at its best, but it is also cataphatic (or positive and affirmative) in that the mystery spoken of in the cloud never ventures from the primacy of love, and specifically a love relationship with a loving God.

The Power of Love

The author says, "All rational creatures, angels and men alike, have in them . . . a knowing power, and . . . a loving power . . . God is always incomprehensible to the first, the knowing power, but to the second, which is the loving power, he is entirely comprehensible. . . . This is the everlasting wonderful miracle of love. Whoever . . . may think that he can . . . achieve it by intellectual labor . . . does violence to his imagination. . . . Such a man . . . is perilously deluded . . . I tell you truly, this exercise cannot be achieved by their labor. . . . When I say 'darkness,' I mean a privation of knowing. . . . For this reason, that which is between you and your God is termed . . . a cloud of unknowing.

"If ever you come to this cloud and live and work in it . . . just as this cloud of unknowing is above you, between you and your God, in the same way you must put beneath you a cloud of forgetting, between you and all creatures that have ever been made . . . I make no exceptions, whether they are bodily creatures or spiritual . . . I say that all should be hid under the cloud of forgetting.

"For though it is very profitable on some occasions to think . . . of certain creatures in particular, nevertheless in this exercise it profits little or nothing. . . . Insofar as there is anything in your mind except God alone, in that far you are further from God.

"In this exercise it is of little or no profit to think of the kindness or worthiness of God, or of Our Lady or the saints or angels in heaven, or even the joys of heaven . . . for though it is good to think of the kindness of God and to love him and to praise him for that, yet it is far better to think upon his simple being and to love him and praise him for himself.

"It is my wish to leave everything that I can think of and choose for my love, and choose for my love the thing I cannot think, because he can certainly be loved but not thought. He can be taken and held by love, but not by thought. Therefore, though it is good at times to think of the kindness and worthiness of God in particular, and though this a light and a part of contemplation, nevertheless, in this exercise, it must be cast down and covered over with a cloud of forgetting. . . . You are to smite upon that thick cloud of unknowing, with a sharp dart of longing love. Do not leave that work for anything that may happen."

Dealing With Distractions

The author then continues with the subject of dealing with distractions, in a way that does not pour fuel on the fire of those same distractions. "If any thought should rise and continue to press in, and if the thought should ask you who God is, you must answer that it is the God who made you and ransomed you and with his grace, has called you to his love, and say: 'You have no part to play.' So say to the thought: 'Go down again.' Tread it down quickly with an impulse of love, even though it seems to you to be very holy; even though it seems that it could help you to seek him. Perhaps the thought will bring to your mind a variety of excellent and wonderful instances of his kindness; it will say that he is most sweet and most loving, gracious, and merciful. The thought will want nothing better than that you should listen to it; for in the end, it will increase its chattering more and more until it brings you lower down to the recollection of his passion. There will it let you see the wonderful kindness of God; it looks for nothing better than that you should listen to it, for soon after that he will let you see your former wretched state of life; and perhaps as you see and think upon it, the thought will bring to your mind some place in which you used to live and soon at the end, before you are even aware of it, your concentration is gone, scattered about you know not where. The cause of this dissipation is that at the beginning you deliberately listened to the thought, answered it, took it to yourself, and let it continue unheeded.

"Yet what it said was nonetheless both good and holy. . . . Men and women who are long practiced in these meditations must leave them aside . . . under the cloud of forgetting, if they are ever to pierce the cloud of unknowing between them and their God. Therefore when you set yourself to this exercise . . . have no other thought of God; and not even of any of these thoughts unless it should please you, for a simple reaching out directly towards God is sufficient."

The Prayer Word

The writer then speaks of a simple prayer word, not unlike the mantras of the East. He suggests some word to, at least, minimally occupy the mind so as not to be led astray. He says, "If you like, you can have this reaching out wrapped up and enfolded in a single word so as to have a better grasp of it. Just take a little word, of one syllable rather than two; for the shorter it is the better in agreement with this exercise. . . . Such a one is the word 'God' or the word 'love.' Use which one you prefer . . . fasten this word to your heart, so that whatever happens, it will never go away. This word is to be your shield and your spear. . . . With this word you are to beat upon this cloud and this darkness above you. With this word you are to strike down every kind of thought under the cloud of forgetting; so that if any other thought should press upon you and ask you what you would have, answer it with no other word but with this one. . . . If you will hold fast to this purpose, you may be sure that the thought will not stay for very long."

Beyond All Good or Evil Thought

The author then speaks of laying aside all thought, whether good or evil, in the time of contemplation. This is in the ancient apophatic tradition of Evagrius Ponticus, and is often a confusing point to those who reach this place of contemplation for the first time.

"But now you will ask, what is this thought that presses upon me . . . and is it good or evil. If it is an evil thing, you say, then I am very much surprised, because it serves so well to increase man's devotion; and at times I believe that it is a great comfort to listen to what it has to say, for I believe that sometimes it can make me weep very bitterly out of compassion for Christ in his passion, and sometimes for my own wretched state, and for many others reasons. All these, it seems to me, are very holy and do me much good, and therefore I believe that these thoughts can in no way be evil; and if it is good, and their sweet consolations do me so much good, then I am very surprised why you bid me to put them down in the cloud of forgetting!

"I say that it must out of necessity be always good in its nature, because it is a way of God's likeness, but the use of it can be both good and evil. . . . The use of it is evil when it is swollen with pride . . . which comes from the subtle speculation and learning such as theologians have, which makes them want to be known, not as humble clerics and masters of divinity or of devotion, but proud scholars of the devil and masters of vanity and falsehood."

The Active and the Contemplative Life

The writer of *The Cloud* then goes on to mention both the active and the contemplative lives, and the two stages of each, and implies that the positive use of thoughts and images is appropriate for the active life and the first stage of the contemplative life, but at that higher stage, he says, "A man cannot come to the higher part of contemplative life unless he leaves full time the lower part. . . . It would be very inappropriate and a great hindrance to a man who ought to be working in the darkness and this cloud of unknowing . . . to permit any thought or any meditation on God's wonderful gifts, kindness, or his work in any of His creatures, bodily or spiritual, to rise up in his mind.

"I bid you put down any such clear and insinuating thought, and cover it up with a thick cloud of forgetting, no matter how holy it might be . . . because it is love alone that can reach God in this life, and not knowing.

"The intense activity . . . of your understanding . . . when you set your souls to this dark contemplation must always be put down. For if you do not put it down, it will put you down."

Mental Pictures and Reality

He then goes on to describe that the mind thinks in pictures, and that if you have a picture of God, you are, by its nature, picturing something below God, so in this sense, like Meister Eckert, he says that you must kill this picture of God to find God. He says, "If you take a close look, you will find that your mind is occupied, not with this darkness, but with a clear picture of something beneath God. . . . Put down such clear pictures, no matter how holy or how pleasant they may be. . . . No man shall ever have such a clear sight here in this life; but the feeling—what a man can have through grace . . . so lift up your love to the cloud . . . draw your love up to the cloud . . . forget every other thing.

"A simple awareness of anything under God . . . puts you further away from God than you would be if it did not exist. It hinders you and makes you less able. . . . If the consciousness of any particular saint or pure spiritual thing hinders you . . . the consciousness of any living person . . . any corporal or worldly thing will hinder you. . . . In spite of goodness and holiness, in this exercise it is more of a hindrance than a help, I mean during the time of the exercise."

Conclusion

As we shall see in the Christian apophatic East, this kind of spirituality is attested to most directly as early as the fourth century with Evagrius the Solitary, or Ponticus, and continues in a long line up until the present time. It is also clearly evident in the more monistic and impersonal religions of the Far East. However, it is also very evident in the Christian West in the theology that is most balanced and developed within the context of a personal love relationship with Jesus Christ. In this, we are arm-in-arm with our Eastern Christian brothers and sisters and close indeed to the psychological and spiritual experiences of the monks of Far Eastern religions, though from a different perspective and understanding of God, the Savior, and the cosmic worldview.

Conclusion

THE CLASSICAL FORMS OF THE PROGRES-
sion to contemplative prayer in the West are sa-
cred reading, vocal prayer, meditation, and contemplation, or simply
sacred reading, meditation, and contemplation. Later we have purgation, illumination, and union. Two analogies from my previous
books, *The Lover and the Beloved* and *The Fire of God,* are helpful: of
the dialogue in *The Lover and the Beloved,* and the building of kindling in *The Fire of God,* represent the first stage of sacred reading
and purgation. Meditation and illumination are represented both by
the roaring fire and by the consummation of the love union. Contemplation and union are represented in the hotbed of coals, and the
afterglow, between the Lover and the Beloved. Lastly, the most important role of all this, in this world, namely evangelization, is represented by the fact that the hotbed of coals exists in order to warm the
cold house in the darkest hours of night, and the impregnated bridge
of Christ is meant to grow fat, to give birth in the fruit of the experience, and to give birth to many children within the Church, who
will, in turn, evangelize all the world and bring it to Christ.

Out of the classical ways in the Christian West, the way of sacred
reading, or *lectio divina,* meditation, or *meditatio,* and contempla-

tion, or *contemplatio,* precede purgation, illumination, and union. They were developed out of the monasticism of the Christian West. In the twelfth century, the *Ladder of Monks,* subtitled a *Letter on the Contemplative Life,* speaks simply on this development in the tradition of St. Augustine, St. Bernard of Clairvaux, and later of St. Bonaventure.

The Ladder of Monks:
Reading, Meditation, Prayer, and Contemplation

Guigo the Second divides the ladder into four rungs, namely, reading, meditation, prayer, and contemplation. He says, "Reading is the careful study of the scriptures, concentrating all one's powers on it. Meditation is the busy application of the mind to seek with the help of one's own reason, for knowledge of hidden truth. Prayer is the heart's devoted turning to God to draw away evil and obtain what is good. Contemplation is when the mind is lifted up to God, and held above itself. . . . Reading seeks for the sweetness of a blessed life, meditation perceives it, prayer asks for it, contemplation tastes it. Reading, as it were, puts food whole into the mouth, meditation chews it and breaks it up, prayer extracts its flavor, contemplation is the sweetness itself, which gladdens and refreshes. Reading works on the outside, meditation on the pith: prayer asks for what we long for, contemplation gives us delight in the sweetness we have found.

"These degrees are joined to each other, one precedes another, not only in the order of time, but in causality. Reading comes first, and is, as it were, the foundation; it provides the subject matter we use in meditation. Meditation considers more carefully what is to be sought after; it digs, as it were, for treasure which it finds, and reveals, since it is not in meditation's power to seize upon the treasure, it directs us to prayer. Prayer lifts itself up to God with all its strength, it digs for the treasure it longs for, which is the sweetness of contemplation. Contemplation, when it comes, rewards the labors of the other three. . . . Reading is an exercise of the outward senses; meditation is concerned with the inward understanding; prayer is concerned with desire; contemplation outstrips every faculty.

"The first degree is proper to beginners, the second to the proficient, the third to devotees, the fourth to the blessed. . . . Reading without meditation is sterile, meditation without reading is liable to error, prayer without meditation is lukewarm, meditation without prayer is unfruitful. Prayer, when it is fervent, wins contemplation, but to obtain it without prayer would be rare, even miraculous. . . . There are commonly four obstacles to these three degrees: unavoidable necessity, the good works of the active life, human frailty, worldly follies. The first can be excused, the second endured, the third invites compassion, the fourth, blame. Blame truly, for it would be better for the man who for love of the world turns his back on the goal, if he had never known God's grace, rather than, having known it, to retrace his steps. . . . Will not the Lord justly say to him: 'What more should I have done for you that I have not done? . . . I created you . . . I redeemed you . . . I called you away . . . I let you find favor in my sight, I wanted to make my dwelling with you . . . It was not my words alone that you repudiated, it was my own self' . . . Never let this happen to us, Lord, and even if we do so fall away from him in frailty, never let us despair on that account, but let us hasten back to the merciful healer who lifts up the helpless ones out of the dust, and rescues the poor and wretched from the mire, for he who never desires the death of the sinner will tend us and heal us again and again."

William of St. Thierry: Animal, Rational, and Spiritual

In the eleventh century, St. William of St. Thierry wrote to the Carthusian community of Mont Dieu, or the Mount of God, in his Golden Epistle, summarizing many of the early Christian monastic teachings of the West. Firstly, he divides the human being into the animal man, the rational man, and the spiritual man or, as it were, body, soul, and spirit. He says: "There are the animals who of themselves are not governed by reason, nor led by affection. Yet stimulated by authority or inspired by teaching, or animated by good example, they acquiesce in the good where they find it, and like blind men, led by the hand, they follow, that is, imitate others. Then there are the rational, whom the judgment of their reason, the discernment that comes of natural learning endow with knowledge of the good and the desire for it, but as yet they are without love. There are also the perfect, who are led by the spirit, and are more abundantly enlightened by the Holy Spirit; because they relish the good, which draws them on, they are called wise. They are also called spiritual because the Holy Spirit draws them when as of old he dwelt in Gideon.

"The first state is concerned with the body, the second with the soul, and the third finds rest only in God. The beginning of good in the animal way of life is perfect obedience; progress for it is to gain control of the body and bring it into subjection, perfection for it is when the habitual exercise of virtue has become a pleasure. The beginning of the rational state is to understand what is set before it by the teaching of the faith; progress is a life lived in accordance with that teaching. Perfection is when judgment of the reason passes into the spiritual affection. The perfection of the rational state is the beginning of the spiritual state; progress in it is to look upon God's glory with face uncovered; its perfection is to be transformed into the same likeness, borrowing glory from that glory, enabled by the Spirit of the Lord."

From here he speaks of the things of the animal man concerning imagination, temptations, and fantastic thoughts, mortification of the weaker impulses, how to deal with boredom, and the absolute need to be directed by obedience, which leads us to bodily sacrifice and bodily training, helps us avoid temptation and idleness, and to grow in the work of the hermit under a spiritual father. He then goes on to speak at length about the rational man and the use of thoughts and will, and the spiritual man and the anointing of the Holy Spirit who transforms one's thoughts, will, and bodily activities.

Between his treatment on the animal man and the rational man, he takes an aside and treats some of the issues proper to the Carthusian eremitical life in the West, namely advice to novices, and another chapter on vocations, poverty, and self support, describing many of the more nuts-and-bolts daily realities of socio-eremitical (solitary, yet in community) life in the Christian monastic West of the eleventh century. Then he devotes a chapter to prayer, in which he speaks of reading, meditation, and prayer. He says: "Now the love of God and man, nourished with the food of meditation, is strengthened and enlightened by prayer. The best and safest reading matter and subject for meditation for the animal man newly come to Christ to training in the interior life is the outward actions of our Redeemer . . . an example of humility, a stimulant to charity, and to sentiments of piety. Likewise, from the sacred scriptures and the writings of the holy Fathers, it is those parts which deal with morality and are easier to understand which should be put before them. He should also be given the lives of the saints and the accounts of their martyrdoms. He should not trouble himself with historical details, but always find something to stir his novice mind to love God, and despise himself. The reading of other narratives gives pleasure but does not edify; rather they distract the mind, and at the time of prayer and meditation, cause all manner of useless or harmful thoughts to surge up from the memory. . . . The reading of difficult works tires the unpracticed mind instead of refreshing it. . . . The novice should also . . . pray spiritually, to keep as far away as he can from material objects or their representations when he thinks of God. . . . Yet it is better and safer, as it has already been said, to put before such a man when he is praying or meditating a representation of the Lord's humanity—of his birth, passion, and resurrection—so that the weak spirit, which is only able to think of material objects and their properties, has something to which it can apply itself and cling to with devout attention."

William then spends a considerable time explaining how the rational power of thought and the affections of the will are stirred up in meditation based upon sacred reading, and then passes into the realm of contemplation. He ends by saying of this contemplative state, "So man begins to know himself perfectly, advances through self knowledge, and ascends to the knowledge of God. . . . He must not think of them otherwise than they are in reality. Therefore when the spirit thinks of its likeness to God, let it first mold its thoughts as wholly to avoid conceiving of itself in terms of a body where God is concerned. Not only must it avoid thinking of him as a body, as if he were in a place, but also as if he could be represented as a spirit and so changeable. For spiritual things are as different from corporal things, both in quality and in nature, as they are remote from all confinement to place. The divine nature, however, transcends both corporal and spiritual things to the same extent that it is free from all restrictions of time and place, and knows nothing of change, remaining changeless and eternal in the beatitude of its own unchangeableness and eternity. . . . What he is in himself, his essence, can only be grasped by thought at all insofar as the perception of enlightened love reaches out to it. . . . Its ineffable reality . . . cannot be seen or apprehended by any means of bodily likeness in sleep, any bodily form in waking hours, any investigation of the mind, but only by humble love from a clean heart.

"For this is the face of God which no one can see and live in the world. This is the beauty for the contemplation of which everyone sighs who would love the Lord his God with his whole heart and his whole soul and his whole mind and his whole strength. Neither does he cease to arouse his neighbor to the same as he loves him as himself."

So we can see that along with a notion of the human being as body, soul, and spirit, or animal, rational, and spiritual man, there is also an understanding of spiritual reading, meditation, and contemplation. This, of course, led many to begin classifying in a new form, namely that of purgation, illumination, and union, which reached its peak and pinnacle, especially with the Spanish mystics of the sixteenth century, and during the era of the Counter Reformation with

the Carmelite Teresean reform and others. This development, however, surfaces as early as St. Bonaventure, the great Franciscan
Seraphic Doctor of the thirteenth and fourteenth centuries.

St Bonaventure: Purgative, Illuminative, and Unitive Ways

Bonaventure says in his *Journey of the Mind to God,* "All scriptures are
about . . . the mystical hierachization of the Church, for they teach
the way of nature, of purgation, illumination, and perfective union,
according to the triple law they express: of nature, of scripture itself,
and of grace, or rather, according to their three main parts: the Mo-
saic law, which cleanses, the prophetical revelation, which enlightens, and the evangelical teaching, which perfects or, better still,
according to their threefold mystical meaning: the tropological,
which cleanses in preparation for a virtuous life, the allegorical,
which enlightens in preparation for clear understanding, and the
anagogical, which perfects through transport of the spirit and the
delightful perception of wisdom; all this, through the said three
theological virtues, the reformed senses, the three levels of elevation
described above, and the hierarchizing of our mind, by which it re-
enters its own inner world, there to see God."

Of course Bonaventure begins this mystical journey of the mind
to God by saying, with St. William of St. Thierry, "It represents the
triple existence of things, that is existence in physical reality, in the
mind, and in the eternal art, according to what is written, let it be;
God made it; and it was. It also represents our presence in Christ, our
ladder, of a triple substance: bodily, rational, and divine. Corresponding to this triple movement, our mind has three powers of perception . . . animal, or sensorial . . . spiritual . . . and supernatural."
He then goes on to speak of the journey of the mind to God through
creation, and in creation to the Creator—from things able to be
sensed and felt with the body and conceptualized with the mind, to
things that can only be intuited with the spirit.

In his work *The Triple Way,* or *Love Enkindled,* Bonaventure speaks further of the purgative, illuminative, and unitive ways. He says, "Now, this threefold interpretation corresponds to a threefold hierarchical action: purgation, illumination, and perfective union. Purgation leads to peace, illumination to truth, and perfective union to love. As soon as the soul has mastered three, it becomes holy. . . . Upon the proper understanding of these three states are founded both the understanding of all scriptures and the right to eternal life.

"Know also that there are three approaches to this triple way: reading with meditation; prayer; and contemplation." He then goes on in chapter 1 to equate meditative reading with the purgative way through illumination of the mind, and affections with the illuminative way, and finally entering into a wisdom beyond all knowledge or emotion in the unitive way. He says finally, "Third, we must raise it aloft, above anything perceptible, imaginable, or conceivable. . . . This beloved cannot be perceived through the senses, since he is neither seen, nor heard, smelled, tasted, or touched: thus, he is not perceptible; yet he is all delight (Song of Songs 5:16). Next, we realize that he cannot be seen through the imagination, since he has no shape, figure, quantity, limitation, or commutability: thus, he is unimaginable; yet he is all delight. Finally, we realize that he cannot be conceived through the intellect, since he is beyond demonstration, definition, opinion, estimation, or investigation: thus, he is inconceivable; yet he is all delight.

"All this makes it clear that meditation about the purgative, illuminative and perfective ways results in attaining the wisdom of holy scriptures. We should be concerned with this triple way, whether we meditate on the scriptures or any other subject. He who is wise will meditate only upon these things."

All of this takes us through the journey from the way of affirmation to the way of negation, from the way that is cataphatic to the way that it is apophatic. St. Bonaventure says there is a way of "the elevation of the mind in the affirmative manner, but there is another, the higher, approach: that is, by manner of negation as Denis says,

'(When applied to God), affirmations are inadequate, while negations are wholly true. Negations seem to say less, but actually they
say more. This manner of elevation consists in using nothing but
negative predications, and that in a way which is orderly, proceeding
from the lowest to the highest, but which also expresses transcendence. For instance, we say: God is not perceptible through the
senses, but is above the senses; nor is he imaginable, intelligible,
manifest, but he is above all these concepts. Then the vision of truth,
having experienced the night of the intellect, rises higher and pene-
trates deeper, because it exceeds the intellect itself as well as every created being. This is the most noble manner of elevation to be perfect.
However, it postulates the affirmative manner, as perfection supposes
illumination, and as negation supposes affirmation: the more intimate the ascending force, the more powerful the elevation; the
deeper the love, the more fruitful the rising. It is beneficial therefore
to practice this manner. Note that on the first level, truth is to be in-
voked by sighs and prayer . . . received by study and reading . . .
communicating by example and preaching. . . . On the second level,
truth is to be sought by recourse and dedication to it . . . grasped by
activity and endeavor . . . and assimilated by sighs of content and
mortification. On the third level, truth is to be adored by sacrifice
and praise . . . admired in ecstasy and contemplation. . . . It is to be
embraced with caresses and love. . . . Note these things carefully for
they hold the fountain of life."

These monastic writings of the Christian West use a system similar to, yet distinct from, the Christian monastic East, using different
language to express the same reality. Both rise to the mystical heights
of the cataphatic and the apophatic experience—of the way of affirmation and the way of negation—of that which can be sensed, felt,
and known, and that which is above all thought, feeling, or sensation
in pure spiritual intuition. Both speak clearly of a highly developed
monastic way, a school of the Lord's service, in which each individual is purified, illuminated and unified in the fire and the love of this
mystical way. Both the East and the West speak of all the mysteries

attained both psychologically and spiritually by the non-Christian monastic of the Far East in the mysticism of Hinduism, Buddhism, and Taoism, to name only three, but in a way that maintains the complete centrality and integrity of a faith in the triune God built on the reality of personal love relationships with and in Jesus Christ, who is the Way, the Truth, and the Life, the door to the sheepfold and to full and abundant life, the truth that sets us fully free.

Later Developments

After these earlier expressions of the mystical, or contemplative life, came the more precise writers of the seventeenth century onwards. St. Teresa of Avila and St. John of the Cross became the foundation stones of the later development of the Christian West. But there was also St. Ignatius of Loyola's *Spiritual Exercises,* and St. Francis De Sales' *The Devout Life,* just to name two of the most popular approaches. In our time, Teilhard de Chardin broke yet new ground with his Cosmic Christ, and a revolutionary marriage between science and mysticism. Catholic textbooks, such as Tanqueray's *Spiritual Directory,* and even Jordan Aumann's more modern *Spiritual Theology,* present these developments in a more or less systematic way.

Aumann uses nine categories of the mystical stages based roughly on the classification of St. Teresa of Avila. They are:

VOCAL PRAYER: attention to what one is saying or reading, and to God, whom one is addressing.

DISCURSIVE MEDITATION: consideration of a spiritual truth, application to oneself, and resolve to do something about it.

AFFECTIVE MENTAL PRAYER: one turns to the "Other," namely, God, and prayer becomes "the language of love."

ACQUIRED RECOLLECTION: also called prayer of simplicity, prayer of simple regard, acquired contemplation, the loving awareness of God.

INFUSED RECOLLECTION: the first degree of infused, mystical contemplation.

PRAYER OF QUIET: the will is totally captivated by divine love; sometimes all the faculties are likewise captivated (sleep or ecstasy).

PRAYER OF SIMPLE UNION: both the intellect and the will are absorbed in God.

PRAYER OF ECSTATIC UNION: this is the "mystical espousal" or "conforming union."

PRAYER OF TRANSFORMING UNION: also called the "mystical marriage" because it is the most intimate union of the soul with God that is possible in this life.

New Expressions

Integrations with both the Christian East and the Far East have culminated in some new and interesting forms in the Christian West. In particular, Centering Prayer, as developed by Abbots Thomas Keating of Snowmass, Colorado, and Basil Pennington of Conyers, Georgia, and the World Community for Christian Meditation with John Main, OSB, and Laurence Freeman, OSB, have done much to spread the use of contemplation in the West through breath prayer and meditation. Both of these approaches use seated meditation adapted to the West, the focusing on the breath as in the Christian East and the non-Christian Far East, and the use of the "prayer word," similar to a mantra in the Far East, as spoken of in *The Cloud of Unknowing* cited above.

These two new expressions both have excellent websites with extensive information. The following excerpts can be found on their sites. I include them here because I believe they are most helpful in popularizing Christian and non-Christian techniques in a way that is compatible with the teaching of the Roman Catholic Church.

The Contemplative Outreach

The World Community for Christian Meditation website lists the following description of how to meditate:

> *Find a quiet place. Sit down with your back upright. Sit still. Gently close your eyes and begin to recite your prayer-word, or mantra, silently, interiorly, and lovingly throughout the time of your meditation: "Ma-ra-na-tha." Say it as four equally stressed syllables. It is an Aramaic word (which is the language that Jesus spoke) and it means, "Come, Lord." It is found in the scriptures and is one of the earliest prayers in the Christian tradition. Do not think about the meaning of the word. Just give your attention to the sound of it throughout the time of your meditation, from the beginning to the end. Whenever distractions arise, simply return to your mantra. Meditate for thirty minutes each morning and each evening, every day of your life. Father John always said: "Just say your word." Meditation is a way of pure prayer marked by silence, stillness, and simplicity.*

Centering Prayer

The official information on Centering Prayer as found on their website is as follows. Its description of the technique is a bit more expansive:

THEOLOGICAL BACKGROUND

> *The grace of Pentecost affirms that the risen Jesus is among us as the glorified Christ. Christ lives in each of us as the enlightened one, present everywhere and at all times. He is the living master who continuously sends the Holy Spirit to dwell within us and to bear witness to his resurrection by empowering us to experience and manifest the fruits of the Spirit and the Beatitudes both in prayer and action.*

LECTIO DIVINA

Lectio divina *is the most traditional way of cultivating friendship with Christ. It is a way of listening to the texts of scripture as if we were in conversation with Christ and he was suggesting the topics of conversation. The daily encounter with Christ and reflection on his word leads beyond mere acquaintanceship to an attitude of friendship, trust, and love. Conversation simplifies and gives way to communing, or as Gregory the Great (6th century), summarizing the Christian contemplative tradition, put it, "resting in God." This was the classical meaning of contemplative prayer for the first sixteen centuries.*

CONTEMPLATIVE PRAYER

Contemplative Prayer is the normal development of the grace of baptism and the regular practice of lectio divina. *We may think of prayer as thoughts or feelings expressed in words. But this is only one expression. Contemplative Prayer is the opening of mind and heart—our whole being—to God, the Ultimate Mystery, beyond thoughts, words, and emotions. We open our awareness to God, whom we know by faith is within us, closer than breathing, closer than thinking, closer than choosing—closer than consciousness itself. Contemplative Prayer is a process of interior purification, leading, if we consent, to divine union.*

THE METHOD OF CENTERING PRAYER

Centering Prayer is a method designed to facilitate the development of contemplative prayer by preparing our faculties to cooperate with this gift. It is an attempt to present the teaching of earlier time (e.g., The Cloud of Unknowing*) in an updated form and to put a certain order and regularity into it. It is not meant to replace other kinds of prayer; it simply puts* *other kinds of prayer into a new and fuller perspective. During the time of prayer we consent to God's presence and action within. At other times our attention moves outward to discover God's presence everywhere.*

THE GUIDELINES

1. Choose a sacred word as the symbol of your intention to consent to God's presence and action within.

2. Sitting comfortably and with eyes closed, settle briefly and silently introduce the sacred word as the symbol of your consent to God's presence and action within.

3. When you become aware of thoughts, return ever so gently to the sacred word.

4. At the end of the prayer period, remain in silence with eyes closed for a couple of minutes.

EXPLANATION OF THE GUIDELINES

I. "Choose a sacred word as the symbol of your intention to consent to God's presence and action within" (cf. *Open Mind, Open Heart,* chap. 5).

1. The sacred word expresses our intention to be in God's presence and to yield to the divine action.

2. The sacred word should be chosen during a brief period of prayer, asking the Holy Spirit to inspire us with one that is especially suitable for us.

    a. Examples: Lord, Jesus, Abba, Father, Mother

    b. Other possibilities: Love, Peace, Shalom

3. Having chosen a sacred word, we do not change it during the prayer period, for that would be to start thinking again.

4. A simple inward gaze upon God may be more suitable for some persons than the sacred word. In this case, one consents to God's presence and action by turning inwardly toward God as if gazing upon him. The same guidelines apply to the sacred gaze as to the sacred word.

II. "Sitting comfortably and with eyes closed, settle briefly and silently introduce the sacred word as the symbol of your consent to God's presence and action within."

1. By "sitting comfortably" is meant relatively comfortably; not so comfortably that we encourage sleep, but sitting comfortably enough to avoid thinking about the discomfort of our bodies during this time of prayer.

2. Whatever sitting position we choose, we keep the back straight.

3. If we fall asleep, we continue the prayer for a few minutes upon awakening if we can spare the time.

4. Praying in this way after a main meal encourages drowsiness. Better to wait an hour at least before Centering Prayer. Praying in this way just before retiring may disturb one's sleep pattern.

5. We close our eyes to let go of what is going on around and within us.

6. We introduce the sacred word inwardly and as gently as laying a feather on a piece of absorbent cotton.

III. "When you become aware of thoughts, return ever so gently to the sacred word."

1. "Thoughts" is an umbrella term for every perception, including sense perceptions, feelings, images, memories, reflections, and commentaries.

2. Thoughts are a normal part of Centering Prayer.

3. By "returning ever so gently to the sacred word," a minimum of effort is indicated. This is the only activity we initiate during the time of Centering Prayer.

4. During the course of our prayer, the sacred word may become vague or even disappear.

IV. "At the end of the prayer period, remain in silence with eyes closed for a couple of minutes."

1. If this prayer is done in a group, the leader may slowly recite the Our Father during the additional two or three minutes, while the others listen.

2. The additional two or three minutes give the psyche time to readjust to the external senses and enable us to bring the atmosphere of silence into daily life.

SOME PRACTICAL POINTS

1. The minimum time for this prayer is twenty minutes. Two periods are recommended each day, one first thing in the morning, and one in the afternoon or early evening.

2. The end of the prayer period can be indicated by a timer, providing it does not have an audible tick or loud sound when it goes off.

3. The principal effects of Centering Prayer are experienced in daily life, not in the period of Centering Prayer itself.

4. Physical Symptoms:

   a. We may notice slight pains, itches, or twitches in various parts of the body or a generalized restlessness. These are usually due to the untying of emotional knots in the body.

    b. We may also notice heaviness or lightness in the extremities. This is usually due to a deep level of spiritual attentiveness.

    c. In either case, we pay no attention, or we allow the mind to rest briefly in the sensation, and then return to the sacred word.

5. *Lectio divina* provides the conceptual background for the development of Centering Prayer.

EXTENDING THE EFFECTS OF CENTERING PRAYER INTO DAILY LIFE

1. Practice two periods of Centering Prayer daily.

2. Read scriptures regularly and study *Open Mind, Open Heart.*

3. Practice one or two of the specific methods for every day, suggested in *Open Mind, Open Heart,* chapter 12.

4. Join a Centering Prayer Support Group or Follow-up Program (if available in your area.)

    a. It encourages the members of the group to persevere in private.

    b. It provides an opportunity for further input on a regular basis through tapes, readings, and discussion.

POINTS FOR FURTHER DEVELOPMENT

1. During the prayer period, various kinds of thoughts may be distinguished (cf. *Open Mind, Open Heart,* chapters 6 through 10):

    a. Ordinary wanderings of the imagination or memory.

    b. Thoughts that give rise to attractions or aversions.

    c. Insights and psychological breakthroughs.

    d. Self-reflections such as, "How am I doing?" or, "This peace is just great!"

    e. Thoughts that arise from the unloading of the unconscious.

2. During this prayer, we avoid analyzing our experience, harboring expectations, or aiming at some specific goal such as:

    a. Repeating the sacred word continuously

    b. Having no thoughts.

    c. Making the mind a blank.

    d. Feeling peaceful or consoled.

    e. Achieving a spiritual experience.

3. What Centering Prayer is not:

    a. It is not a technique.

    b. It is not a relaxation exercise.

    c. It is not a form of self-hypnosis.

    d. It is not a charismatic gift.

    e. It is not a para-psychological phenomenon.

    f. It is not limited to the "felt" presence of God.

    g. It is not discursive meditation or affective prayer.

4. What Centering Prayer is:

    a. It is at the same time a relationship with God and a discipline to foster that relationship.

    b. It is an exercise of faith, hope, and love.

c. It is a movement beyond conversation with Christ to communion.

d. It habituates us to the language of God, which is silence.

Conclusion

As we shall see later on in the sections on the Christian East and the Far East, these above new expressions have borrowed much without doing violence to the legitimate traditional contemplative expressions of the Christian West. While coming from our own Western tradition of works like *The Cloud of Unknowing,* there are great similarities with the Jesus Prayer of the Christian East, and the entire Hindu, Buddhist, and Taoist traditions of seated meditation in the Far East. We will discuss these further in the next sections.

It has been said that Christianity is the best religion of words but is sometimes short on actual meditators. It has also said that Christianity is strong on building institutions of corporal works of mercy and social action but is short on presenting great mystics and holy men and woman as a more normative expression of the faith. I must agree that this is largely true.

I am reminded of a story told to me by a friend who converted to Christianity from Taoism. He went to tell his Taoist master of his decision. The master said Christianity is the best religion on earth as a religion of words. But that is only a paper reality. Finally he said to his young student, "You show me, boy!"

Likewise, I am reminded of what the Dalai Lama once told a group of Christian meditators. He said that if we really believe that Jesus is who we say that he is, then he would not want Christians to become Buddhists. He would want us to really follow the one who is the fullness of rebirth and awakening. Then the Dalai Lama gave an ever-so-subtle challenge. He said that if Jesus is really who we say that he is, we should be the ones leading the other religions in the way of meditation and prayer. I must say that I agree with him, too.

Christianity is an illusion if it only stays a religion of words and ideas, no matter how wonderful those may be. It must become a reality in our life. It is not enough to simply talk about meditation. We must do it. Otherwise, it remains substantially ineffective in our life. So I encourage you to take the words of the Christian West on meditation and put them into practice. Otherwise they remain only a good idea that is never realized.

Part Two

THE
CHRISTIAN
EAST

The Christian East

MONASTIC TRADITIONS

AND THE FOUNDATIONS

OF OUR FAITH

T HE TRADITION OF THE CHRISTIAN EAST actually precedes that of the West. As we discussed in the last section, the Christian West grew out from the Christian East. Christianity began as a Middle Eastern religion, and grew both to the East and West from this cradle of civilization. The western expansion was heavily documented in the Acts of the Apostles, and the writings of St. Paul. Since the western expansion of Christianity was better documented, we often think of Christianity as a western religion. But, in fact, Christianity is neither eastern nor western. Christianity is universal, or Catholic, including both East and West, but exclusively neither. Nonetheless, we owe a great debt of gratitude to the Middle Eastern beginnings of a faith that has now encompassed the world.

Triad System of Threes

Like the West, the tradition of the Christian East builds on a system of triads, or threes. As Orthodox and Catholic Christianity see the reality of God as a Trinity, so do they see human anthropology as a trinity as well. This, in turn, affects their mysticism, and the stages of ascent to pure contemplation. The human being is seen as a body, soul, and spirit. This is also true in the West, but the West quickly developed a more dualistic anthropology of body and soul, subdividing the soul into a lower, or animal, and a higher, or rational and spiritual, soul. In the West, this understanding is firmly cemented in place with St. Thomas Aquinas in the late thirteenth and early fourteenth centuries.

Corresponding to this trinitarian anthropology of body, soul, and spirit is the East's use of the incensive, rational, and intellective powers of the soul, or human being. While impossible to find a strict definition and use of these terms, in general they would mean the following: the incensive power would equate to the emotional and sensual faculties, and would correspond to the body. The rational power would apply to the faculty of cognition and general self-awareness, and would correspond to the soul. The intellective power would correspond to the faculty of pure spiritual intuition beyond senses, emotions, or thoughts, and would correspond to the spirit. The incensive and rational powers, and the corresponding body and soul, would be energies of the human being, and would be knowable through both objective and subjective means. The intellective power, and corresponding spirit, would be the essence of the human being and, while working in conjunction with the other two, would be beyond objective or subjective knowing and could only be known through pure spiritual intuition.

These would find a loose correspondence to the descriptions of the methodologies and stages of the Christian West. The incensive power, and tools used at that level by the Christian East, would correspond to the same tools discovered in *lectio divina* and the asceticism of the purgative stage in the West. The rational power would correspond to sacred reading moving on into meditation and the illuminative stage of the West. The intellective power would be the equivalent of the contemplative and unitive stage in the mysticism of the Christian West. The incensive and rational powers could be described and encouraged by the positive means of thoughts, emotions, and senses, which is called the cataphatic way. Knowable concepts of faith and morality, or the ascetical or meditational means of your own growth, would fall into this category. The intellective power can only be described by negative means beyond all thought, emotion, or sense perception, or the apophatic way. The way of "unknowing," or "divine darkness," would fall into this category.

Environment

As we discussed in our treatment of the Christian West, setting a proper environment is most important to prayer and meditation. This environment includes personal and communal dimensions. Specifically, it includes monastic community, and the various stages and degrees of solitude and silence, which this environment makes possible. Of course, this is applied to all lay Christians by way of inspiration and symbol, rather than in literal imitation.

Every Christian is called to a total renunciation of possessions, relationships, and self. Jesus says, "You must renounce all your possessions if you are to be my disciples," and, "You cannot serve God and money." More radically, he says, "You must renounce your very self," and, "Take up your cross each day and follow in my footsteps."

This call of Jesus to total renunciation is what inspired early monastic movement in the deserts of the Middle East. As Evagrius says, "Renounce all, to gain everything," and, "A monk is one who is separated from all and united with all." In our treatment of the Christian West we've already explored the various inspirations and rationales for the monastic impetus in the early Church. Suffice it to say here that it was to provide a good environment for radical prayer, to get to the very core of the spiritual sickness that afflicts the secular world, and to have the courage and humility to begin not by pointing to someone else but to oneself.

Moderation

This way of renunciation, or asceticism, is to be radical but not fanatical. It is to be self-critical, rather than self-righteous and judgmental of others but not scrupulous with others or oneself. There must be a certain moderation to its zeal. As St. John Cassian (c. 360–435 A.D.) says, "All extremes are equally harmful. It is as dangerous to fast too much as it is to overfill the stomach; to stay awake too long as to sleep too much; and so on." Evagrius says similarly, "start out walking at a gentle pace until they've gotten accustomed to walking, in the end they will not get tired, even though they walk great distances. . . . Train yourself gently, until you finally reach the perfect state . . . do not be in a hurry. Be patient." This way of moderation is positive for yourself, and for all of those who live and work with and around you. It bears good fruit in one's life.

The positive effect of entering into this "school of the Lord's service" is a change in both interior attitudes and external actions for the better. St. Neilos the Ascetic (d. 430 A.D.) says of the early monks: "They did not seek excessive gain by exploiting each other; nor do they bring lawsuits against one another. One was not rich while another was destitute, nor did one overeat while another starved . . . establishing equity and fairness." Of interior attitudes he says, "Envy, malice, arrogance, and haughtiness were banished, along with all that leads to discord. . . . They showed everyone how simple it is to escape unharmed from the provocation of the passions."

Three-Tiered Monastic System

As in the monastic environment for meditation and prayer in the Christian West, a classical three-tiered system is also used in the Christian East. This amounts to the cenobium, the skete, or Laura, and the isolated hermit's cell. One begins monastic life within the cenobium for cenobitical monasticism. Here one undergoes the intensive training of finding the way of prayer and meditation within the responsible relationships established and nurtured within community. After ten years or so, one may petition the abbot and the elders to retire into semi-eremitism, or social eremitism, with a handful of monks, in a Skete or Laura, gathered around the spiritual father. After another ten years or so of training in greater solitude, without neglecting the responsibility of brotherly relationships, one may petition to enter into strict reclusion as a full-time hermit. This three-tiered system insures that neither community nor solitude are escapes from reality. Community cannot be an escape from solitude, nor can solitude be an escape from community.

Hesychia

One of the great goals of this "royal" monastic way is the establishment of "stillness," or "hesychia." The point of attaining stillness within the body and soul is so that the spirit might be reborn. When disordered senses, passions, and thoughts become still and quiet, the spirit can be set free. Once the spirit is reborn, the thoughts of the mind, or soul, and the senses and passions of the body can find their rightful place in service of the spirit. In this new hierarchy, the spirit leads the way and is served by the soul, which in turn is served by the body. Consequently, nothing is lost, but all is reordered, and used in a way that is truly beneficial and peaceful for everyone and everything.

In the Christian East, a great example of hesychia is the spider. After the spider spins its beautiful and symmetrical web, it must sit in perfect stillness in order to discern the slightest stirring on the web. Only then can the spider find nourishment and live. If it moves too much, it cannot discern the stirring on the web, and it will starve to death. Likewise, in our spiritual life, if we find the gift of hesychia, or stillness, we will find great spiritual nourishment. If we are too agitated and anxious in our bodies, senses, emotions, and thoughts, we will never break through to the abundance and rebirth of the spirit but will remain in an unhealthy spiritual hunger.

Another example that is often used is the pond. When the pond is agitated, it becomes muddy, and you cannot see to the bottom. When the pond is still, the mud and debris settle, and you can see all the way to the bottom. Furthermore, the surface can perfectly reflect whoever gazes into it. When the pond of our body and soul become still, then we can look clearly into our own being, and can reflect all of creation, and the Creator most perfectly. Of course, this was the original purpose of the rightly ordered and fully peaceful human being.

Time and Place

Setting aside a place and time for silence and stillness is most important in the Christian East, and for us as well. This universal principle applies to both the East and West, and also in a proportional manner to both monks and laity. The importance of making one's whole dwelling a sacred space is seen in the emphasis of the Fathers on the monastic cell. As Thomas à Kempis says in his Western classic *The Imitation of Christ*, "If you will withdraw from unnecessary talk and useless running about and listening to the latest gossip, you'll find the time to occupy yourself in devout meditation. . . . Saints . . . preferred to be alone with God. One man has said, 'As often as I have been among men I've returned less a man'. . . . Unless you like solitude, it is not easy to appear in public. . . . The cell becomes dear to you, while if you are seldom in it, you will grow tired of it. . . . If only you would never have left yourself, or listened to idle rumors, you would have remained in peace of mind."

We need to set aside times and places for meditation prayer within our homes and dwellings. We can have times for silence within our families, or for ourselves. I have suggested twenty to thirty minutes in the morning and the evening, if possible, for private and personal devotion. A short but meaningful family time of devotion is most strengthening on a daily basis. This may consist of husband and wife saying a simple prayer before retiring to bed at night or upon rising in the morning. It may be something as simple as thanksgiving before and after meals, or a short scripture reading or rosary at other convenient times.

One of the more interesting things we've seen with our families at Little Portion Hermitage is that children take to sacred silence like bees to honey, if the parents approach it as something positive and fun and do not become too scrupulous or judgmental in carrying it out. For the more courageous and advanced family or couple, extended times for meditation are sometimes possible. But you will never know about any of these things unless you try, and if you do not give up upon experiencing the inevitable initial discomfort of the new activity or exercise. As the saying goes, "The family that prays together stays together." And for personal prayer, "Seven days without the word of God makes one weak!"

Places for prayer are also important. The personal or family altar are most sacred in Christian tradition, as well as in other major religions of the world. A prayer corner with suitable sacred images, such as a cross, or crucifix, or icons, or other sacred pictures, and candles, can be most beautiful and inspirational without losing an ultimate simplicity or intruding upon the normal functions of the rest of the house. This is a most sacred tradition in the Christian East, and can also be found in the earlier traditions of the Christian West in Christian Europe and in the founding stages of the United States. Certainly, it would not be out of place, or without sociological precedent, to reinstate such a practice of prayer within our Christian families all around the world today.

These are just a few suggestions for providing a good environment for prayer and meditation within one's life. They range from joining a monastery, or community, which is set up to make all of life into a prayerful environment, to personal things we can do while living for God out in the secular world. Both involve personal change and sacrifice. Please make the changes in your life that will help you to live more fully in the peace and right order of the Ultimate Reality of God through Jesus in today's world.

The Incensive
Power

THE POWER OF THE
SENSES AND
EMOTIONS

THE INCENSIVE POWER CORRESPONDS TO the faculties of the body of sense and emotion. In a most specific sense, the Christian East speaks of the passions when referring to the incensive power. The passions may be used in a positive or negative way, but in this fallen era they are more inclined to be used in a negative and destructive sense. Today, instead of the spirit being primary and leading and served by the soul and body, the body, with its senses and passions, leads the way. Now it makes the soul its servant, leaving the spirit abandoned and forgotten. This means that sensual appetite and emotion rule over the thought and mind of the soul. When the thoughts of the mind are shackled by the senses in the passions, the soul is unable to truly set the spirit free so that all can be awakened and reborn in the true freedom of the sons and daughters of God. This means humanity is trapped in the mere energy of itself, rather than being able to break through to its true essence, which is the very core of its true personhood and identity in the reality of eternity.

St. Hesychios the Priest says, "The incensive power by nature is prone to be destructive. If it is turned against demonic thoughts, it destroys them; but if it is roused against people, it then destroys the good thoughts that are in us. In other words, the incensive power, although God-given as a bow against evil thoughts, can be turned the other way and used to destroy good thoughts as well, for it destroys whatever it is directed against."

Based on this train of thought, the Eastern Fathers learned how to use the incensive power, especially at the beginning of their conversions to Christ and monastic life, against the enemy of God. Specifically, they used the incensive power against sin and the devil. As St. John of Karpathos (present at the Sixth Ecumenical Council in 680–681 A.D.) says, "How can we overcome the sinfulness that is already firmly established within us? We must use force . . . we're not forbidden to resist force with force."

Holy Anger

St. Isaiah the Solitary (d.471 or 491 A.D.) is more specific when he says, "Anger is in accord with nature. Without anger a man cannot attain purity. . . . Resistance is rebuttal to Jesus Christ. The foundation is the incensive power."

Holy Hatred

The Fathers actually speak of a holy hatred and godly anger against the devil and sin. As St. Isaiah the Solitary continues, "If your heart comes to feel a natural hatred for sin, it has defeated the causes of sin and freed itself from them. . . . Unless a man hates all the activity of this world, he cannot worship God." As a local pastor and friend of mine once preached, "Unless you hate what God hates, you cannot love what God loves."

Holy Fear

The Fathers also speak of holy fear. Of course, scripture tells us clearly that, "The beginning of wisdom is the fear of the Lord." Jesus tells us to have a healthy fear of both God and the devil (Luke 12:4). Yet we are also told, "Be not afraid," and, "Perfect love casts out all fear" (1 John 4:18). So a journey, beginning with wholesome fear and ending in love, is part of scriptural spirituality.

As St. Diodochus says most succinctly, "No one can love God consciously in his heart unless he has first feared him with all his heart." The various Fathers then go on to explain the different kinds of fear for beginners, the advancing, and the perfect in spiritual development. They also differentiate between wholesome fear of God as the Almighty, a fear of the devil and his limited, but nonetheless real power, and a fear of hell. In today's society we seem to lack a wholesome fear of all these things. In an attempt to overcome an unhealthy fear we have often done away with all fear in a way that only makes us presumptuous. This presumption fails to motivate us properly in loving God and hating anything that stands against God. Consequently, most of us in Western civilization today remain stuck in our negative patterns of behavior, emotional responses, and thoughts in reaction and response to the normal realities of daily life.

For myself, I have found one simple way to discern the difference between healthy and unhealthy fear. Healthy fear motivates. Unhealthy fear cripples. Healthy fear motivates us to change the negative patterns of our life in favor of the positive things of God's truth and love. Unhealthy fear cripples us so that we are unable to move from the negative patterns of our life. We are simply too afraid to move. Healthy fear is from God. Unhealthy fear comes from the enemy of God, who desires power and destruction.

Rebuke

Related to this is the Eastern Fathers' teaching on rebuttal. We are to use the incensive power of rebuttal and rebuke in the face of the devil and sin. In scripture, Jesus frequently rebukes Satan, demons, or the destructive powers of nature. The apostles are empowered to do the same in the name of Jesus. St. Michael the Archangel had the courage to rebuke Lucifer, or Satan, when he said, "The Lord rebuke you" (Jude 9). He also has the humility not to do so in his own name, despite his own power. He realized that even his inherent power comes from being a creature of God.

St. Isaiah the Solitary says, "The city is prayer. Resistance is rebuttal to Jesus Christ. The foundation is the incensive power. . . . At the time of prayer, we should expel from our heart the provocation of each evil thought, rebutting it in the spirit of devotion." And St. Hesychios the Priest says, "Never relax . . . your power of rebuttal."

The Fathers of the East use the experience of a serpent trying to get into one's house as an example of how to rebut evil. They would say that it is easier to chop off the head of the serpent before the body gets in the house. Once the entire snake is inside, it is most difficult to capture, kill, and remove. Likewise, they would say that if you take a snake to your bosom under your shirt, it will surely bite you, and you will die. Likewise in the spiritual life: If you rebuke evil and sin at the very moment you notice its entrance through the door into the house of your soul, it is easy to kill. If you wait until it is inside fully, it is more difficult to remove. If you allow it to get close to your heart in the secret places of your soul, it can easily strike with a fatal bite.

In the West, St. Augustine uses a different analogy to make a similar point. He says that sin must be "nipped in the bud" if it is to be removed easily. If we wait until the young sprout grows into a new branch or limb, then we must pull out the shears and clippers to trim it clean. Then the job is more difficult. This means that sin must be removed as soon as we notice it within our soul. If we dally with it, it can grow so strong that it becomes more difficult to remove. But even this can be done in Christ.

Personal Life

For myself, all of this reminds me of an example from my earlier childhood. When I was learning how to swim at the local YMCA in Oklahoma City, Oklahoma, I had to learn how to push off from the side of the pool with great force in order to build up enough momentum to get me swimming on top of the water. Even accomplished swimmers begin the race by diving forcefully into the pool. Likewise in the spiritual life: At the beginning of our journey we must make a forceful break with negative things of this world in order to find the real freedom and proper working of the things of God in our life. Jesus calls us to "renounce everything." St. Paul tells us that we must view all of the things of this world before Christ "as rubbish," or garbage. This is strong and forceful language. Behind the language must be a proper use of the incensive power against anything that stands between God and us.

For God

But the Fathers do not only speak of the use of the incensive power against negative things. They also speak of using the incensive power for positive things, most especially for the most positive Reality in eternity—God. This means stirring up the emotions in a positive way for God and for the things of God. We should get enthusiastic and excited about our spiritual life. Without this enthusiasm, very few people have the motivation to keep going, especially at the beginning of their spiritual journey.

St. Hesychios the Priest speaks of the journey of the soul to God and says, "Because the taste of the divine and ecstasy desire to make their longing ever more intense and insatiable as they ascend, they do not stop until they reach the seraphim, nor do they rest from their watchfulness of intellect and the intense longing of their aspiration until they have become angels in Christ Jesus our Lord." As St. Peter of Damascus says, "Desire should long constantly and entirely for God alone and never for anything else." This is quite a statement if taken seriously!

Penthos

The paradoxical combination of both the positive and the negative use of the incensive power can be found in what the Eastern Fathers call "penthos," or "deep compunction." This is a sorrow for sin, and a joy and thankfulness for forgiveness and the experience of God's love that is beyond all words. In penthos, this is all happening at once! It is too much for the mind to understand. It can only be experienced in the heart. This includes the emotions of the incensive power, and the understanding of faith within the rational power, but goes beyond them all to pure intellection in the contemplative intuition of the spirit. Penthos comes to be experienced constantly within the totality of one's very being. It is a constant reality in the monastic way of life, and for the serious layperson as well.

The Gift and the Way of Tears

Related to penthos and the use of the incensive power is the Eastern Fathers' emphasis on the gift and Way of Tears. Of course, this way can be seen in the East and the West. It began in scripture itself with Jesus and his disciples, especially in the story of the penitent woman who washed Jesus' feet with her tears and dried them with her hair, or in Jesus' own tears over the death of his friend Lazarus, or over ancient Jerusalem and, most especially, in the face of his own passion and death. Both St. Benedict and St. Francis of Assisi, who is said to have cried himself into blindness, speak of tears. There are numerous quotes from the Christian East emphasizing the importance of tears in spirituality. Suffice it to say here that the gift of tears overwhelms a person during prayer in a way that is uncontrollable. This happens only occasionally, especially at the beginning of one's conversion, or other new stages of spiritual development. The Way of Tears is something that can be experienced daily, and may be physically expressed with sweet and gentle pure drops, or with interior tears of the heart. This latter way of tears is said by the Eastern Fathers to be possible for all Christians, especially when receiving Jesus in Holy Communion.

The Prayer of the Heart

Penthos and the Way of Tears lead us to the Eastern Fathers' emphasis on the Prayer of the Heart. They considered the heart as the center of the human being. Physiologically, they believed the heart is found right under the navel. When they prayed, they gazed at their navel in order to concentrate on dropping the prayer from the head to the heart. They did this by sitting on a low stool in a slumped position. This is where we get our term "naval gazer!" While this prayer position has not become popular among Christians in general, the Prayer of the Heart has become very popular.

The Prayer of the Heart consists in dropping prayer from mere intellectual ideas and images into a full and complete experience of the entire human being—body, soul, and spirit. As with penthos, it begins with an awakening of the incensive power in a paradoxical way, including, and going beyond, positive or negative senses, emotions, and thoughts. It becomes a pure intuition of the spirit that builds on, and includes, the subjective emotions and passions, and sensual sensations of the body's incensive power, as well as the cognitive thoughts and images of the soul's rational power, yet goes beyond the incensive or the rational powers of body and soul to pure intellection and contemplation in spirit.

Conclusion

How do we use the incensive Power? Do we use it for God, or for self, or even for evil? Do we feel trapped by emotion, or does it empower us to do the good things so needed in today's world? Do we use the appropriate spiritual tools to turn negative and destructive emotions around and turn them into good? Lastly, do we sometimes even feel addicted, or trapped, even to a good use of emotions in our spiritual life, whereby we always need a new spiritual high to keep us going? If so, we are not alone. But there are ways out of all of these negative traps. Let us now go on to the rational power, and the right use of the thoughts and images of the soul, to help us on our way.

EMOTIONS (INCENSIVE) EXERCISE

1. Sit in your meditation place, and breathe deeply.
2. Be aware of your negative emotions with each inhale, and simply let go of them with each exhale.
3. Now, allow a good use of your emotions with each inhale of God's Spirit and the rebirth of your spirit.
4. Allow deep compunction for past sins against the love of God.
5. Allow deep gratitude for God's love and forgiveness, no matter how far you have fallen.
6. Stir up enthusiastic praise for God for the simple wonder of his being.
7. Allow yourself to pass over into the Prayer of the Heart, or the deepest prayer from the very center of your being, to the very center of the Heart of God. If this takes the form of songs, tongues, tears, or awesome silence, allow it to go on for the rest of the period.
8. Conclude as usual.

The Soul and the
Rational Power

A FTER THE EMOTIONS AND SENSES OF
the body in the incensive power come the thoughts
of the mind, or soul, in the rational power. This is the human faculty
of cognition and awareness. It is the place of images and concepts. It
is directly connected to the preceding incensive power, for there is an
inherent connection between senses, emotions, and thoughts.

Interconnectedness of Thoughts, Feelings, and Actions

As St. Theodorus the Great Ascetic says, "Many people wonder
whether thoughts stimulate passions, or the passions stimulate the
thought. . . . My own view is the thoughts are stimulated by the passions." However, thoughts have the ability to direct and strengthen
the emotions. St. Maximos the Confessor says, "The intellect receives impassioned conceptual images in three ways: through the
senses, through the body's condition, and through the memory. . . .
The demons fight against us either through these things themselves

or through our impassioned conceptual images of these things." In other words, they can reach all of the other faculties through our thoughts.

As the Old Testament Book of Proverbs says, "Whatever you think, you become." Or as the Buddhist text, the *Dhammapada,* says in utmost simplicity, "You are what you think." Jesus says, "Wherever your treasure lies, there will you find your heart," and, "The mouth speaks what fills the mind." St. Paul says, "Confession on the lips leads to salvation," and the New Testament is filled with teachings that emphasize the connection between the emotions, thoughts, words, and actions of life. The principle is easy: Emotions affect thoughts, thoughts have an effect on words, and words confirm emotions and thoughts so that they eventually become actions. Therefore, the thoughts of the mind, or the cognition of the soul, have an effect on our whole life.

Imagination

It's also good to remember how the thought process actually works. It has been said that we think in pictures. In other words, when I think of Jesus, or the Buddha, or any person at all, I see a picture, or an image, of them in my mind. When we think of mathematical formulas, we see pictures of the numbers and letters in our mind as we work the formula. This is called "imaging." It is a simple use of the imagination. Recall that in the West, St. Bonaventure said to meditate with "vivid representation" in one's mind. This is a simple use of imaging, or the imagination.

It is this creative use of imagination that constitutes genuine meditation. Only later will passive contemplation, beyond all images and forms, be entered into naturally, without contrivance. So the use of thought is not relegated to some abstract and speculative use of the mind. Thought is manifested in images within the mind, and has a profound effect in actualizing images and mental forms within real life.

It is because of this connection that meditation has played such a central part in any religious or spiritual awakening. As the Old Testament encourages, "Meditate on the law of the Lord day and night." As we have said, meditation consists of the positive use of the thoughts and images of the mind to focus on God, or the things of God. The New Testament is filled with injunctions to experience "the spiritual renewal of the mind" by filling the mind with "all that is true, all that deserves respect, all that is honest, pure, admirable, decent, virtuous, or worthy of praise." Other religions of the world likewise emphasize filling the mind with positive and wholesome images.

But it is not only the positive things of God that affect the mind. Negative things also affect the mind. As disordered senses and emotions run wild, they entrap the thoughts into equally disordered patterns. The mind is imprisoned by the disorder of the senses and emotions. This is negative. Anything that is negative is ultimately destructive if left unbalanced and unchecked.

INTERCONNECTEDNESS: BODY, SOUL, SPIRIT EXERCISE

1. Sit in your meditation place, and breathe deeply.
2. Be aware first of the senses of your body. Notice that if they are satisfied, our emotions are positive. When our emotions are positive, our thoughts are happy and good. Conversely, if our senses are not satisfied according to our desires, then our emotions are agitated and negative. When our emotions are negative, then our thoughts become negative as well. The problem, of course, is that we cannot always satisfy our carnal desires, and the more we satisfy them, the more they demand. We are

trapped in a negative pattern. Biblically, this is called being a carnal person.

3. Let go of your senses, emotions, and thoughts, as in the cross meditation on p. 66.

4. With each breath, allow your spirit to take priority in your awareness of your being and in your life. Allow yourself to be happy with the simple union with God available with every breath. Biblically, this is called being a spiritual person. Your thoughts now become focused, clear, and positive. Allow them to lead the emotions and the senses. If your spiritual mind and cognition is positive, your emotions are positive. If your emotions are positive, then your senses are healthier. The body becomes the vehicle for the soul and the spirit. The emotions become the empowerment of the thoughts, and the thoughts become the servants of the spirit. This is right order, peace, and harmony in Christ.

5. Simply *be* in this place of right order for the rest of the meditation period. This few minutes of right order practiced daily will prepare you for all that would threaten to turn you upside down again in daily life.

6. Conclude as before, thanking God for any graces received.

Watchfulness

Because of this negative pattern in the thoughts of the soul, the Fathers of the Christian East have encouraged the art of watchfulness. This is sometimes called attentive watchfulness. In the Far East, it is sometimes called mindfulness, though they mean what we call the contemplative experience as well. Here it simply means to be aware of the stirrings in one's thoughts, emotions, and senses. This is accomplished through stilling the senses and emotions of the body through hesychia, so that the thoughts of the mind, or soul, will follow suit. Once all is still, then one can truly detect the thoughts, emotions, and senses. While all is active, and in anxious turmoil, it is difficult to discern the truth of the activities of these faculties. So hesychia and watchfulness are inherently linked. When properly linked, they are a powerful tool in overcoming negative and disordered thoughts, which lead and confirm the heretofore misled senses and emotions. Then all is brought back into harmony, peace, and restful order.

St. Hesychios the Priest says, "Watchfulness is a spiritual method which . . . completely frees us from impassioned thoughts, impassioned words, and evil actions. . . . Watchfulness is a continual fixing and halting of thoughts at the entrance of the heart . . . and consists in closely scrutinizing every mental image or provocation . . . in freeing the heart from all thoughts, keeping it profoundly silent and still, and in prayer. . . . Our intellect's great gain from stillness is this: all the sins which formerly beat on the intellect as thoughts and which, once admitted to the mind, were turned into outward acts of sin are now cut off by mental watchfulness."

Evagrius says, "Sometimes thoughts are cut off, and sometimes they do the cutting off." And St. Maximos the Confessor says, "It is in the intellect's power to make good or bad use of conceptual images. Their wrong use is followed by the misuse of the things themselves."

So we use good thoughts to fight bad thoughts. We fill our mind with good images to overcome bad images. It is like the example of oil and water. It is said that oil and water do not mix. If a vessel is filled with oil, pouring water into it will displace the oil from the bottom, and the inside out. If you try to pour oil into water, it floats on the surface and cannot penetrate. Likewise, if the mind is filled with the oil of negative and disordered images, then filling the mind with the water of positive images will, of itself, displace the oil. Furthermore, if the mind is filled with the water of positive images, you cannot fill it with the oil of negativity. So if we concentrate on good thoughts through meditation and prayer, this will, of itself, displace negative thoughts and keep them from reentering the soul.

Three Categories: Godly, Demonic, and Human

Thoughts are categorized into three groups according to the Fathers of the Christian East: human, demonic, and angelic, or godly. They use the example of gold to demonstrate the difference. Human thought would simply see the precious metal as a fact, with no negative or positive value. It simply is. The demonic thought would see gold with attachment and greed, or with negative moral value. Angelic, or godly, thought would see gold with detachment, and a positive moral value; for instance, how it can be used in sacred art, or to help the plight of the poorest of the poor. It simply is, and can be used according to its needed function, without the attachment of selfishness and greed.

It is negative, or demonic, thought that concerns us next. Here, we will not treat the theological issue of the reality of spiritual beings, called angels, and their positive and negative position in the cosmos through their own choices regarding their relationship with God. Let us simply recognize that the Eastern Christian Fathers, and the Roman Catholic Church in the East and West today, formally recognize the existence of such beings, and their effect on humanity and creation for good or evil. This is especially relevant when studying the meditation and prayer of the Orthodox and Catholic Christian East.

According to the sacred tradition of Christianity, demons are personal spiritual beings that have the power to stimulate our senses and make suggestions within our thoughts. It is up to us, through the power of free will under the sovereignty of God, to choose whether to go along with these temptations and give birth to sin, or to combat and rebuke these negative stimulations and suggestions through rebuttal, as described in the last section. Everyone is tempted. Even Jesus was tempted. Scripture says he was "tempted in every way we are, yet without sin." It is what we do with it that constitutes whether or not it is righteousness or sin, whether we remain in the right order and harmony of God, or whether we fall into the discord, confusion, and destruction we call sin.

Sin

Let us keep in mind the actual definition of sin. "Sin" is a Greek word that was used during archery tournaments. Hitting the target but missing the perfect centeredness of the bull's-eye was called "sin." The arrow would go in the right direction. It would even hit the target. But it would miss total centeredness, or balance. This is the original meaning of the Greek word for "sin."

Likewise with us. We are created in the image of God. Therefore, the divine seed remains within us to seek the things of goodness, truth, beauty, and all the things of God, whether we know to call God "God" or not. It is part of our humanity. Very few people are doing a 180-degree turn from God toward pure evil when they sin. Most of us are seeking to do the right thing, but we are doing it in the wrong way. We want to do good but end up doing bad things because we are not in the total balance and harmony of God. So most "sinners" are not bad people, but good people who have lost their way.

This does not mean that sin does not have radical negative effects in human life and throughout all of creation. Scripture teaches us that "the wages of sin is death, but the gift of God is eternal life in Christ Jesus." In his epistle, James tells us that "the tug and lure of passion leads to sin, and when sin reaches maturity it begets death." St. Paul tells us that all of creation is affected by our negative choices and accomplishments, and awaits the revelation of those who truly follow God's way to be released and set free.

So sin is neither as bleak as what many evangelists would like us to believe concerning our basic human nature, nor is it as innocuous, or harmless, as many New Age teachers would have us believe. It involves basically good people who do some terribly bad things. It has affected the entire created order in nature, but it is not untreatable. It can be fixed. It can be set right and healed through Jesus. As usual, the truth lies between two extremes.

THOUGHTS (RATIONAL) EXERCISE

1. Sit in your meditation place, and breathe deeply.
2. Be aware of your unruly and negative thoughts. The masters say that such thoughts are like a caged monkey that jump from place to place to find a way out. The monkey must be quieted before it can be safely set free. Simply let go of your unruly and negative thoughts at the foot of the cross. They will become quiet on their own.
3. Focus your thoughts on the positive things of God. This can be done most effectively through the use of sacred reading of the Fathers and the scriptures. When you become cognitively aware of a disordered sense or emotion, simply bring them to the cross, and let them go with each breath. Quietly continue to focus on the things of God.
4. When the senses and emotions are noticed *after* they gain habitual control of the mind, bring them *and* the thoughts to the cross, and gently let them go. Giving any of them too much attention often causes them to grow stronger. The author of *The Cloud of Unknowing* says to see these negative distractions as an object slowly coming toward your head. When it gets to you, slowly move the head to one side, and let it pass. It will then go away of its own.
5. Conclude as usual.

Temptation

The temptation that leads to sin happens in progressive stages according to the Eastern Christian Fathers, and according to the Western Fathers as well. The Eastern Fathers divide the stages in anywhere from five to seven, or even nine, stages. The stages are quite well defined and helpful for the experienced discernment of good or evil. However, for the average person, they seem too complex to be understood, much less remembered. Therefore, I prefer the threefold division of St. Augustine in the West. It accomplishes the same end with greater simplicity.

According to St. Augustine, the first stage of temptaion is demonic suggestion and temptation in the thoughts. This does not involve our will but is placed involuntarily within one's thought processes. This is not sin. It is only temptation. The second stage is playing with the thoughts of temptation within our own thought processes. This rouses the emotions. This has not yet given birth to action but does constitute sin, since it involves an act of the will to dwell upon the demonic thought. Third, comes action. This is the exterior manifestation of the interior sin in private or public word or deed. This is where sin really begins its negative and destructive work.

Interestingly enough, the Eastern Fathers would say that, while the first stage does not constitute sin, it does constitute a propensity to sin. In other words, the more one actually sins in thought or deed, the more temptations one is open to. Conversely, the more one trains the mind and the body, through positive meditation and self-discipline, the less one is susceptible even to the temptations of the evil one. It is like a computer that opens a circuit for the first time. After that first time, it is more apt to go down that circuit in the future. The same is true of opening the circuits of sin and tempting thoughts.

All of this is relevant to the art of watchfulness. The more one is able to enter into attentive watchfulness through the practice of hesychia, the more one is able to discern the cognitive stirrings of the thoughts and images within the mind, or the soul. The more still one is in hesychia, the more one is able to discern whether these stirrings are good or evil. Furthermore, the more one stills the thoughts, especially the negative ones, the less apt they are to trouble us in the future.

Spiritual Direction and Discernment

Here the issue of discernment and spiritual direction comes into play. It is sometimes very difficult to discern the genuine working of the Spirit as contrasted to the forgeries and imitations of evil spirits. As St. Paul says, "Angels of darkness can come as angels of light." The stories and sayings of the Desert Fathers are filled with warnings against being spiritually deceived, and tragic stories about those who were. Some monks even end in death because of their stubborn unwillingness to open their spiritual life to the genuine discernment and input of a true elder.

To help with discernment, the entire Christian and monastic tradition has emphasized the need for placing oneself under the direction of a spiritual father or mother. These are experienced men and women who have walked the way before us and know the spiritual, mental, and emotional pitfalls and minefields that could easily harm or destroy us along the way. In the monastic tradition, placing oneself under a spiritual father or mother, who had already experienced the solitude and silence of the desert, was the foundation and beginning of monastic community as we know it today.

This general principle applies to monks and laypeople alike. All of us need some form of communal support in this spiritual journey, and we do best when we find a good spiritual father or mother to serve as our director beyond the general norms and teachings of the Church. No doubt, the search for good spiritual directors is on in the modern Church. After that comes the challenge to really follow their advice, even when it is different from our own opinion concerning a particular matter of faith or spiritual life.

The actual form of spiritual direction is a little different from our modern western culture, which likes to talk a lot but often communicates very little. For the Eastern Christian monks, direction was sought during the revelation of thoughts. This takes place as a very brief, but brutally honest, session that lasts only a few minutes, sometimes just before public prayer in a semipublic/private place in the church. During the session, the younger monk confesses not only sins but also temptations to the spiritual father or mother. This happens very quickly, with no attempt to rationalize or justify. It is pure honesty, with readiness to take responsibility for the temptation and act upon it without blaming others. After the frank confession, the spiritual parent gives some equally brief and bottom-line advice and encouragement, and then lightly taps the monk on the forehead as if to say, "Get your thinking straight." The whole thing is over in a matter of a few minutes.

This is very different from our Western concept, which thinks in terms of hours of counseling. We also do our best to rationalize and justify our own point of view as the most desirable path before our confessor or spiritual director. In the East, this is simply not tolerated. It is seen as a waste of everyone's time. Real spiritual growth requires an attitude of humility that does not always seek to blame an outside person or situation for our own problems. It has the humility to begin with ourselves.

It is also good to distinguish the roles of spiritual director, or father and mother, from a confessor and a counselor. A confessor only deals with actual sin from the perspective of the Church's sacrament of penance. A counselor uses an hour-or-so session of dialogue to get to the point of advice. A spiritual director deals with the inner thoughts and temptations relative to the spiritual life in Christ.

Our job is to take the spiritual son or daughter to the point of totally letting go of the old man or woman, in order to be totally reborn a new person in Christ. This takes honesty, but usually not a lot of words. It takes the Word, which is sometimes heard in silence. It takes eternity, which can be experienced in just a few moments, in this case. All of this requires courageous honesty on the part of the spiritual son or daughter, or directed, and on the part of the spiritual father or mother, or director. If the son or daughter wants this kind of bottom-line honesty and spiritual help, there is no better way to get it. If all we really want is, at worst, to justify ourselves or, at best, to seek inexpensive counseling, then this process is guaranteed to fail.

A word of caution is in order here. Following the example of all the Eastern Fathers before him, the great eighteenth century St. Seraphim of Serov, called "the St. Francis of Russia," encouraged obedience to one's spiritual father very strongly. But he also recognized that a good spiritual director is not always available. Therefore, he said, "Better no spiritual director than a bad one." This wisdom is echoed in the mystical and monastic traditions of major religions of the world. In this case, Seraphim said that it is better to read the Fathers and the scriptures under the general guidance of the Church than to be under the direction of a bad spiritual father or mother.

Today, it is also often hard to find a good spiritual director. There are many who go to a six-week seminar, or course, on how to give spiritual direction, but few have actually lived the life necessary to give the genuine spiritual authority needed to guide souls in this spiritual art. This means there is greater burden laid upon those who seek direction. The knowledge of the monastic and mystical fathers and mothers, and the general teaching of the Church, is indispensable in finding a suitable spiritual director, and in spiritual growth in Christ.

Discerning God's Will

Generally, five things are needed to fully discern the will of God, which, in turn, helps us to discern the identity and character of the spiritual entity, passion, or idea we're dealing with in our thoughts and emotions. First, is the suggestion in accordance with the teaching of sacred scripture and apostolic Tradition within the Church regarding faith and morality? Second, is it in accordance with the norms of the community or ministry within the Church that we are part of, and have made a commitment to? Third, is it in accordance with the teachings of one's spiritual director or one's spiritual father or mother? Fourth, does it line up with the input of tried-and-tested community members, spiritual friends, and family? Fifth, does it bear good fruit, or the fruit of the Spirit (love, joy, peace, patience, kindness, generosity, mildness, chastity, and faith), within our life, and the lives of those around us?

If these five things line up, then we can be relatively certain of God's will as it pertains to a particular suggestion or thought within our emotions and thoughts. Unfortunately, in today's individualistic and self-willed society and culture we see that very few have the patience, or humility, to go through this process; therefore, very few break through to the greater benefits of real spiritual awakening and rebirth in Christ and his Church.

Scrupulosity

Finally, I would offer another word of caution about scrupulosity. Using the Latin word "scruple," or "pebble," St. Augustine likens scrupulosity to having a pebble in one's shoe or sandal. It causes us to focus on the pebble rather than the large rock, and can keep us from either walking correctly or running freely. Likewise in spiritual life, scrupulosity involves focusing on the little things while overlooking the big. Watchfulness without proper spiritual direction and discernment can easily degenerate into scrupulosity and can become harmful rather than helpful in one's spiritual life. Scrupulosity is considered one of the devil's greatest tools in sidetracking the saints from the real goal of their spiritual journey in Christ.

Conclusion

These are some of the general teachings concerning the rational power of the thoughts and images of the soul. No doubt, the old saying that "the battle for the soul is in the mind" holds true today. Many, or most, seem trapped in negative and destructive thought patterns. No matter how hard we try, we just cannot seem to get set free. But there are ways that are time-tested and sure. They do take patience and effort. But they work. Let us now look at some of these ancient tools that can still help us today.

The Eight Vices,
or Demons

FROM THIS EMPHASIS ON WATCHFUL-
ness of the positive and negative spiritual stirrings
in the body and the soul, the Eastern monastic fathers and mothers
of Christianity soon developed a system and categorization of the
positive and negative things of the spirit based on their own metaphysical training from Greek philosophy. The positive things were
called "virtues." The negative things were called "vices." The positive
things came from the Spirit of God or the angels. The negative things
came from Satan and his demons.

Traditionally, there are three theological virtues, and four moral
virtues. The three theological virtues are faith, hope, and charity. The
four moral virtues are fortitude, justice, prudence, and temperance.
The Eastern Fathers also have alternate and more primitive lists of
the four moral virtues. St. Hesychios the Priest speaks of moral judgment, wisdom, righteousness, and fortitude but asserts ultimately
that "virtue is one."

There are eight vices, coming from eight demons. Out of the
eight there are three that are considered leaders to the other five.

These eight demons, or vices, come to us in the West through St. John Climacus of the famous St. Catherine's Monastery in the Sinai, and from St. Gregory the Great, who speaks of the seven cardinal sins of pride, avarice, envy, wrath, lust, gluttony, and sloth, or ascedia. Because of their awareness and expertise in spiritual combat, an emphasis on the eight vices and the tools to overcome them became a special area of teaching in the Christian East.

The list of the eight vices first comes to us from Evagrius, but is solidified and commented on in the teachings of St. John Cassian. Cassian's list is as follows: gluttony, unchastity, avarice, anger, dejection, listlessness, self-esteem, and pride. The three principal leaders out of this list of eight are gluttony, avarice, and self-esteem. Evagrius would say that dejection precedes anger. In certain instances both are correct.

The logic of the progression of these demons is as follows: gluttony awakens the misuse of the senses, which leads to sexual unchastity. Avarice stirs the need to possess and control other people, things, or events in a negative way. When we, inevitably, do not get all of the sensual gratification we want, the sexual gratification we want, or the control we want, we get angry. When anger continues over a long period of time without genuine healing, we become dejected. Many people think that because the anger has seemingly subsided, it has healed. But this is not true. It has simply settled more deeply into the inner recesses of the soul into a deep-seated bitterness. Bitterness slowly begins to poison every relationship, every task, and even every prayer if left untreated and unhealed. When all is poisoned by bitterness, we become listless and bored with everything in our life. Listlessness can also occur when everything is going quite well spiritually, and all the previous vices have been conquered. Listlessness, sometimes called "the noonday devil," or "ascedia," is considered one of the fiercest and most destructive of all the demons encountered in the heat and stillness of the monastic desert. Self-esteem then stirs an unhealthy need for self-affirmation based on poor self-image. When this reaches maturity, it manifests in full-blown egotism and pride, which is considered the mother and root of all sin.

It is interesting to note that the other major religions also have a rather developed demonology. If anything, religions such as Buddhism have a much more frightening depiction of hell and demons, even though they are viewed as temporary (meaning hundreds of thousands of "kalpas," or worlds, lasting hundreds of thousands and millions of years each). In particular, the Buddhist work on the fifty demon states from the *Shurangama Sutra,* or the three primary personal demons (pride, anger, and attachment to emptiness) listed in *Dhyana for Beginners,* are very similar to this treatment of the eight demons from the Christian East. It shows that the human experience of the more interior and mystical aspect of religion has some strikingly common elements throughout the world and its ages. Based on this chorus of religious agreement, we should take it all the more seriously, especially when confirmed through Jesus and the Church.

Self-Discipline

These eight demons are overcome through rigorous, yet moderate, self-discipline. This self-discipline is found primarily in the areas of the redirection of thoughts through meditation and the subjection of the senses though physical asceticism. Combined, they become a powerful remaking of the entire human person according to a spiritual and Christlike model, rather than a sensual, emotional, and egoistical precedent and priority in one's life.

Gluttony is overcome by moderate fasting. Unchastity is overcome by vigils at night, manual labor in the day, and filling the mind with positive thoughts and images through spiritual reading. Avarice is overcome by intentionally embracing simple living in the context of obedience to an abbot within a community. Anger is overcome through forgiveness, thankfulness, and humbly avoiding casting blame on others by admitting one's own fault and responsibility in conflict from a general perspective. Dejection is overcome through hope and thankfulness. Listlessness is overcome through staying active in manual labor or one's assigned work, and by meditation on death, or by realizing the fact that this very day could be our last day on earth. Self-esteem is overcome by not allowing oneself to become conceited in spiritual progress, and particularly in successful ministry. Pride is overcome by meditating on the humility of Jesus, the Son of God, in his passion and crucifixion. The specific tools are applied with wisdom and moderation. Extremes are avoided. Stages of development are gone through at a slow and steady pace. The goal is something that is truly helpful and doable in one's daily life.

Let us now look more completely at the eight vices and the classical spiritual tools used to overcome them.

Gluttony

Moderate fasting excludes the extremes of eating too much, or too little, especially for extended periods of time. The monastic fast involves moderate eating on a daily basis, with only occasional periods for greater, or even complete, abstinence. I have seen many at the monastery destroy their physical and emotional health through immoderate fasting and fad diets. I have also seen people make up for the lack of sensual gratification in the area of sex, or just plain old hard monastic work, through overeating when so much food is available on a table set out to feed a whole community rather than just one small family.

Traditionally, there are two kinds of fasting within monastic and Catholic Christianity. The first, coming from the ancient Christian writing, the Didache, indicates that the early Christians fasted on Wednesdays and Fridays, in contrast to the Jewish fast on Mondays and Thursdays. The recent reports of apparitions of the Virgin Mary in various places, especially Medegorje, Yugoslavia, have revived this ancient practice of fasting on bread and water on Wednesdays and Fridays. The monastic fast recommends a daily moderation that, in its earliest Eastern expressions, involved beginning with only two meals a day regularly, with a third light meal added on special liturgical feast days. As the monk progressed, fasting could become more intense under the direction of one's spiritual father or mother.

Both of these traditions would not encourage extreme measures, or passing fads, concerning food, drink, and fasting. Here at the monastery of the Little Portion Hermitage we have seen many go off into extremes. Some have done serious harm to their health through self-diagnosis without a doctor's help, and the implementation of various dietary trends and fads. This not only has physiological effect, but can have serious psychological consequences as well. All of this can have an eventual effect on the well-being of one's overall spiritual life in Christ. Many who have gone down this path are unable to return to health on a physical, emotional, psychological, and spiritual level.

We have also seen many become obese through overeating. This happens for two reasons. First, we have to set out enough food for a whole community, rather than for just one person or family. Some simply cannot control themselves when so much organically home-grown food is right there in front of them. But more deeply, monastic life calls for real renunciation and sacrifice in many areas. Some are external and obvious. Some are internal and very private. All are very difficult. Sometimes a person will miss the more perfect plan of God by compensating for these sacrifices through overindulgence in food and drink. It is always tragic to witness, and a bit of a scandal to outsiders, who expect that we, above others, should be able to control such a basic and common abuse and sin. A fat monk is really a contradiction in terms, though we do not expect that all body sizes be identical or unrealistically perfect.

Unchastity

Vigils simply involve rising at three or four in the morning after six to eight hours of sleep, keeping in mind that the early monks retired at sundown. There is also a tradition that interrupts sleep at midnight for a one- to three-hour vigil, going back to bed until Morning Prayer at six or seven in the morning. Manual labor involves a six- to eight-hour workday, broken up with appropriate breaks for meals, study, and liturgical and private prayer. Spiritual reading involves hearing the Word of God and the Fathers during the lessons of liturgy, and in private times in one's monastic cell. It is considered the source leading to the thoughts and images of meditation which, in turn, lead to passive contemplation beyond all concepts or thought.

There are two traditions of vigils within Catholic Christianity. The first is monastic, and involves rising eight hours after sunset, at two to four A.M., depending upon the season of the year. The second dates back to the early cathedrals of the Church, and the later monastic and religious tradition of consecrated life, and involves interrupting sleep at midnight to keep a vigil from one to three hours, and returning to bed until a reasonably scheduled Morning Prayer. Both of these traditions are an excellent way to overcome sexual temptations, which so frequently occur in the middle of the night.

Manual labor is an excellent way to humble our pride, and to get us back in touch with the most basic, or earthy, realities of life. Here at Little Portion Hermitage, we always give our newest participants and members, called postulants and novices, assignments to manual labor in the garden. Only later do we allow them to begin doing more office-oriented, and administrative tasks. This initial time of getting back in touch with the basics of human existence are most healing, though they are quite difficult for the average aspirant who has been raised in a typical American city and has held down a typical American job. After the example of the entire contemplative tradition, it is also apparent that manual labor is most suited to maintaining an authentic contemplative life. Concerning sexual temptations, manual labor is an excellent way to simply work off any excess energy in our physical body, making illicit sexual behavior something we are often simply too tired to engage in. Spiritual reading has been addressed under *lectio divina* in our section on the

Christian West. However, it is good to reiterate that there is not a much better way to redirect negative thoughts into positive thoughts than by this time-tested jewel of monastic spirituality. Since illicit sexual behavior must first manifest in our thoughts, the redirection of our thoughts from negative sexuality to the things of God through spiritual reading is most beneficial in overcoming this most common of human temptations and sins.

Avarice (Control)

Simple living and community, in obedience to a spiritual father or mother, are considered a natural cure for the desire to control and possess people, things, or situations. Cassian's depiction of the avaricious monk is a tragically humorous description of the unhappy psychological tailspins people can get into when they become disobedient, and self-willed, in community. It starts with little things, leads to big things, and eventually seeks justification through the support of others. Unless healed, it almost always leads to the departure of the avaricious monk.

Living in a community dedicated to simple living is a great tool against avarice. But even here, avarice usually strikes in the least expected places. We all take the vow of poverty, and divest ourselves of the major material possessions of our life when we come to the monastic expression of The Brothers and Sisters of Charity at Little Portion Hermitage. But it's the little things that catch you off guard. We discover quickly our possessiveness of our own ideas and agendas, as well as the few remaining possessions we recollect, or bring with us to monastic community. They are all overcome through what St. Francis called the greatest poverty. This greatest poverty is obedience. As St. Francis says, the greatest poverty is "to renounce one's will into the hands of a Superior through obedience."

Likewise, it's amazing how much importance we place on little items that would have been insignificant to us out in the world. Our own personal coffee cup in the kitchen, or our usual "personal" seat in chapel, our portable CD and cassette players, and the like, all become major possessions once one's major worldly possessions, such us homes, cars, or fancy wardrobes, are no longer available. But the problem of avarice remains. Monastic community—living in common with brothers and sisters in obedience to a spiritual father or mother—is an expert and time-tested way to rout out this more deeply ingrained avarice within our lives. But it takes real courage to persevere. Most give up and leave before they get the real reward, even though they hopefully received some good gifts from God anyway. As we usually say when people leave, "We do not send out failed community members but better Christians."

Anger

Detachment from the disordered and immoderate use of the senses regarding food, sex, and possessiveness of things, people, and situations is usually enough to substantially diffuse the emotional explosion of anger. The monastic fathers also encourage the redirecting of the thoughts by the conscious and willful forgiveness of anyone with whom we have conflict, thanking God for the good and bad situations in our life as means for spiritual growth, and making a concerted effort not to blame others for the bad things in our life but to take personal responsibility. These are powerful means for healing.

As with avarice, in monastic community little things can become big things if left untreated and unhealed. Small infringements upon our own avaricious possessiveness that would have been quickly overlooked out in the world become major obstacles in relationships within a monastery. Learning real detachment from things, ideas and opinions, and relationships allows us to "let go and let God." Then our use of things, our presentation of creative ideas, and our relationships with others can truly begin to prosper in a way that is free from possessiveness and anger.

Consciously learning to ask and offer forgiveness, even when, in our old self-centered opinions, we're convinced that we did no wrong, and the blame belongs to someone else, is a powerful tool in overcoming anger. It helps us to realize that we exist spiritually within the very people we think have offended and wronged us. This happens in the natural order of creation, as understood within the New Physics, and most certainly within the gift of the Holy Spirit, in whom all believers now operate in tangible spiritual communion.

Of course, giving thanks for all things is a most powerful tool for climbing out of the deep and dark pit of negative thoughts and emotions. To realize that God has a lesson for us even in the things we see as most negative empowers us to thank God even for the things we perceive as "bad." This kind of thanks can only operate in a faith that is stronger than the immediate negativity of thoughts and emotions about a particular situation we may perceive to be bad or evil.

Last, in the ancient novice instruction for monks, Dorotheos of Gaza introduces a concept that is almost shocking to the modern reader, yet most effective in overcoming anger. The concept is self-accusation. It means that even in a particular situation where we have been unjustly blamed, or wronged, we look from a more universal and spiritual perspective in order to keep from getting trapped into anger. From the perspective of the particular situation, we may have been treated unjustly. But Dorotheos would encourage us to look further in order to see our own responsibility for the situation. Though our actions in words may not have been wrong, what about our body language, which is so subliminally affected by the interior attitudes of thoughts and emotions from the body and soul? Furthermore, perhaps we have offended this individual or group earlier, perhaps even years ago, and the relationship is still suffering as a result. Even further, what if we have been wrong in our treatment of someone else long ago and far away, and only now is God using this particular circumstance to get us to look at the wrong in the past particular action? Dorotheos is adamant that the primary reason for bad relationships in monastic community is because monks have not learned to see offenses against themselves by others in this more universal and spiritual perspective.

What about us? Do we always want to be right? Do we always seek justice, especially when it is we who have been wronged? Despite our vision for "justice," are we often angry and upset internally? If so, perhaps we need to try this ancient way of Dorotheos of Gaza.

Dejection (Bitterness)

A conscious and willful redirecting of our thoughts to thank God for all things, both good and the bad, and to intentionally have hope for the future based upon our faith in God are most trustworthy tools. This involves an intentional and courageous act of the will to choose the positive over the negative, even when we feel overwhelmed by the negative. At this point, the charismatic gift of praying in tongues, or the contemplative practice of breath prayer, can be most helpful. How does this work? Sometimes we cannot bring ourselves to offer positive thanks and praise genuinely, even when we know we should. We know that words of praise will cause thoughts of positive praise, which will affect our emotions as well. Yet, when we make the choice for God with an act of the will, our mind still goes back to negativity. This occurs right in the middle of a mental exercise that is supposed to be positive!

With tongues, we temporarily bypass the mind in order to cleanse the mind. We include the voice and the emotions, keeping in mind the connection between emotions, thoughts, and words. We speak forth praise in words of seeming nonsense in order to stir the incensive power of emotions, and stir up the Spirit of God. In turn, God reaches out to cleanse the mind of negativity by his power, not ours, when we are seemingly powerless to overcome the surge of negative thoughts and emotions. Once this is done, we can use the mind in objective thoughts of positivity again.

Breath prayer is similar but works in an opposite direction. Instead of directing our spiritual energies out and up through positive thanks and praise, we are letting go, out and down, of every thought, emotion, and sensual perception with every breath. We breathe in the good things of the Breath, or Spirit of God, and breathe out the negative things in our life in a systematic, meditational way, which eventually takes us beyond thought, emotion, or sense yet renews them all. It is a powerful tool of "letting go and letting God." We will discuss it more fully in later chapters.

It is easy to become negative in monastic community. Things close in on themselves. Mountains are made out of molehills. If we lose the broader perspective of both earthly and spiritual life, we do not remain truly grounded in prayer. It is most important to hope against hope, even in the midst of what we perceive as a most desperate and dark situation. I have seen many people lose hope and quit their vocation prematurely because they could not have the faith to continue in hope and go forward to the greater things in Christ.

Listlessness (Boredom)

Simply getting to work and getting our mind off of our boredom and ourselves can solve most of this problem. Furthermore, realizing that this might be our last day on earth and that every moment is precious becomes a most powerful tool for rising up out of this mire of the enemy and getting busy with the many good things of God's work in creation. There's an old saying, "If you want to stop doing the don'ts, start doing the do's!" Likewise with listlessness, simply getting busy with the positive work we've been assigned to, and the good results of its faithful execution, or the belief that these will come, will pull us out of negativity and boredom nine times out of ten.

For the other one time out of ten, meditation on death usually works well. This is not some kind of morbid preoccupation with death. It is meditating daily that death could come to us at any moment of any day in a way least expected. This means that today may be our last day on earth. As scripture says, "Today is the day of salvation." And St. Paul says, "Make good use of the time that remains." Buddhist monks, and monks of many other traditions, have a similar meditation. For all of us, it can prove to be the motivation to use every waking minute and hour in a truly beneficial and constructive way.

Self-esteem (Unhealthy vs. Healthy)

Consciously humbling oneself in thought and action after successful ministry or times of spiritual progress is a most helpful tool. This is one that I had to learn early on, especially in light of my public ministry of sacred song and teaching. For myself, this means offering the glory to God internally and, if appropriate, externally as well, every time I am praised for a particular ministry or work, or even for when I feel I'm making spiritual progress. As scripture says, "It is you have accomplished all we have done." The scripture is clear that it is God who accomplishes the good within us, for he is the author of all that is good. Often, when receiving a compliment after a talk or concert, I internally offer the praise to my God, though it is not always socially appropriate to interrupt the person to do so. Finding the balance is a matter of wisdom that can only be learned with experience through the passing of years.

Pride

There is no greater tool against pride than simply meditating on the passion and crucifixion of Jesus, the King of kings, the Lord of lords, to get us to realize that if Jesus was not too good to suffer this kind of pain and humiliation, neither are we! Furthermore, Jesus' self emptying on the cross can inspire us to let go of self and to be truly detached from our own self-centeredness and ego. Only then do we really discover what it is to be "born again" as a new person substantially free of such selfishness.

This meditation on the crucifixion and resurrection of Jesus supplies us with all the motivation and empowerment we need to overcome pride, or any other of the eight vices. In the cross the greatest becomes least, the highest becomes the lowest of all, and the master becomes the servant. Yet through this great condescension we find the greatest ascension in all of the cosmos. The way to greatness is through the least, the way to the heights is by taking the lowest road, and the way to rule and lead is by becoming the servant of all. Yet even beyond these dualities, the highest is in the lowest, the great is in the least, and leadership is in humble and lowly service. This is the way of mystery and paradox through the cross and resurrection of Jesus Christ. It is the doorway to contemplation.

All of these tools are most valuable and have been tested for almost two thousand years in the context of monastic communities, which have sought to provide supportive environments for true spiritual growth in Christ and God. They provide the ascetical and meditational rationale for the whole structure of monastic life. Once understood, these tools cease to be external or mental ascetical burdens too heavy to carry, as often described by those who have been poorly instructed, or who have given up on this way. They become a true means for liberation and genuine human freedom. This is the whole point of monastic and Christian life.

Conclusion

To conclude, let's go back to Evagrius, with whom we started. He says, "As stated in the beginning, there are three chief groups of demons opposing us in the practice of the ascetical life, and after them follows the whole army of the enemy. . . . They are the demons set over the appetites of gluttony, those who suggest avaricious thoughts, and those who incite self-esteem in the eyes of men. If you long for pure prayer, keep guard over your incensive power, and if you desire self-restraint, control your belly, and do not take your fill even of bread and water. Be vigilant in prayer . . . avoid all rancor. Let the teachings of the Holy Spirit be always with you; and use the virtues as your hands to knock at the doors of scripture. Then dispassion of heart will rise within you, and during prayer you will see your intellect shine like a star."

THE EIGHT VICES EXERCISE

1. Sit in your meditation space and breathe deeply.
2. Allow yourself to be aware of the leading three of the eight vices. They are gluttony, avarice, and negative self-esteem.
3. Begin with gluttony. With the inhale of breath, be aware of an area in your life where you are attached to little sensual pleasures, including gluttony, that can lead to bigger sensual addictions such as sexual sin. Also be aware of any other major sensual addiction such as substance abuse, etc. Do not judge these things now or be scrupulous about the little things. Just be aware of their existence in your life.
4. Bring these areas to the cross of Christ, and release them to Jesus as you exhale. Let them go. Visualize them detaching themselves from your sensual appetites. By letting them go, they will release the hold they have upon you. Residual results of addiction are resolved through repeated meditation of this kind.
5. Now move to avarice. As you inhale, recognize any attachment to your control of things, people, or agendas. Also recognize any anger or deeper bitterness that results when these, or other desires, are not satisfied, or when anger is not healed. Again, now is not the time to become upset or too scrupulous about these things. Simply acknowledge that they are in your life, and cause negative results for you and others.
6. Bring these areas to the cross of Jesus, and let them go as you exhale. Especially visualize your need to control as it leaves your soul and body.
7. Now we move to the heart of all others. As you inhale, be aware of your disorder, illusion, and delusion—your false self. Also, see how feeding this false self has given birth to pride

in its many forms in your life. Simply acknowledge it being in your life.

8. Bring the false self to the cross of Christ, simply release it to God's judgment, and let it go. *Really* doing this will free you of most other vices in your life, including pride. See your attachments from disordered priorities in the senses and emotions of the body, and the cognitions and thoughts of the spiritual mind, or soul, simply fall away from your true being through the cross of Jesus.

9. With the next inhale, allow the essence of your being to emerge, your spirit. Allow your spirit to emerge and join fully with God's Spirit. Now allow your spirit in God's Spirit to transform every other aspect of your life so that they will be used properly for your and everyone else's highest good in God through Christ.

10. Thank God for the graces of this meditation through the cross of Jesus.

11. Conclude as usual.

The Spirit and Intellection

FOLLOWING THE SENSES AND PASSIONS of the body, and the thoughts and images of the mind, or soul, comes the pure spiritual intuition of intellection. Contrary to its name, this does not involve the use of the intellect as a faculty of the mind. On the contrary, intellection builds on, yet surpasses, both the thoughts and images of the soul and mind, and the senses and passions of the body. Thus, intellection builds on, and includes, both the incensive and the rational powers but surpasses them both.

Spiritual Intuition

Intellection is the place of pure spiritual intuition. It is beyond all sensual perception, all emotions, and all concepts or images. It cannot be described, understood, or felt. It can only be experienced. This is called knowing in unknowing, yet it is not the absence of knowledge. It is light in darkness, yet it is beyond both darkness and light. This kind of experience can only be called pure spiritual intuition. This cannot be understood if it has not been experienced.

Energy and Essence

Intellection builds on the energies, or that which can be known and perceived about God and creation, and breaks through to pure essence, or that which is beyond all sensual, emotional, or conceptual knowing, which can only be known through pure spiritual intuition. Yet it is the essence that constitutes the deepest Reality of God, humanity, and all creation. The energies, though truly part of the identity of any object or entity—human, angelic, or divine—remain the more external part. The energies can be known through senses, emotions, and concepts. Essence is known only through pure spiritual intuition, spirit to Spirit, essence to Essence, as it were.

In God, energies are the part of him that can be called loving, good, true, or just, etc. In God they are called "uncreated energies." God's more traditional divine attributes of omnipotence, or all-powerful, omniscience, or all-knowing, and omnipresence, or the ability to be present everywhere, as well as his being eternal, or infinite, are all part of God's energies, and are part of his immanence, or his ability to be known by creation. But God's essence is beyond all these things, yet is his deepest reality and being. It represents his transcendence, or his being, "wholly other," or beyond the grasp of humanity or creation. Energies reveal a part of God and are very really he, but they remain only part of God, not God in absolute fullness. In pure transcendence, God remains unknowable. Essence is the fullness and deepest Reality of God and is beyond all description of sensual, emotional, or conceptual knowing by humanity or creation. Yet, this essence can be known through a communion of pure spiritual intuition in contemplation.

This knowing is direct knowledge, beyond any intermediary of creation. It is spirit to Spirit, essence to Essence, and being to Being.

It is the knowing of All through intuition beyond all knowledge. It appears to be stupid and stammering, yet it knows All that Is in a mystical flash of intuition in spirit. It is, as says St. Paul, "able to judge all things, yet can be judged by none."

This also applies to the rest of creation. Humanity also has energies and essence. So does all the rest of creation. In human beings, our body and soul, our senses and emotions, and images and concepts of the mind are our energies. They are truly part of us, but they are only part. Our essence is the deepest and eternal reality of our being, and it enlivens all the parts of the whole. It is pure spirit.

The best analogy I can use for this is within my own human person. If I were to lose my hand, or even part of my brain, I would no longer be able to play guitar to make the music I'm known for, or to write books and teach as I am doing here. My music and my teaching are a very real part of me. They communicate the reality of my being in a way that cannot be done elsewhere in normal daily life. Yet, if I were to lose these faculties, I would be no less "John Michael Talbot." The "meness" of me would remain untouched, and my life would be equally as precious as it was before.

My hand or my brain are my energies. My senses, my emotions, and even my conceptualizations and ideas are part of me, and a very important part, but they remain something extrinsic to my essence, or my spirit, though my spirit thoroughly enlivens my body and my soul when it is fully reborn and awakened in Christ. Even that which I call my "personality" is something extrinsic yet enlivened by the essence of my personhood. Many times my personality fails to express that which is deepest within my being. In this sense, personality fails to fully capture the reality of my person. My true person is something much deeper, existing in the realms of the spirit and pure essence.

Once we break through to this realm of spirit and pure essence, the body and the soul begin to express the realities of the spirit as their first priority. This does not mean the negation of senses, emotions, or ideas. If anything, it means the fulfillment of their original purpose in God's plan. Senses, emotions, and conceptual ideas of the body and soul become even more fine-tuned under the leadership of the spirit. Energies become more expressive and effective under the leadership of essence.

The Human Will

Nor does this mean the negation of the importance of the human will. In the medieval spiritual anthropology of memory, intellect, and will, the human will was the seat of divine love. In modern times we say that "love is a decision" and, therefore, an act of the will. In the anthropology of body, soul, and spirit, of energies and essence, the spirit would be the seat of the human will working in full harmony with, and directing, the body and soul. But as I have said before, it would be a great mistake to overly divide the human person into compartments by the use of these formulated categories. The human person, as is God himself, remain an integrated trinity and whole. Thus, both love and choice become an act of the entire integrated person.

Creation

But essences exist not only in humanity and God but in the rest of creation as well. Sentient beings, such as animals of various kinds, have energy and an essence, though we would be improperly speculating if we tried to compare them identically with the body, soul, and spirit of human beings. There's a clear difference between humanity and the rest of sentient life that has been recognized by the Judeo-Christian heritage, as well as by all the major faith traditions of the world, though we express it in different theological terms. Nonetheless, that same Judeo-Christian heritage, especially in the monastic expression of the Orthodox Christian East, recognizes that all creation has both energies and essence. So even nonsentient life, such as flowers and trees, and even nonliving objects, such as rocks or metals, have both external energies and interior essence. It is possible to intuit the inner essences of all the things of creation, and of creation as a whole, through what the Eastern Christian Fathers call "intellection."

The best example I can use for us is the example used earlier of the two Franciscan friars watching the sunrise or sunset. One says, "Notice his use of color here." This statement perceives the energies of God in the energies of the sunrise or sunset through the energies of the human faculties. This is all done with spiritual motivation and appreciation, but it remains on the level of energies.

Yet we have all had times when we have looked at the sunrise or sunset, or the flower or the tree, and have broken through beyond the external energies to the true interior essence of God, and of the thing itself, through the use of our own spiritual intuition, or essence. These are decisive moments where we break through from the things of space and time to Eternity, from the finite to the Infinite, from objective or subjective truth to pure Reality. For those who follow the path of contemplation as a way of life, these moments become more frequent and soon become a whole new way of intuitively seeing and perceiving all of our life.

Infinite Spirit

Perhaps it is for this reason that the Eastern Orthodox monastic fathers say that, while the body and the soul are finite, created realities, the human spirit is created for infinity and is actually infinite! While the body and soul definitely exist in space and time, and under the cognition of concepts and ideas, the spirit exists in Eternity and Infinity even now. The scriptures say that we are already seated "at the right hand of God the Father in Christ Jesus." This means that our spirit is already in eternity and infinity through our communion with Christ in the Holy Spirit. We are already existing with God in the past, the present, and future, all in an "eternal now," though our body and soul still sojourn in space and time. At the end of the world as we know it, even our body and soul will be transformed in this Ultimate Reality in a way beyond what we can possibly understand now. We begin to break through to that reality in Christ through contemplation, or what the Eastern Christian and monastic fathers and mothers call intellection.

Self-Control and Dispassion

This breakthrough to the true human spirit in God's Spirit does not happen automatically. It cannot just be read in a book, listened to on a teaching tape, or watched on a video or DVD, and then suddenly become a reality in one's life. It must be implemented in one's whole life. This means embracing a way of self-discipline in the human faculties of the body and soul before the awakening and rebirth of the spirit is possible in Christ. These human faculties, as we have seen, involve the senses, emotions, and thought processes. As we discussed earlier, the tools of self-discipline, or self-control, are fasting, vigils, meditative reading, manual labor, simple living and renunciation in community in obedience to a spiritual father and/or mother, and the mental disciplines of devotion, which lead to attitudes of thanksgiving and praise, forgiveness, hope, and humility.

The fathers and mothers of the monastic Christian East call this self-discipline "self-control." It is fundamental to both monastic and authentic Christian spirituality. It is not something that one does only for a period of time, even though more intense liturgical periods of self-denial are also part of the general religious practices of the major religions of the world. In addition to these liturgical periods, like Advent and Lent in the Christian tradition, or Ramadan in the Moslem tradition, self-control must become a way of life.

This self-control leads one's whole life into a way of great tranquility and peace, substantially unaffected by the ups-and-downs of the external circumstances of daily living. It is not intended to be an ascetical competition of physical endurance, or a masochistic exercise in an erroneous understanding of creation and God. On the contrary, it is intended to bring the things of creation back into the harmony and peace of God. This brings an abundant and full understanding and an appreciation, awareness, and sensitivity to their true worth. Self-control brings true abundance to creation when properly understood and lived.

As St. Diodochus says, "With regard to self-control and eating, we must never feel loathing for any kind of food, for to do so is abominable and utterly demonic. It is emphatically not because any kind of food is bad in itself that we refrain from it, but in not eating too much or too richly we can to some extent keep in check the excitable parts of our body. . . . It is in no way contrary to the principles of true knowledge to eat and drink from all that he is set before you, giving thanks to God. . . . But gladly to abstain from eating too pleasurably or too much shows greater discrimination and understanding."

Ilias the Presbyter says, "Combine simplicity with self-control, and unite truth with humility, and you will keep house with Justice, at whose table every other virtue likes to gather. Having united simplicity and self-control, you will experience the blessing that their union produces. . . . No one can pray purely if he is constrained by the passions. . . . The intellect cannot be peaceful during prayer unless it has acquired self-control and love." This implies real work and determination. Ilias says, "Many ascend the cross of mortification, but few consent to be nailed to it." St. Thalassios the Libyan says, "If you wish to be in control of your soul and body, forestall the passions by rooting out their causes. . . . Curb the impulses of desire by means of self-control. . . . Self-control and strenuous effort curb desire; stillness and intense longing for God wither it."

St. Peter of Damascus adds, "Where is the gentleness . . . the all-embracing self-control that restrains each member of the body and every thought and desire? . . . I will speak of the trees of the spiritual Paradise. . . . Of these, the most all-embracing is self-control, by which I mean abstinence from all the passions. There is also another, more partial, form of self-control that applies to bodily actions. . . . Self-control needs to be cultivated and guarded ceaselessly. . . . The two forms of self-control are not identical. . . . The first curbs our chastity and the other shameful passions; the second controls even the slightest thought. . . . Self-control is a sure and unfailing sense of discretion. . . . Without self-control, the soul's three powers are carried either upwards toward licentiousness or downwards toward stupidity. . . . Self-control disciplines all things and bridles mindless impulses of soul and body, directing them toward God." And St. Theodorus the Great Ascetic concludes, and leads us to the next section on dispassion when he says, "Self-control together with humility withers passionate desire. . . . Dispassion is born from self-control and humility."

Dispassion

Dispassion is the result of a reordered and harmoniously peaceful function of body and soul, or the senses, emotions, and thoughts. That reordering occurs through self-control, or ascetical self-discipline. But dispassion is the goal, for dispassion is the attitude of Jesus Christ, who is our ultimate goal. He is the archetypal Human Being, as well as God. It is God who shows his human creation how to be truly human. And it is this Human, who leads all of humanity back to the original divinity, or deification, which was originally ours. Dispassion is one of the greatest characteristics of this mystery of divinity and humanity being one.

Dispassion is a holy detachment from the incensive powers of the senses and emotions of the body, or the rational power of conceptual images or thoughts, which would disturb our stillness, or hesychia, which leads us into union with Reality, or God. At first, it is detachment from the obviously evil, or negative, things in life that keep us from the godly use of these human faculties. As one grows in Christ, this dispassion ironically includes detachment from any stirring of the incensive or rational powers within the body or the soul. This leads us to the highest form of intellection, or contemplation, which builds on, yet is beyond, any sense, emotion, conceptual image, or thought. It is pure intuitive union with God and All on the level of the spirit.

It is good to caution, however, that this is not the Quietism of Christianity nor the "stinking Zen" of Buddhism. These refer to those who enter into an unhealthy detachment from reality in their attempt to reach holy dispassion. True dispassion is detached from everything in a way that unites us more fully to All. False dispassion detaches us from everything in a way that separates us from all, and makes us functionally dysfunctional. People who enter into false dispassion lose touch with reality, and eventually become very inefficient and insensitive in any job, task, or relationship they engage in. Holy dispassion is selfless, while false dispassion is really just selfish indifference in godly and religious disguise.

St. Peter of Damascus sums up most of what can be said about dispassion when he says, "This is a sign of dispassion: to remain calm and fearless in all things because one has received God's grace and strength to do anything. . . . We should not be distracted by anything . . . rather, with humility we should strive to maintain a state of stillness, free from all distraction. . . . In short, we should be detached from all things, whether good or bad, so that nothing perturbs us and we reach a state of stillness.

"Dispassion is a strange and paradoxical thing. . . . For though a person who has attained the state of dispassion continues to suffer attacks from demons and vicious men, he experiences this as if a gift were happening to someone else. . . . When he is praised, he is not filled with self-elation, nor when he is insulted is he afflicted. For he considers that what is pleasant comes to him by the grace of God . . . of which he is unworthy, while what is unpleasant comes as a trial:

the former is given to encourage us . . . while the latter is given to increase our humility. . . . Such a person is impassable, yet because of discrimination is acutely aware of what gives pain. . . . Dispassion is not a single virtue, but is a name for all the virtues." St. Diodochus speaks of a priest who has attained this dispassion when he says, "This man does not think of what he is, even when others praise him . . . does not think of his priestly rank . . . strips himself of any thought of his own dignity . . . sees himself in his own mind as a useless servant. . . . He is both present in this life, and not present in it." This is also a sign of great humility.

Essence of Creation

After we have exercised self-control and entered into dispassion, then we are ready for the pure intuitive spiritual perception of the essence of creation leading to the essence of God. While still under the control of the senses, passions, and conceptual thought, we can only dimly perceive the energies of either creation or the Creator. Before the senses, passions, and conceptual images are purified through ascetical self-control and discipline, they remain as negative influences of illusion and delusion concerning our perception of the created world, and of the Creator. After purification, they can be used in a positive way for godly things, and for God. However, this is still not breaking through to the level of intellection and contemplation beyond sensual perception, emotional stimulation, or conceptual thought concerning either creation or the Creator. While operating on the level of energies can be both positive and godly, it is only the beginning level in the stages of contemplative enlightenment and rebirth.

Contemplating the essence of creation through intellection takes us beyond space and time through the things of space and time into the eternal and infinite. It is a breakthrough from seeing reality into Reality itself. It is knowing that which is beyond knowledge through, what the mystics called, "unknowing." Yet it is the deepest knowing possible for the human being within the human existence. It is the closest thing to the reality of what we call "heaven," while remaining here on earth.

St. John Cassian says, "God may be perceived and understood in many ways. God is not only to be known in his blessed and comprehensible being. . . . He is also to be known from the grandeur and beauty of his creatures." This reality is possible on both the level of the energies and the essence in body and soul, and spirit, respectively. St. Maximos the Confessor is more specific regarding contemplating the essence of creation when he says, "The intellect, once totally free from passions, proceeds undistracted to the contemplation of created things, making its way toward knowledge of the Holy Trinity. When in a pure state, the intellect, on receiving the conceptual images of things, is moved to contemplate these things spiritually. . . . When the intellect is engaged in the contemplation of things visible, it searches out easier than natural principles these things, or the spiritual principles which they reflect."

Ilias the Presbyter says of the difference between energies and essence, "The man engaged in ascetic practice can readily submit his intellect to prayer, while the contemplative man can readily submit prayer to the intellect. The first restricts his perception of visible forms, while the second directs the soul's attention toward the inner essences concealed in such forms. Alternatively, the first compels the intellect to apprehend the inner essences of corporal realities, while the second persuaded to grasp those of incorporeal beings. The inner essences of corporal realities are also incorporeal."

St. Peter of Damascus relates this to his threefold division of demonic, human, and angelic thought. Demonic thought is the misuse of the senses, emotions, and conceptual forms. Human thought consists solely in the abstract conception of some created things. He says, "Angelic thought, finally, consists in the dispassionate contemplation of things, which is spiritual knowledge proper. . . . We should look on man with wonder, conscious that his intellect, being infinite, is the image of the invisible God. . . . When we come to consider the body, we should marvel . . . that it is not its own animated principle but is, at God's command, co-mixed with the noetic and deiform soul, created by the Holy Spirit breathing life into it. . . . By thus contemplating the dispassionate way, the beauty and use of each thing, he who is illumined is filled with love for the Creator."

Ironically, it is Evagrius, the first monastic and Christian commentator on such things, who states most clearly the unique reality of the contemplation of the essence of creation. Again, with irony, he does this by stating it in the negative when compared to pure prayer, and the contemplation of the pure Essence of God. He says, "One who has attained dispassion has not necessarily achieved pure prayer. For he may still be occupied with thoughts which, though dispassionate, distract him and keep him far from God. . . . It has not necessarily reached the realm of prayer, for it may still be contemplating the inner essence of things. And though such contemplation is dispassionate yet sensitive of created things, he impresses their forms upon the intellect and keeps it away from God. If the intellect has not risen above the contemplation of the created world, it has not yet beheld the realm of God perfectly."

So for the first rugged monks and solitaries of the desert even the high level of the dispassionate contemplation of the inner essence of created things was not enough. They pushed on past creation to the Creator, through the inner essence of created things to the very essence of God. Both of these realities lie within the spirit's faculty of intellection, or the pure spiritual intuition of contemplation, beyond even the positive use of the senses, emotions, or conceptual images and forms of thought. But for the seeker of God, even breathing the rarefied air of contemplation of the essence of creation is not enough. They must move from in and through this level to the final level; pure prayer and contemplation of God.

The Essence of God

Once we have purified the senses, emotions, and thoughts of the body and the soul, and experienced something of the contemplation of the essence of creation through pure spiritual intuition, then we can move on to the pure contemplative experience of the essence of God. Here, our essence becomes one with the Essence who is the source of every essence of creation, human and nonhuman, living and nonliving. Here, spirit is one with the Spirit who Is One. This is unknowing beyond knowledge, yet clarifying all that can be known among the knowable. It is sensing beyond senses through "off-sensing," yet clarifying and awakening all the senses in perfect harmony in balance. It is passion beyond all passion through dispassion in a way that frees us from negative passions and clarifies and frees the positive emotions to function in a noncontrived and holy way in our life.

The monastic Christian mystics of both East and West call this "contemplation." The Eastern Christian mystics also call it the intellection of God. Whatever you call it, the experience is the same and is beyond all attempts at complete description. That's why the mystics call it "unknowing," or "divine darkness." Instead of calling it what it is, we call it what it is not, aware that what we can say about it is almost nothing when compared to what it truly Is. Therefore, it is safer to call it what it is not, rather than what it Is.

What we can say about God concerns his energies, which he has chosen to reveal to creation and humanity. Theologically, this is called the way of affirmation, or cataphatic theology. What is beyond our descriptions about God concerns his essence, which remains transcendent beyond the full grasp of creation or humanity. This is called the way of negation, or apophatic theology.

All through history there have been those within every religion who have criticized this contemplative way in favor of an approach more simplistic and understandable. Within Christianity, there have always been those who have criticized this contemplative, apophatic way as a carryover from Greek philosophy. To some degree, the criticism is correct. However, apophatic mystical theology exists in every religion and philosophy, including the Judaism from which Christianity came. Therefore, our personal lack of understanding of this higher and deeper mystical way cannot be justified by placing blame on a non-Jewish influence on a Christianity that was, itself, reaching out beyond the Jewish world. No, this apophatic way of contemplative prayer and meditation is common to all religions of the world. Therefore, we must take it all the more seriously when we see it arising from our own Christian tradition, having been confirmed, fulfilled, and completed in Christ.

In his work *On Prayer,* we have seen that Evagrius says, "The state of prayer is one of dispassion. One who has attained dispassion has not necessarily achieved pure prayer. He may still be occupied with thoughts, which, though dispassionate, distract him and keep him far from God. It has not necessarily reached the realm of prayer, for it may still be contemplating the inner essences of these things."

He then goes on to speak directly of contemplative prayer and the essence of God. "When you are praying, do not shape within yourself in the image of the deity . . . but approach the Immaterial in an immaterial manner, and then you'll understand. . . . Never try to see a form or shape during prayer. Do not long to have a sensory image of angels or powers or Christ, for this would be madness. . . . Blessed is the intellect that is completely free from forms during prayer. . . . Blessed is the intellect that has acquired complete freedom from sensations during prayer."

St. Hesychios speaks of this contemplation beyond all image and form in his work *On Watchfulness and Holiness*. He says, "One type of watchfulness consists in closely scrutinizing every mental image or provocation. . . . A second type of watchfulness consists in freeing the heart from all thoughts, keeping it profoundly silent and still, and praying."

St. Diodochus says, "Let no one who hears us speak of the perceptive faculty of the intellect imagine . . . we mean that the glory of God appears to man visibly. . . . No visible reality appears to it in invisible form, since now 'we walk by faith, not by sight,' as St. Paul says (2 Cor. 5:7). . . . The perceptive faculty of the intellect . . . leads us toward invisible blessings." For those who complain that this division between energies and essence, or body, soul, or spirit, overly separates the human being into compartments, he explains, "The perceptive faculty natural to the soul is single, but . . . it is split into two distinct modes of operation as a result of Adam's disobedience." He then goes on to give a clear discernment between the false prayer experiences sent by the enemy to distract us from deeper contemplative prayer, and the ones genuinely sent by God to lead us deeper into his very being and Ultimate Reality.

St. Peter of Damascus concludes by saying, "Apply the counsels of the holy fathers: that during times of prayer we should keep our intellect free from form, shape, color, and not give access to anything at all, whether light, fire, or anything else. . . . The fifth form of discipline consists in spiritual prayer . . . free from all thoughts. . . . For the contemplative, there are yet higher forms of prayer."

Aware that it is difficult to maintain this state throughout the day, the Fathers encourage an alternation between physical and mental activity and stillness. St. Peter of Damascus continues, "Those who are advanced in the spiritual way should direct their intellect now to the contemplation of sensible realities, and now to the cognition of unintelligible realities and to that which is formless; now to the meaning of some passage of the scriptures, and now to pure prayer. On the bodily level, they should engage sometimes in reading, sometimes in prayer."

St. Diodochus says, "Our intellect often finds it hard to endure praying because of the straightness and concentration which this involves: but it joyfully turns to theology because of the broad and unhampered scope of its speculation. . . . To keep the intellect from expressing itself too much in words, or exalting itself unduly . . . we should spend most of our time in prayer, in singing Psalms and reading the scripture, yet without neglecting the speculation of wise man whose faith has been revealed in their writings. . . . In the time of contemplation we must keep the intellect free of all fantasy and image. . . . There is . . . a prayer which is above the broadest scope of speculation."

The Jesus Prayer

TODAY THERE'S MUCH EMPHASIS ON meditation techniques involving the use of breath. This is seen especially in light of the New Age movement, and a rediscovery of the prayer techniques of Hinduism, Buddhism, and Taoism. Each of these Far Eastern religions has a developed system of meditation, and an intricate understanding and use of the breath in calming and focusing the body and mind.

But there is also a breath prayer tradition from ancient Christianity. This tradition is called the Jesus Prayer. It involves a few phrases constructed from biblical texts, united with the breath in order to achieve constant, intuitive prayer based on genuine relationship with Jesus Christ and good theology as understood by the Orthodox and Catholic churches.

The actual content of the prayer is very simple. It consists of the words "Lord, Jesus Christ, Son of God, have mercy on me, a sinner." Each of these words and phrases has deep theological and mystical significance. Let's take a moment to look at this deeper significance.

Lord

The word "Lord" is deeply significant. It comes from two biblical sources. "El" refers to "God," or a compound such as "Almighty God." "Adonai" is "Lord," as in "Lord God." Some earlier sources also include "El" in the compounds, according to some scholars. "Lord" also comes from an English word that was used for the head of the feudal castle/village, as in "the lord of the manor." This individual was the leader of the castle and the village that grew up around it. The peasants could produce the wheat, but only the lord had the wealth and the technology to turn the wheat into bread for the whole village. So the English word "lord" literally means "the keeper of the bread." This all means, first, that the Lord is one who is beyond the normal human classifications of a single person of a particular sex, yet works in and through the things of creation, including individual human leaders. Second, the Lord is one upon whom we all depend to take the particular gifts and talents of each individual and family and transform it into something beneficial for all.

Jesus

The name "Jesus" means "salvation," or "salvage." Jesus means "savior." To fully appreciate this word, one must first need saving. Only those who have been lost at sea, or who have nearly lost their lives in some catastrophic natural event, or have nearly died through illness, can fully appreciate its meaning. But we all need saving in some way. Talk to the recovering alcoholic or drug addict, or the one who has lost their family through death or divorce, or their job and sense of self-worth, and this becomes self-evident. But the fact remains, as in the first step of Alcoholics Anonymous, that we must recognize that our life is out of control, and totally unmanageable without divine assistance, before we can truly appreciate the person of Jesus. Many are not there yet. But everyone gets there sooner or later in the course of their life. Some get there and are too proud to admit their basic human need. This is not an interfaith reference but a simple comment on human nature. Others get there and go through true conversion to Jesus through their humble recognition of their own need for a savior.

Christ

"Christ" simply means "anointed." Anointed by whom, or what? Anointed by the Spirit of God. But what does it mean to be anointed by the Spirit? Sometimes we think we were anointed, but were only excited! Anointed by the Spirit certainly includes enthusiasm, but it is not limited to it, nor is it the only means of determining the authenticity of that anointing. The real test for a genuine anointing from the Spirit of God is spiritual fruit. What is that fruit? Is it learning how to recite scripture, or lead in the liturgy or in the Church, or learn a particular prayer or meditation technique? I think not! The spiritual fruits that come forth in one's life when truly anointed by the Spirit of God are listed in St. Paul's Letter to the Galatians. The list is not exhaustive or exclusive, but it's a good place to begin. They are love, joy, peace, patience, kindness, generosity, mildness, chastity, and faith. These characteristics only surface in the person's life when the old man or woman has passed away, and the new person, after the image Christ, and the child within originally created and planned for us by God, are allowed to be reborn, awaken, and surface. If we try to manipulate these fruits into our life without dying to the old person, we will fail. It is only by totally letting go of the old man and woman that the new person in Christ can be resurrected and reborn.

Son of God

"Son of God" implies many deep theological mysteries. The first is the eternal begetting of the Son from the Father in the Holy Spirit in the eternal reality and realm of heaven. Jesus is "eternally begotten of the Father, God from God, light from light, true God from true

God." Also implied in the title "Son of God" is the mystical reality of the Blessed Trinity, whose wonders are beyond human comprehension and all description, though it includes a two-thousand-year-old tradition of great theological richness. Last, "Son of God" implies Jesus' birth on the earth through the Blessed Virgin Mary. This mysterious revelation in human history is known as the Incarnation. Related to this is the mystery of the mix and imbalance of humanity and divinity within the person of Jesus Christ known as the Hypostatic Union. It, too, is a great mystery beyond full human comprehension or description, yet includes a theological balance and richness virtually unmatched anywhere else on earth. All these things have occupied the minds and meditations of the greatest mystics, monks, and theologians of the Church throughout the ages.

Have Mercy on Me

"Have mercy on me" builds on the whole notion of the mercy of God. Again, anyone who has not known their own need for mercy cannot fully appreciate the depths of this word and its meaning. Anyone who has known their guilt is deeply appreciative when guilt is forgiven and its consequences taken away. Yet the heart of justice is mercy, not revenge. As Jesus says, "The heart of the law is mercy." In the Old Testament, justice was not a matter of getting even. The "eye for an eye, and tooth for a tooth" is not even a matter of getting even through socially moderated revenge. To the contrary, it was a matter of minimizing revenge from the usual destruction of entire families and tribes as a consequence of an offense against a single individual or family in favor of a more clement and benevolent justice. The heart of justice is mercy. It has been said that mercy is forgiveness plus compassion and empathy. Mercy occurs when the person giving forgiveness truly gets inside of the person who is receiving forgiveness. Therefore, mercy is a matter of understanding the offender from the inside out and bringing true healing to the source and cause of their offense.

A Sinner

Originally, the Jesus Prayer concluded here. In later years the monks added the phrase "a sinner" to "have mercy on me" for the younger monks who have not yet grown in the deeper spiritual way of Jesus Christ. We have discussed the meaning of the word "sin" in previous chapters. Suffice it to say that this addition personalizes one's own awareness of one's own sin, and our responsibility for it. Therefore, a humble confession of sin, a true repentance for it, and a deep appreciation for forgiveness and mercy are implied in this seemingly small and insignificant addition. Yet the addition is powerful and profound.

The Sources

The Fathers are very clear on the Jesus Prayer. St. Hesychia says, "The single-phrased Jesus Prayer destroys and consumes the deceits of the devil. For when we invoke Jesus, God and Son of God, constantly and tirelessly, he does not allow them to project in the mind's mirror . . . their provocation, or any form. . . . The heart will be empty of evil thoughts. . . . The intellect cannot conquer a demonic fantasy by its own unaided powers. . . . But when we call upon Jesus Christ, they do not dare play their tricks with us even for a second."

St. Diodochus says that the prayer is used as a tool to enter into contemplation: "Continuity of attention produces inner stability . . . succeeded by . . . the Jesus Prayer . . . in which the intellect, free from all images, enjoys complete quietude. . . . Extreme watchfulness and the Prayer of Jesus Christ, undistracted by thoughts, are the necessary basis for . . . unfathomable inner stillness of soul, for depths of secret and singular contemplation. . . . These gifts are the guarding of the intellect with the invocation of Jesus Christ . . . , stillness of mind unbroken by thoughts which even appear to be good, and that capacity to be empty of all fault." Diodochus was aware that we could never be entirely empty of thoughts, but can simply minimize them. He says, "When we have blocked all its outlets by means of the remembrance of God, the intellect requires . . . some task which will satisfy its need for activity. . . . Give it nothing but the prayer, 'Lord Jesus.'"

Ceaseless Prayer

This prayer is to be continuous. St. Hesychia says, "We have learned from experience that for one who wishes to purify his heart it is truly a great blessing constantly to invoke the name of the Lord Jesus. . . . The Apostle says: 'Pray without ceasing.' A certain God-given equilibrium is produced in our intellect through the constant remembrance and invocation of our Lord Jesus Christ." Aware that this sounds most difficult, he says, "To human beings it seems hard and difficult to still the mind so that it rests from all thought. . . . But he who, through unceasing prayer, holds the Lord Jesus within his breast will not tire."

Breath

One of the tools for praying ceaselessly is to unite the Jesus Prayer with the breath. Hesychia continues, "Attentiveness is the heart's stillness, unbroken by any thought. In this stillness, the heart breathes and invokes, endlessly and without ceasing, only Jesus Christ. . . . To be still and calm . . . let the Jesus Prayer cleave to your breath, and in a few days you'll find that this is possible. . . . Let us live every moment in . . . continually breathing Jesus Christ."

The Fathers are clear about the method of uniting the Jesus Prayer with the breath. In their work *Directions to Hesychasts,* Saints Calistas and Ignatius say, "Sitting down in your cell, collect your mind, lead into the path of the breath along which the air enters in, constrain it into the heart together with the inhaled air, and keep it there . . . do not leave it silent and idle; instead give it the following prayer: 'Lord, Jesus Christ, Son of God, have mercy on me'. . . . One utters the name 'Lord Jesus'; another of 'Jesus Christ'; the third of

'Christ, Son of God'. . . . Thus was our divine prayer composed. . . .
As regards the words: 'have mercy on me' . . . it was added by the
holy fathers chiefly for those who are still infants in the work of
virtue. . . . For the advanced and perfect in Christ are content with
anyone of these forms."

Traditional Form or Abbreviated?

Yet Calistas and Ignatius cautioned against changing the words of the
traditional form too much. "Beginners may at times say all the words
of the prayer and at times only part of them, but must pray constantly and within the heart. . . . Refrain from changing the words of
the prayer too often lest this frequent dropping and changing . . .
should accustom the mind not to concentrate." St. Gregory of Sinai
concurs. "How to say the prayer: Some of the Fathers taught that the
prayer should be said in full . . . others advised saying half . . . or to
alternate. . . . Yet it is not advisable to pander to laziness by changing
the words of the prayer too often, but to persist in a certain time as a
test of patience."

My personal experience is based upon these counsels. I divide
the prayer into two sections, corresponding to my in breath, and my
out breath. Breathing in, I say, "Lord, Jesus Christ, Son of God."
Breathing out, I say, "have mercy on me, a sinner." There have been
times when I only pray part of the prayer like, "Lord, Jesus Christ,"
or "Lord, Jesus," and so on. I have also just used one word like "Jesus," or "mercy." I usually do this when I am very physically or mentally tired and exhausted. At those times this is about all I can muster!

Normally, however, I prefer to pray the entire prayer. At the beginning of my spiritual life I concentrated on the objective content
of the words. But as I have grown older, I now go in and through the
words to their deeper intuitive meaning. The objective meaning of
the words is most important and guards one from falling into theological and spiritual error. But once this objective theological foundation is in place, it is possible to build upon that firm support and

go into the heights of contemplation beyond all concepts and knowledge. In this, the words serve as a tool to keep one at the prayer in a disciplined way. But to truly enter into the prayer of the heart, which is the purpose of the prayer, one must travel beyond the knowable meaning of the words to a simple intuition that includes, yet surpasses, their objective and subjective realities, into reality Itself.

Posture

It would be good to also mention the topic of posture. The Fathers sat on a low stool with their knees pulled up to their chest in order to gaze at their navel, which they believed was the physical locality of the heart. The purpose of this whole posture was to focus the eyes on the heart, to help drop the prayer from the head to the heart. Dropping the prayer down into the heart, which we have treated in another chapter, was the point of the posture.

This is in contrast to many Far Eastern traditions that use posture as a preparation for meditation. For them, the point of the posture is a stability that will keep one from getting distracted in the middle of meditation by an ache or pain in the body. So they focus on the body temporarily at the beginning of meditation in order not to be distracted by the body once meditation is engaged in, and achieved. Therefore, when praying the Jesus Prayer, any good posture will work. Personally, I like the Far Eastern approach, since the motivations for the posture of the Christian East are no longer viable. However, other traditional prayer postures, such as kneeling, standing, prostrations, or outstretched arms in the form of a cross, are all acceptable, as long as they do not become distractions from the very prayer they are trying to aid.

THE JESUS PRAYER EXERCISE

1. Sit in your meditation place, and breathe deeply. Let go of your faculties of sense, emotions, and thoughts.

2. With your inhale, gently say, "Lord Jesus Christ, Son of God." With your exhale say, "have mercy on me, a sinner." Repeat this ten, then fifty, then one hundred times, using the one-hundred-knot prayer rope of the Eastern Church. Later you may pray this prayer more continuously with or without the prayer rope, one thousand and more times a day, until you pray it constantly as an intuition while daily life continues.

3. As you say the words, first use your senses to sit in the proper posture and finger the prayer rope. Use your mind and emotions to meditate on the meaning of the words. Eventually, move beyond mind and emotions to a pure spiritual intuition of the full meaning of the words in the person of Jesus and our place as his disciples. This is called dropping the Prayer from the mind to the heart.

4. At first, stay with saying the classical form of the Prayer. As you progress, you may want to use only part of the Prayer, such as simply repeating the word "Jesus," or "mercy." But you should only do this as you have mastered the classical Prayer under the direction of an experienced teacher.

5. Conclude as usual.

Part Three

THE FAR
EAST

The Far East

AS THE EARTH HAS BECOME A SMALLER place due to increased opportunities in transportation and communication, the East and the West have begun coming together. This has occurred culturally, economically, and also with religion. Early in the twentieth century, adherents of various Far Eastern religions began coming to the western shores of the United States, and from there on to Europe. Earlier, in the days of the British Empire, proponents from Far Eastern religions came to England, and from there to Europe, and to the eastern United States. Another similar migration occurred in the days of the hippie movement in the 1960s, when there was such an interest in Far Eastern religion. Today, many are again looking into the ancient religions of the Far East to try to find spiritual answers.

Of course, Christianity had reached out to the Far East centuries earlier. This occurred first with the earliest forms of Christianity, including the Arian and Nestorian heresies, which denied the deity of Christ. Later on, the Franciscans went to the Orient within a hundred years after the death of St. Francis, as the orthodox gospel of Jesus Christ was brought for the first time to China with any serious effect. Later, the Jesuits followed suit, and still later the missionary movement within Protestantism sent scores of missionaries into China, Japan, and throughout the Orient.

All of these Christian missionary efforts created cross-pollination with the religions of the Far East. Both Franciscans and Jesuits frequently wore the apparel of the sages and holy men of Confucianism and Taoism in order to reach the Confucians and the Taoists. Jesuits, in particular, sought to master the system of Confucianism in the East as the earlier Church Fathers of Christianity had mastered the philosophy of Aristotle and Plato in the West, in order to bring the gospel to each particular culture and society. All of these missionary efforts also brought the wisdom of each respective society back into their own Christian faith in some way. Even the more separatist and militant evangelical missionaries brought back a great love and respect for the good things that could be found in the religions of the Far East. The Franciscans and the Jesuits wrote similarly of their great respect for the good, beautiful, and spiritual things found in the religions of the Far East, without in any way compromising their own Christian faith and the need to bring the message of Jesus to all the earth.

Today, we see another movement of renewed interest in Far Eastern religion. This is partially due to a disenchantment with the inherent superficiality and individualism of the New Age movement, which frequently neither has solid roots nor a properly communitarian orientation in lived reality. This interest in Far Eastern religions also is a result of a disenchantment with Christianity, specifically, since the form of Christianity that has been so apparent in the media is so greatly lacking regarding the real rich and beautiful tradition of Christian mystical and contemplative prayer, as well as radical communal lifestyle. Many have looked elsewhere in order to find these legitimate things they long for from the depths of their soul.

Cardinal Ratzinger has said that the greatest challenge to Catholic Christianity in the West in the near future will be Buddhism. I agree with him. This is partially because we Catholic Christians have not sufficiently brought out the fullness of our own mystical and contemplative tradition and placed it upon the table for the spiritual nourishing of the people of God everywhere. Furthermore, we have not brought to the table of the faithful the very real and appropriate integrations, in theory and in practice, of the meditation techniques of the religions of the Far East with our own Catholic Christian and Orthodox tradition of meditation, while maintaining our complete and unquestioned focus on Jesus as the Alpha, the Omega, and the center of our whole faith.

Great strides have been made in dialogue on the level of the monastics of each respective tradition. The Catholic Church has actively pursued a monastic dialogue with the monks of other Far Eastern religions, such as Hinduism, Buddhism, and Taoism. Furthermore, there has been a more general interreligious dialogue fostered between the Catholic Church and the leaders and clerics of these Far Eastern religions concerning not only meditation and contemplative prayer but the social concerns which affect all religions of the Far East, and all of their disciples and adherents. On this level, such issues as human rights, women's rights, justice and peace, and the like come under the purview of the moral teachings of each respective religion. Each religion has found it advantageous to join one with the other as we find our morality overlapping and supporting each other in many but not all areas of moral teaching. We can share that common morality with society so as both to raise the moral standards of these societies in which we all find ourselves and to head off any subtle or overt persecution of religion in those same societies.

On the level of the monastic dialogue, there has been great common ground established in the actual meditation methods used by each respective monastic tradition in their own meditations and prayers. On the level of faith, a great difference in worldview and view of God remains. However, even on this level, we have discovered that there are many semantic differences that in the past have proven to be barriers but which are now coming down in our efforts to dialogue rather than argue with or proselytize each other. These dialogues require that each participant has a mature understanding of their own tradition so as not to be overly defensive in dialogue, and the humility needed to be able to truly listen to, hear, and learn from one another regardless of our faith or persuasion.

For the Christian, this means that we must have the sure foundation of the apostles and the prophets with Christ Jesus as the cornerstone of our whole faith. When this foundation and cornerstone are sure and firm, then we are able to enter into real dialogue with the confidence and humility necessary in such a process. If any of the participants lacks the confidence or humility, the whole structure of interreligious dialogue begins to shake, to lean, and ultimately threatens to collapse.

For the Christian, we view the other religions of the world in general as natural religion, or part of God's inspiration. Inherent in our being created in his image is the natural desire for both God, and the many good things he brings to the created order. This inspiration to reach toward God has enabled many religions to discover the many wonderful and beautiful realities of the things of God and to experience and possess them in a way that is most commendable, and even perfect. Formal Revelation occurred first in the Old Testament with the law and the prophets, and culminated with the coming of Jesus in the New Testament, the Word made flesh, in a way that is clearer, more understandable, and also far more mystical. In this, we would see Jesus as the fulfillment of both Old Testament Revelation, and the inspiration of the religions of the world. In Christ, the Church possesses all of the gifts that can be found in any other faith expression. In pastoral experience, we do not always use them in a way that is most commendable or perfect. Therefore, other faiths often use the gifts that we ourselves have but have neglected. So dialogue enables us to share not only the fullness in Christ with other faiths but to receive those same gifts from the other faiths that might use them better than we do.

Interfaith: False Gods

The Old Testament gives us many indications of not mixing the worship of false gods with our worship of the true God. This is seen strongly in the life of the great King Solomon. Some have applied that warning to interfaith ministry. This warning is well taken, and needs to be seriously considered by those who take the scriptures seriously.

From the interfaith perspective, we do not necessarily see working with other religions as working with false gods. It is commonly held that the one God of Judaism, Islam, and other monotheistic expressions are expressions of searching for, and natural revelation of, the one God. Even polytheistic religion is an expression of isolated aspects of the one God. Only when clearly and militantly against the teaching of the gospel and the Church on faith and morality are they seen as enemies. I have dealt with the interfaith issue on a more theological level in my book *The Music of Creation*.

The greatest false gods are the gods of selfishness, which lead to all the other ills of this world. These are the blatant untruths and illusions that cause clear delusion and negative results in the human relation to the divine, and his creation.

The New Testament also says to be on the watch for false prophets and angels of darkness that come as angels of light. It says that we will know them by their fruit. What is this fruit? A life changed to become more like Jesus. It is not just a matter of doctrine. Only when the teachings of religion keep one from letting go of the false self and becoming more like Jesus do we see it in more adversarial terms.

So we heed well the warnings of the Old Testament regarding the worship of false gods. Interfaith dialogue and meditation actually takes us further on our journey of worshiping the one true God, and of destroying the false gods and demons of the false self in our life, and in the lives of all those we meet.

The Catholic Church teaches that we reject nothing of truth that is found in any other religion, and it recognizes the work of the

Holy Spirit in other faiths. Likewise, it teaches that nothing should be rejected out of hand simply because it comes from a non-Christian source. It affirms, however, that only Jesus and the Church contain the fullness of God's Revelation for humankind's salvation in this era. Other faiths may contain truth and salvation, and may even use a gift we possess better than we do, but they do not contain the fullness of Revelation in the same way as is found in Christ and his Church.

But we must personally know and share the *real* Jesus to be believable. We don't have to enroll in esoteric seminars, or find some kind of gnostic, or hidden-knowledge, approach to Christ in order to do this. The real Jesus is right there in the traditional four gospels, if only we would really take them seriously. This Jesus is radical and mystical, indeed!

Jesus probably was a whole lot more like a Buddhist Bodhisattva, a Hindu sannyasi, or a Confucian or Taoist sage than he was like a tele-evangelist, gospel radio preacher, or mega-Church pastor! Certainly, he more resembled the great saints of our history, such as St. Francis Assisi, St. Benedict or, in modern times, Mother Teresa of Calcutta. There's no question that Jesus falls into the holy-man tradition that is known to every major religion of the world. This tradition calls the holy man, or woman, to renounce home, possessions, and family, and to live a life of itinerant wandering while in the state of contemplative prayer and sharing the good news of spiritual enlightenment and rebirth with anyone who will listen or follow. In this, Jesus is complementary to the many, and the most, of other major founders and faiths of the world.

But Jesus is also unique. For example, the Buddha said that he was only a finger pointing at the moon, but he was not the moon. This is a most appropriate thing for any ordinary religious teacher or prophet to say. To say more would be arrogance. Jesus, in his humanity, would share the Buddha's statement, for Jesus is priest, prophet, and king. But in his divinity, he would say that he is not just a finger pointing to the moon, nor is he even the moon, but he is the

Light which illumines the moon! Indeed, it is now the Church, after the image of Mary, who is the moon reflecting the light of Jesus her Son.

Therefore, the Catholic Church teaches a theology of both complement and fulfillment regarding the relationship of Jesus Christ to other religions. Insofar as he is a prophet and a holy man, Jesus complements and confirms all that is good and holy in the other traditions. In so far as he is the unique incarnation of the Word as the eternally begotten Son of God, Jesus fulfills all other traditions in a way not unlike his fulfillment of the law and the prophets of the Old Testament. This means we confidently proclaim Christ to all, but in a way that is humbly open to the unique gifts of all.

In this it is good to remember Cardinal Ratzinger's letter encouraging proper interfaith dialogue, but warning that we not lose the primacy of Jesus Christ as Christians in the midst of a world of religious pluralism. Specifically, he guards against various abuses that are most common today, such as seeing Christianity as a mere compliment to other religions without fulfilling its role as well, or of seeing the role of the Spirit in other religions as separate from the work of Jesus Christ and the unity of the Trinity, or the work of the cosmic Christ in other faiths as separate from the historical work of Jesus on earth. Likewise, some would see Jesus and his salvation in only cosmic terms, thus erroneously isolating his incarnation in history, space, and time from his saving work. These are all excellent points to call to mind for the Christian. According to the same letter, they are not intended, however, to stop legitimate interfaith dialogue, humble respect for the faith of another, and the ability to learn and share even from those of other faiths about God. They are only warnings for us who are Christians not to lose the uniqueness of our own faith in an attempt to relate to those of other faiths.

The Dalai Lama warns against putting a yak's head on a camel's body, or vice versa, and challenges Christians not to lose our own belief about the uniqueness of Jesus in an attempt to make him relatable to other believers. If anything, he challenges us to take the forefront regarding things like meditation and contemplation, as well as peace and justice. As Jesus said to those who found themselves in a Jewish religious environment, "Your holiness must surpass that of the scribes and pharisees." Likewise, our holiness must surpass that of the holiest traditions of other major world religions. Until we do that, we really have little believable authority from which to speak.

The Basics of
Eastern Religions

EVEN THOUGH I WISH TO FOCUS MY sharing from a personal perspective, it might be good to look at some basics regarding Far Eastern religions. The religions that will concern our topic of meditation here are Hinduism, Buddhism, Taoism, and Confucianism. We could also look at the mystical traditions of the Essenes of Judaism and the Sufis of Islam. We could also mention Zoroastrianism from the Middle East, and Jainism and Shintoism from the Far East. There are, of course, many more religions for the serious student of religion. The primitive and aboriginal religions indigenous to the various regions of the world are also of special interest today, especially the Native Americans, the Aborigines of Australia, and the Celts of northern Europe. For now we will focus on Hinduism, Buddhism, Taoism, and Confucianism, and their respective traditions of meditation.

Hinduism

Hinduism is not a single religion but a conglomerate of many primitive folk religions, which slowly developed into a more sophisticated and advanced spirituality. "Hinduism" is a word that Westerners used to describe the religion of India. Indians use different words to describe different aspects of the whole. It began with a polytheistic folk religion, and developed, first into monism, which sees the oneness of all things, and then into a full monotheism, which believes in one ultimate God behind and beyond all the other gods, goddesses, or spirits.

For our purposes, let us understand the basics of "yoga." The word simply means "yoke," or "union." It is very similar to the definition of the word "religion," which means "to bind," or "to yoke." It is not some kind of mystical word with esoteric meanings. It is a simple word with meanings shared in common with most religions of the world.

There are four general kinds of yoga. "Jnana," or the yoga of "knowledge." "Bhakti," or the yoga of "love and devotion." "Karma," or the yoga of "work." And "Raja," or the yoga of "meditation." Jnana yoga, or the way of knowledge, includes going from the study of scripture, or the sutras, to enlightenment through meditation. Indeed, both Bhakti and Karma yoga would also include aspects of meditation, even though the emphasis is on their respective specialty. Raja yoga is the one that will primarily concern us here, and it is called "The Royal Way."

The Royal Way of Raja yoga, or meditation, includes eight steps. They are: 1) yama; 2) niyama; 3) asana; 4) pranayama; 5) pratyahara; 6) dharana; 7) dhyana; and 8) samadhi. These eight steps take us to a similar progression that we find in the asceticism and mysticism of the Christian West and Christian East.

Yama consists of processing the Five Desire Killing Vows, or abstinence. They consist of: 1) ahisma, or no killing; 2) no lying; 3) no stealing or greed; 4) no unchastity, and 5) brahmacharya, or no acquisitiveness, or curiosity to possess or control.

Niyama consists of Five Observances, or self-discipline. They are: 1) cleanliness; 2) contentment, or calm; 3) mortification, or self-control; 4) study, and 5) prayer, or contemplation of the divine.

Asana means proper posture. Perhaps the most common asana is the typical seated position of India, or the lotus position, upon a tiger skin to signify energy, and a deer skin to signify calm.

Pranayama means the control of the breath. The breath is to be even and slow. It is to be so refined that a goose-down feather will not be moved if placed in front of the nostrils. It's learning how to breathe in one nostril and out the other to clear the energy passages, or to hold the breath in order to descend the nerve currents down about the spine, etc.

Pratyahara means to withdraw the senses from sense objects. They use the example of becoming like tortoise in a shell.

Dharana means concentration. It begins by focusing on a single object in order to still the mind, while still giving it something minimal to focus on. Through this, the mind is to become as still as a quiet lake, reflecting the moon, or reality. Here we notice that our uncontrolled thoughts become like "crazed monkeys" in a cage. The point is to still them one by one as they arise. This is not esoteric, just hard work.

Dhyana means meditation. It is a half conscious state that makes one more conscious. This is a transitional state that moves quickly to the next, or samadhi.

Samadhi means meditational absorption. In real samadhi, the object of meditation vanishes. One becomes one with the infinite and the formless. One enters into a state of Supreme Reality, yet beyond object or subject. This is pure contemplation.

These four types of yoga and eight stages of meditation mirror much of our Christian ascetical and mystical tradition, both in the East and West. Today, many are seeking an easy way for spirituality. They want all of the rewards without any of the labor. Classical disciplines of meditation and prayer teach us that this simply is not possible, except in the most extraordinary of cases. Therefore, it is good for us to embrace a discipline of meditation and prayer, and to patiently work through it under the direction of the teacher, in order to reap the bountiful harvest of abundant spiritual fruit.

Hinduism also speaks of Four Stages of Life. This applies to male Brahmins but, as we shall see, has relevance for us all. The four stages are: 1) Religious / Monastic Student; 2) Householder; 3) Forest Dweller, or hermit, and 4) Sannyasin, or wandering ascetic, or holy man.

The Student lives a monastic life in the home of his guru, or teacher. In the tradition of the Hindu holy man, he must live on alms or donations collected by begging door-to-door. This is considered a time of rebirth for the Student. It lasts an indefinite period of time, but usually is concluded by the twentieth birthday.

After monastic training as the Student, one is expected to marry and raise a family as a Householder. This stage is considered the most important stage for the building of society, but it is the later meditational stages that are considered the most important for the individual's soul.

After one has raised their family, and has become a grandparent, a husband and wife may go together, or separately, to live as hermits, or Forest Dwellers. This is not an easy life. One must renounce all their possessions and their craft or trade, and their ability to make a living, to develop holy dispassion, or indifference. They are to wear poor, tattered clothing, or the traditional rugged deerskin of the Forest Dweller. Privately, they are to study and recite the Vedas, or scriptures. They practice compassion for all creatures through ahisma. If the wife is still living, she can make the determination as to whether or not the man has matured enough to pass on to the next stage of becoming a Sannyasin.

The Sannyasin is the wandering holy man of India. In a meditational state of union he is to set off in a straight line from his hermitage and wander alone until the day he dies. He is to possess nothing and desire nothing, neither to live nor to die. He may beg once a day, live in makeshift dwellings, wear worn-out garments, and see the Supreme Soul in all living organisms. Through this, he gains eternal Brahmin. This last state of becoming a Sannyasin is considered the highest goal for one's personal spiritual life. To die penniless and poor in the state of spiritual rebirth and awakening is the greatest way to make real progress in eternal life after we die.

These last two stages have significance to our modern Western society. Many times we see retired men and women searching for a deeper spiritual way of life. They have raised their children, and frequently become grandparents. They are ready for something new. They are ready to focus in their last years more intently upon their spiritual life. From a secular perspective, sociologists, and psychologists are now calling this the Generative Stage of Life. No doubt, this ancient four-staged progression through life still has much to teach us today.

It is also interesting in light of our existing monastic and mendicant expressions of consecrated community life. It has been said that, of our expressions, it is the monastic way of life that most resonates with the meditational or contemplative expressions of the Far East. However, it is the mendicant, or religious begging tradition, such as the Franciscans and Dominicans, that most resembles the Sannyassin and Sadhu way of life within Hinduism and Buddhism.

Buddhism

Buddhism is based on the life of the Siddhartha Gautama, who was born in 560 B.C. into the "kingly" caste of the Gautama clan in northern India. He was married with a newborn son, and in line to inherit the throne of his father, who had protected him from the suffering of life during his upbringing. One day, upon seeing the "Four Passing Sights"—an old man, a diseased man, a dead man, and a calm ascetic in the yellow robe of the Sannyasin—he became dissatisfied with his life of materialistic happiness and success. One night, while everyone was sleeping, he left the palace, renounced all of his possessions, cut off his hair, donned the yellow robe of the ascetic, and went to the forest to join a group of mendicant monks. He spent the next six years seeking enlightenment.

After six years of failed ascetical rigors and intense studies under the masters of Hinduism, he sat down under the Bodhi tree and experienced enlightenment through the "Middle Way" between extreme asceticism and extreme worldliness and pleasure. After his enlightenment, he spent the next forty-two years wandering across India and teaching this Middle Way. This is called "the dharma," or "the teaching."

The dharma consists primarily of the Four Noble Truths and the Holy Eightfold Path. All of the rest of Buddhist teachings flow out from these basic truths. The Four Noble Truths are: 1) the existence of suffering; 2) the cause of suffering: 3) the cessation of suffering, and 4) the path of cessation.

To become a Buddhist, or one who seeks to be enlightened in a way after the example of the Buddha, one makes the Triple Refuge in the Buddha, the dharma, and the sangha. We have already explained the Buddha and the dharma. The sangha is simply the community of those who embrace Buddhism. In the early days, it was primarily monastic, as was the Buddha himself. Later, it expanded to include more of the laity.

The Holy Eightfold Path is the fourth Noble Truth that constitutes the path of cessation. It is made up of: 1) right belief; 2) right aspiration; 3) right speech; 4) right conduct; 5) right livelihood; 6) right effort; 7) right mindfulness, and 8) right meditation.

The Holy Eightfold Path is subdivided into three groups of; 1) prajna, or wisdom; 2) shila, or morality, and 3) samadhi, or meditation. prajna, or wisdom, includes 1) right belief and 2) right aspiration. shila, or morality, includes 3) right speech; 4) right conduct; 5) right livelihood, and 6) right effort. samadhi, or meditation, includes 7) right mindfulness and 8) right meditation.

Right belief, or understanding, includes an understanding of the Four Noble Truths and all related Buddhist teachings. These would include the Ten Roots of Merit and Demerit. The ten positive and negative roots are: 1) killing; 2) stealing; 3) unchastity; 4) lying; 5) tale bearing; 6) harsh words; 7) frivolous words; 8) covetousness; 9) ill will, and 10) right and wrong views. The Ten Roots of Merit and Demerit are also divided into three major groups of: 1) greed; 2) delusion, and 3) anger.

Right aspiration, or resolve, includes overcoming sensuality and lust, having right love for others without ill will, doing no harm to living creatures through cruelty, and overcoming desires that cause suffering.

Right speech includes being against loose and harmful talk, speaking ill will, and speaking love for all creatures, as well as prohibitions against tale-bearing, harsh words, or frivolous words.

Right conduct includes the three primary prohibitions against killing, stealing, and unchastity, as well as all of the other Five Precepts.

Right livelihood encourages making a living through the good use of time, in energy that is consistent with Buddhist principles.

Right effort includes an untiring and constant effort to: 1) avoid and 2) overcome things against Buddhist teaching, and to 3) develop and 4) maintain all that is good. It includes a watchfulness for the elements of enlightenment, which are: solitude; detachment; extinction; and deliverance through attentiveness; investigation of the law; energy; rapture; tranquility; concentration, and equanimity. It also involves discernment of the wise and unwise, desires and attachments.

Right mindfulness involves well-disciplined thought habits, and long hours of study meditation. It involves the development of the Four Foundations of Mindfulness in the: 1) body; 2) feelings; 3) thoughts, and 4) phenomenon.

Right meditation, or absorption, is similar to the Hindu concept within a Buddhist cosmology. It is the road to becoming an arahat, or fully enlightened Buddha, or saint, the way to nirvana, and the experience of complete peace and stillness.

Buddhism must always be seen against the backdrop of Hinduism. Consequently, many of its doctrines that sound unreasonable, or extreme, to Western ears, make much more sense when seen against this backdrop in a historical setting. Siddhartha Gautama, the Buddha, was one among many new founders and ascetic holy men wandering India at the time. All were protesting, in one form or another, the monopoly that the Hindu Brahmins, or cast of holy men, were exercising over the rest of the people. For instance, only Brahmins were permitted to undertake the fully ascetic life, and only at a certain time in their life. Furthermore, all people from the other castes—kings, workers, and unclean peasants—had to go through the Brahmins in their ritual worship. Since so much depended upon the Brahmins and the Orthodox teachings of Hinduism, the ascetic protesters like the Buddha showed that one could find enlightenment in any caste, and without either the doctrines or the hierarchy of Hinduism.

It is from this protest that it is easier to understand the Buddhist teaching of anatman, or "no self." So much of Hinduism was based on the teaching of atman, or Self. This Self was seen as running through everything. [Though the way we treated all things affected the awakening to this Self,] the Self itself was seen as autonomous, transcendent, and independent. This teaching was essential to the Brahmin's hold on the laity of Hinduism; therefore, the Buddha rejected this foundational teaching and showed that everyone, not only Brahmins, could attain to enlightenment.

Related to this is the Buddhist teaching of impermanence. Since there is no independent Self, all will eventually pass away, including our current perception of our own Self, or even God. What remains is what was in the beginning, namely, nirvana. Nirvana is not nothing or nihilism. It could be described as a living absence of any disturbance of any kind on any level—physical, emotional, psychological, or spiritual. It could be described as a living, peaceful, flat line. It is not nothing, but to call it something would be to disturb this fundamental intuitive reality. It simply is.

Related to this is the Buddhist teaching on interdependence, or dependent origination. This basically means that anything is ultimately affected by everything. The scientific truth of this teaching is profound. But it affects the psychological and emotional aspect of the human being, as well as the physical. Certainly, on a scientific level, we are learning that within the human body are also the particles that used to be in other living beings and objects, both on earth and from the stars themselves. But it is also true on the emotional and psychological level. Our emotions are affected by the circumstances in which we find ourselves, not to mention the chemical reactions of our own physical bodies. The same is true of our thoughts. They are affected by the circumstances in which we find ourselves. All is defined in terms of relation with another, or conditions. All that is based on condition is impermanent. Since all is impermanent, the circumstances come and go, and our physical, emotional, and psychological Self rises and falls. When all is said and done, what remains is nirvana. Only it is unaffected, though to call it "it" is to destroy its pristine purity, and ultimate character.

Formally, this is stated in the belief of the skandhas, or aggregates, and the Twelve Conditioning Links. The Five Aggregates are: 1) Matter. The body [in] its four elements of solidity, fluidity, heat, and motion, and the five sense organs of eye, ear, nose, tongue, and body; 2) Feeling and sensations; pleasant, unpleasant, and neutral kinds; 3) Perception [through the five sense organs and the mind]; 4) Mental formations, and 5) Consciousness, dependent upon the preceding four aggregates.

The Twelve Conditioning Links are: 1) Ignorance gives rise to 2) volitional action, which gives rise to 3) conditioned consciousness, which gives rise to 4) name and form, which give rise to 5) the six bases (the five senses, plus mind), which give rise to 6) sense impressions (through contact), which give rise to 7) feelings, which give rise to 8) desire or craving, which gives rise to 9) attachment, which gives rise to 10) becoming, through the life-rebirth process, which gives rise to 11) birth and or rebirth, which gives rise to 12) old age, death-grief, limitation, illness, sorrow, and despair.

Also related to the Buddha's dependence upon Hinduism is his teaching on karma and rebirth. Hindus believe in reincarnation, or the transmigration of souls. This means that the Self, or soul, of the human being transfers from one line to the other after death. With transmigration of souls, the soul can transmigrate from animal to human, and from human to animal bodies. In this transmigration, the very personality, or personhood, of the Self is transmigrated from one life to the other.

The Buddha rejected some aspects of this Orthodox Hindu teaching as presented by the Brahmins. He adhered to rebirth rather than reincarnation, teaching that, while some dimension transferred from life to life through interdependence, the Self, with its sense of personality and personhood, did not do so due to its impermanence.

Both Buddhists and Hindus teach Karma, or what we Christians would call "reaping what you sow, "applying this principle beyond the realm of one lifetime. In a sense, it is the spiritual version of the scientific principle that "for every action there is an equal and opposite reaction." For the Hindu and the Buddhist, this applies to an endless round of birth and death and rebirth, through literally countless lifetimes.

The Buddhist would believe that there are hundreds of millions of "kalpas," or worlds, and hundreds of millions of lifetimes for each of us within each world. In each life, we would be learning lessons, and righting wrongs to rectify the failures and sins of past lives. Somewhere along the way we are reborn through enlightenment, and the end to this sorrow of birth and rebirth finally comes to a close, and we enter the final peace of nirvana.

For the Hindu and the Buddhist, rebirth is not a blessing but a long and seemingly endless sorrow and suffering from which one seeks to be set free. That is why the Buddha's "good news" was that this could be your last life if you followed his teaching. It is also why Christian missionaries present Jesus in the same way, only with even more grace due to his actually *being* the paradoxes the other great faiths speak of to help us get free.

For the Christian, rebirth and reincarnation are not fully relevant issues. To the Hindu, they are simply accepted, as with the Buddhist reform, but for the Christian, Jesus is the immediate way to the heights of heaven, brahmin, or nirvana. It no longer really matters whether or not there is such a thing as rebirth or reincarnation. What matters is that in this very life of ours we can accept the ultimate way to freedom and spiritual enlightenment and rebirth.

The early Church addressed this issue in connection with Origenism, which, following the Greek philosophers, believed in the transmigration of souls. The Church condemned this belief on the basis of its violation of the human soul being created in the image of God, in distinction to animals simply bearing God's traces. Today, the Church frequently mentions the scripture that, "It is given to man once to die, and then the judgment." Other scriptures mentioned in support of reincarnation are frequent but weak. In the final analysis, reincarnation is really an unnecessary belief for the Christian. As a doctrine, it was seen not as a blessing, or curiosity, but as a source of great suffering by the ancient beliefs and faiths that adhere to it. Jesus shows all people a final, and unquestionable, way to be free of this way of suffering.

Buddhism developed into two major streams; Theravada, or Hinnayana, and Mahayana. Theravada, or the "teaching of the elder," is the earliest expression and is most faithful to a literal translation of the Buddha's words and lifestyle. It is expressed primarily through a monastic lifestyle for monks and nuns, with some involvement by the laity. Its primary concern is for the individual's attainment of nirvana. Those who attain the highest level in this life are called arahats, or saints. Mahayana, "the great vehicle," developed later and expands the Buddha's words to apply in a more mystical, yet practical, way for the laity as well as to monks and nuns. Their highest expression is the Bodhisattva, who is one who could go on to nirvana, but chooses to keep being reborn in this world until all beings are enlightened.

The Mahayana expression includes both Zen and Tibetan Buddhism, which are both popular in the West today. Tibetan Buddhism is seen as a third type unto itself by some, called Vajrayana. It is based on Tantraism, and builds on the Hinnayana and Mahayana, and is seen as the highest form of Buddhism by those who practice it. Tantraism came originally from India, and includes a complex approach to union with the absolute under the direction of a guru. Tibetan Buddhism has been popularized by the much-publicized plight of the Dalai Lama, and represents a Buddhism highly influenced by the tantric tradition of Hinduism, and one that has had one of the most complete effects on an entire people and culture. Zen Buddhism traces its origins back through Bodhidharma, who first brought Zen Buddhism to China in the ninth century, which spread to Korea and Japan. Zen is said to represent an integration of the Taoism of China with a mystical expression of Buddhism from India.

Taoism

Taoism is the study of the "Tao" or the "Way." It is the mystical side of the coin of the Tao, the practical side being Confucianism. It is said that Taoism is the mystical expression of China, and that Confucianism is the ethical and social side. Both place the Tao at the beginning, center, and end of all that is.

It is said that one gives birth to two, and two gives birth to three. From three flow forth all the five elements of creation. So, after the Tao comes "yin and yang," or "the sunny side of the mountain" and "the shadow side of the mountain." Sometimes, this is spoken of as the masculine and feminine side of all creation. Yin and yang flow from the Tao.

From yin and yang flow energy, essence, and vitality, or soul, spirit, and body. From energy, essence, and vitality flow the Five Elements of wood, fire, earth, metal, and water. These five elements correspond to the five major organs of the liver, heart, spleen, lungs, and kidneys. Corresponding to these five elements and organs are various colors, such as green, red, ocher, silver-white, and dark blue, for visualized meditation, foods for good health, and virtues and corresponding vices for good living. From this developed the whole system of Tai Chi, or moving meditation and martial art, and Chi Kung, or a complete system for spiritual, emotional, and physiological health.

Taoism emphasizes the experience of "wu wei" as the means to attain the Tao and perfect balance in one's life. "Wu wei" simply means "stillness," or "non-contrivance." For the Taoist, getting back to original simplicity is a matter of stilling one's complex, false self, in order to peacefully arrive back to the perfect balance of the original self in a non-contrived way. This is done through what we call meditation, breath prayer, and a moving meditation and health program called "Tai Chi" and "Chi Kung."

Taoism began with the legend of Lao-tsu, the older fifth- to sixth-century contemporary of both Confucius in China and the Buddha in India. It joined together with Buddhism at the Shaolin Temple in the ninth century under the direction of Bodhidharma, the monk who brought Zen Buddhism to China from India. Legend has it that it was here that the martial arts were born, as peaceful monks combined the graceful movements of the animals around their wilderness monastery with meditation and the attainment of balance and harmony for overall good health.

Taoism has developed into both a philosophical and religious expression. Religious Taoism combines the folk religions of China with an ultimate belief in the supremacy of the Tao. It adheres to a complex system of thousands of spirits and lesser gods, leading ultimately to the Tao. Philosophical Taoism believes in the ultimate supremacy of the Tao, and the above-mentioned principles at work in creation. Taoism has given birth to Tai Chi and Chi Kung, not to mention the rest of the martial arts, which are so popular in the West today. Beyond these basics, there are many schools of religious and philosophical Taoism, many forms of Tai Chi and Chi Kung, and many methods of meditation too numerous to enumerate and elaborate on here.

As Taoism, Hinduism and Buddhism become more popular in the West—due to health and spiritual benefits—more of their complete tradition slowly becomes available to us in English translations of their scriptures and other source texts, and with truly qualified and trained teachers. For now, it is good to remember that much of what we hear in the West is still rather limited in its scope and application from a perspective of the cultures from which they come, and the languages through which they have been taught. With time, we will build up a more complete tradition of each and a more balanced integration with our existing religion and disciplines of meditation.

Hindu Sources

THE BHAGAVAD GITA

From the Hindu tradition, the *Bhagavad Gita,* or the scripture on yoga, says,

Let the student of spirituality try unceasingly to concentrate his mind; let him live in seclusion, absolutely alone, with mind and personality controlled, free from desire, and without possessions.

Having chosen a holy place, let him sit in a firm posture on a seat, neither too high nor too low, and covered with a grass mat, a deerskin, and cloth. Seated thus, his mind concentrated, its functions controlled and his senses governed, let him practice meditation for the purification of his lower nature. Let him hold body, head, and neck erect, motionless, and steady; let him look fixedly at the tip of his nose, turning neither to the right nor to the left.

With peace in his heart and no fear, observing the vow of celibacy, the mind controlled and fixed on me, let the student lose himself in contemplation.

Meditation is not for one who eats too much, nor for one who eats not at all, nor for one who is over much addicted to sleep,

nor for one who is always awake, but for one who regulates
food and recreation, who is balanced in action, and sleep, and
in waking, it shall dispel all unhappiness.

When the mind completely controlled is centered on the Self,
and free from all earthly desires, then is the man truly spiritual.
The wise one who has conquered his mind and is absorbed in
the Self is as a lamp which does not flicker, since it stands shel-
tered from every wind. The whole nature is seen in the light of
Self . . . He enjoys bliss which passes sense. . . . There is no
possession so precious. . . . It should be practiced with determination, and with a heart which refuses to be depressed,
renouncing every desire which imagination can conceive, controlling the senses at every point by the power of the mind;
little by little . . . let him attain peace; and, fixing his mind on
the Self, let him not think of any other thing. When . . . the
mind would wander, let him restrain it.

Supreme bliss is the lot of the sage, whose mind attains peace,
whose passions subside, who is without sin, and who becomes
one with the Absolute. The saint enjoys without effort the bliss
which flows from realization of the infinite.

He who experiences unity of life sees his own Self in all beings,
and all beings in his own Self and looks on everything with
impartial eye. He who sees me in everything and everything in
me, him shall I never forsake.

The mind is fickle . . . with practice and renunciation it can be
done. It is not possible . . . if one does not know how to control one's Self; but for one who . . . learns such self-control, it is
possible.

I will now state briefly how he who has reached perfection finds
the eternal spirit . . . guiding always by pure reason, bravely
restraining himself, renouncing the objects of sense, and giving
up attachment and hatred; enjoying solitude, his body, mind,

and speech under perfect control, absorbed in meditation, he becomes free—always filled with the spirit of renunciation. Having abandoned selfishness, power, arrogance, anger, and desire, possessing nothing of his own, and having attained peace, he is fit to join the eternal spirit. . . . He feels no desire, no regret, he regards all beings equally.

On the chapter of the Yoga of Wisdom, the Bhagavad Gita says,

One who can see inaction in action, and action in inaction, is the wisest among men. He is a saint. The wise call him a sage; for whatever he undertakes is free from the motive of desire . . . having surrendered all claim to the results of the actions, always contented and independent. In reality, he does nothing, even though he is apparently acting. Expecting nothing, his mind and personality controlled, without greed, doing bodily actions only; though he acts, yet he remains untainted. Content with what comes to him without effort of his own, mounting above the pairs of opposites, free from envy, his mind balanced, both in success and failure. . . . One who is without attachment, free, his mind centered in wisdom, his actions, being done as a sacrifice, leaving no trace behind.

Some sages sacrifice to the powers; others offer themselves on the altar of the eternal. Some sacrifice their physical senses in the fire of self-control; others offer up their contact with external objects in the sacrifice of their senses. Others again sacrifice their activities and their vitality in the spiritual fire of self-abnegation, yet others offer as their sacrifice wealth, austerities, and meditations. Monks, wedded to their vows, renounce their scriptural learning and even their spiritual powers.

There are some who practice control of the vital energy and govern the subtle forces of the outgoing breath and the incoming, thereby sacrificing their outgoing breath unto the incoming breath, and their incoming breath unto outgoing breath. Others, controlling their diet, sacrifice the worldly life to the spiritual fire. All understand the principle of sacrifice and by its means their sins are washed away. The sacrifice of wisdom is superior to any material sacrifice, for the climax of action is always realization.

Buddhist Sources

THE BUDDHIST TRADITION, TOO, SPEAKS of seated meditation. In a collection called *A Buddhist Bible,* compiled by Goddard, the word of the Buddha on the seventh of the Eightfold Path within the fourth of the Four Noble Truths says, "How does the disciple dwell on the contemplation of the body? (Or the feelings, the thoughts, or the phenomenon). There the disciple retires to the forest, to the foot of a tree, or to a solitary place, sits himself down, with legs crossed, body erect, and within attentiveness fixed before him. With attentive mind he breathes in, with attentive mind he breathes out. When making a long inhalation, he knows: I make a long inhalation; by making a long exhalation, he knows: I make a long exhalation. In making a short inhalation, he knows: I make a short inhalation; When making a short exhalation, he knows: I make a short exhalation. Clearly perceiving the entire (breath) body, I will breathe out. Thus he trains himself, calming himself."

From the Chinese sources for *Dhyana for Beginners* it says, "Seek an open and quite place, sitting up with determined and concentrated mind, reciting Mahayana sutras." It then goes on to speak of a regulation of clothing, food, shelter, contact with the world, living in community, and a watchfulness over the eyes, ears, smell, taste, touch, and the mind, including memory and imagination. It then speaks again of regulating and readjusting the food, the sleep, and the body, and in this section it speaks of "its physical state, its breathing, and its mental state." Before we begin Dhyana, we must keep close watch over our physical activities and states, which is walking, working, standing, sitting, etc., lest we become overtired, excited, or our breathing become rapid and forced. The mind will then not be in good condition to begin practice. It will be disturbed, vexed, and clouded. We ought to take precautions against such a state at all times. We should also take careful thought as to the place where we are to carry out the practice. We should find a place that will be free from disturbance and will not offer any unnecessary difficulties.

"Next, we should consider the position of the body. We should cross the feet, with the left foot on the right, draw the legs close to the body, so that the toes are in line with the outside of the thighs. This is the half position. If you wish to take the full position, simply place the left foot on the right thigh and the right foot on the left thigh, and at right angles to each other.* Next we should loosen the girdle and arrange the garments so that they will not become disarranged during the practice. Next we place our left palm upon the right hand and place the hands on the left foot, which we draw close to the body. Next we straighten up the body, swaying it several times to find its center, the backbone neither too bent nor too straight. Next we straighten the neck so that the nose is in a perpendicular line with the navel. Next we open the mouth and breathe out all bad air from the lungs slowly and carefully so as not to quicken the circulation. Then close the mouth and breathe in fresh air through the nose. If the body is well regulated, once is enough, otherwise do it two or three times.

"Next, close the lips with the tongue resting against the upper palate. Close the eyes easily, simply to shut out unnecessary light. In this position, sit firmly, as if you were a foundation stone. Do not let your body, head, hands, or feet move about. Do not be hurried about it, nor unduly sluggish.

*This full position is often impossible for Europeans and Americans.

"The fourth lesson relates to the regulation of breathing. There are four kinds: blowing, panting, audible, and silent, only the last of which can be said to be in a regulated, adjusted state. By silent breathing is meant that there is no sound, no compression, no force, simply the slightest feeling of the tranquility of our breathing, which does not disturb the mind, but rather gives to the mind a pleasant feeling of security and peace. We can attain samadhi only with silent breathing."

To paraphrase, the fifth lesson speaks of the regulation and adjustment of the mind and three stages for it. In entering into the practice, practicing it, and retiring from it, the mind is to be empty and tranquil and prevented from again arising or entering into bad states, such as discouragement, aimlessness, lack of control, too great a tension, and the like. It is to be focused so as not to fall into bad mental states or drowsiness. It also recommends focusing on a single object if that is helpful, such as the tip of the nose or the navel. It would also caution against too much mental strain, so that the brain becomes tired or fatigued, or a pain in the head or chest occurs, encouraging relaxing the effort slightly if this occurs, but the relaxation should not lead us to looseness, dullness, or dispersion through laxity.

The second part of the fifth lesson, mainly regulating the mind, speaks of three kinds of body breathing, and mind. Of the first, we should deal with time, namely, learning how to extend the time "from one hour to two, to four, to even six out of twenty-four." The body and the breathing might in these time periods begin to drift, and we are simply encouraged to correct it, again and again, in a way that is "gentle, continuous, and silent." The same is true for the mind. It may begin to drift or sink or become too lax or too constrained. "As soon as we are conscious of it, we simply bring it into adjustment as before."

The third teaching of the fifth on withdrawal is most important. It says, "In the third teaching of the fifth lesson—how to withdraw from Dhyana—there are three things to be attended to. First we should gently relax the mind, open the mouth, and exhale the air as though to empty it from every part of the body and arteries and veins. Then we should move our body little by little; next our shoulders, hands, and neck; next our feet until they become flexible; then gently rub the body, next rub the hands until blood circulates warmly; and not until then should we open our eyes and rub them with our warm hands. Finally, sit quietly for a moment or two and then get up quietly and go away. If we proceed otherwise, if we break in suddenly upon our meditation and hurry away, the conditions of the body in Dhyana, being different from the conditions of active life, there will be disharmony, perhaps a feeling of headache or of paralysis in the joints, which will linger in the mind as a feeling of annoyance and uneasiness, which will prejudice the mind against a following sitting. Therefore we should be attentive and careful in retiring."

As to the preference for sitting or walking meditation, it says, "In the practice of Dhyana there are two aspects. The first relates to the sitting, and the other relates to the circumstances and conditions of life.

"First, as to the right practice of sitting; Dhyana can be practiced when one is walking, standing, sitting or reclining, but the position of sitting being the best for practice that is considered first." There follows a complete treatment of the various movements of the mind and the body in both states.

Dogen

Dogen's manuals of Zen meditation from the thirteenth century are also very helpful. Though there are many different versions and translations, the paraphrase is as follows: "For studying Zen, one should have quiet quarters, be moderate in food and drink, and cast aside all involvements and discontinue all affairs. Do not think of good or evil. When you sit in meditation, spread a thick mat in a quiet place, loosen your robe and belt, and assume a proper demeanor. Then sit in the full cross-legged position. First place your right foot on your left thigh; then place your left foot on your right thigh. You may sit in the half cross-legged position: simply rest your left foot on your right thigh.

"Next, place your right hand on your left foot, and your left hand on your right palm. Press the tips of your thumbs together. Slowly raise your torso and stretch it forward. Swing it to the left and the right; then straighten your body and sit erect. Do not lean to the left or the right, forward or backward. Your ears should be in line with your shoulders, and your nose in line with your navel. Press your tongue against the front of your palate and close your lips and your teeth. The eyes should remain open. Breathe gently through your nose.

"Once you have settled your posture, you should regulate your breathing. Whenever a thought occurs, be aware of it. As soon as you're aware of it, it will vanish. If you remain for a long period, forgetful of objects, you will naturally become unified. This is the essential art of zazen. Zazen is the dharma gate of ease and joy.

"If you grasp the point of the practice, the four elements of the body will become light and at ease, the spirit will be fresh and sharp, thoughts will be correct and clear, the flavor of the dharma will sustain the spirit, and you will be calm, pure, and joyful. Once you achieve clarification of the truth, you may be likened to the dragon gaining the water, or the tiger taking to the mountains. When right thought is present, dullness and agitation cannot intrude. When you arise from sitting, move slowly and arise calmly; do not be hasty or rough. At all times protect and maintain the power of samadhi, as though you were protecting an infant. Then your samadhi power will be easily developed.

"This one teaching of meditation is our most urgent business. Transcending the profane and surpassing the holy are always contingent on the condition of Dhyana. Shedding this body while seated and fleeing this life while standing are the power of sumati. If you let go of the six senses, you can see and turn the whole path. If you do not produce a single thought, you sit and cut off the ten directions."

Personal
Experience

I N MANY OTHER BOOKS, THE PHILOSOPHI-
cal, theological, and historical similarities and differences of Christianity with the other religions of the world have
been treated. We will not repeat this here. Perhaps it would be best
for me simply to share some of my own personal experiences from
the perspective of the Catholic Christian monastic experience of integrating various methods and techniques from other religious meditation and prayer techniques into my own personal prayer life. For
myself, I have found that I can do this in a way that in no way threatens the absolute primacy of Jesus in all that I am about. He remains
the Alpha, the Omega, and the center of my faith. However, since he
completes all that is good and holy and true from any faith tradition,
I can also use anything that is good and holy and true from any other
faith tradition, in and through Christ, in a way that does not
threaten my own experience as a Catholic Christian monastic.

For myself, I begin my days with a regimen of prayer movement,
meditation, and contemplation, which prepares me for the liturgical
prayer and community responsibilities of the day. I begin reasonably
early at about 4 or 5:00 A.M., in preparation for a liturgical prayer

time at 6:45 A.M., which begins the communal monastic day. After rising, I shower and get dressed. Then I go to a particular prayer space in my hermitage where I can begin to awaken my body, soul, and spirit to greet the new day in Christ.

Christian Yoga

I begin with some simple stretches, taken from Christian yoga. These are done primarily in the standing position, and they simply stretch the back, legs, arms, and get the blood moving, and are easily incorporated into a prayer of greeting the day in and through Christ, with my whole being. Many years ago I did a more extensive Christian yoga routine, but with Tai Chi I have opted to focus more primarily on the latter discipline.

Tai Chi

From this, I do a series of warmups, taken from Tai Chi in the Taoist tradition. Tai Chi was basically developed over a long and complicated history from the monastic experience at the Shaolin monastery, where Buddhist and Taoist monks studied together. These movements were first patterned on what they observed in nature in various animals, incorporating the best from each into human movement. Each movement is united with the breath, which through visualization moves the basic physical energy of the body called "chi" from the earth through the body, and then back into the earth, thus harmonizing the body with all of God's creation.

On the ideological level, the Taoists follow the Tao, which simply means "the way." This way is the simple balancing and harmonizing of the various and seeming opposites of life, such as the yang and the yin, or the male and the female, the active and the passive, the light and the dark, etc. The balancing of seeming opposites is easily incorporated into the Christian experience, and is completed both through the incarnation of Christ and through the paschal mystery, which likewise balance, harmonize and unify all of these seeming opposites in a way that builds on proper faith and morality, but goes beyond any duality to mystical and contemplative experience.

For the Taoist, there are three basic powers at work. One is "chi," which simply means "an invisible energy," and which flows from the Tao through all creation, and through every human person. It also means "breath and life." It is through the proper and unrestricted flow of chi, through creation and through the body, that things are brought back to the way of the Tao. Deeper than chi is "shen," or "spirit." When chi is balance and harmonized, and is flowing in an unrestricted and free manner, then shen is awakened to bring the individual to the even deeper mysteries of Tao. "Jing" is the "physical power" of the human being. Again, when chi is harmonized and unrestricted, it can be converted into physical power and strength. These three are sometimes spoken of as vitality, energy, and spirit, in classical Taoist writings and teachings. When all three come together, the person experiences good health, both interior and exterior, and longevity of life. This is also the point both of Tai Chi meditation practice, for one or for two people, or even for the martial arts, though this has frequently been misunderstood both by participants and observers.

I am not an expert or a teacher of Tai Chi. I am only a simple Christian monk who has incorporated certain aspects of this teaching into my own daily routine exercise and meditation from the perspective of the centrality of Jesus. I, myself, use only a few of the simple Tai Chi warmup moves, which incorporate the eight basic positions of Tai Chi. While I have friends who are formal Tai Chi practitioners and masters, as Christians, I do not live in a situation where I am able to either study with them or under them.

For myself, my simple Tai Chi movement does three things. It gets the body and the blood moving in a way that is neither violent nor forced, first thing in the morning. By combining the movement with my breathing, I am able to harmonize both my bodily movement and the flow of chi throughout my body. This means that the movements become rather graceful and harmonious, and also greatly invigorating and energizing. With my mind, I simply thank the Lord for creation, and for my body, soul, and spirit rising to a new day, and I try to bring all of the actions, words, thoughts, and intuitions of the whole day into harmony, balance, and union in Christ. While this is my conscious thought at the beginning of the exercise, I soon move beyond this thought, into the simple intuition of the practice.

In Tai Chi and Taoist meditation, the practitioner is taught to incorporate the breath with a visualization of chi moving throughout the body. This happens in three stages. The first stage is simply visualizing chi, or energy, flowing in with each life breath, and descending into the lower abdomen, right around and below the navel. This area is called the "tan t'ien," pronounced, "dan ti'en." This deeper form of breathing is the way that infants and little children breathe, and the way all of us breathe when we relax in sleep. During the conscious hours of the day, many degenerate into a breathing that only involves the upper chest, thus limiting our intake of oxygen, the oxygenation of our blood, and the resulting health of our organs and tissues. This more normative shallow breathing is the result of the activity and the anxiety of our daily life. Deeper breathing occurs when we are more relaxed, which causes greater relaxation without diminishing sensitivity or awareness. In fact, since this deeper breathing fills the lungs with more oxygen, and creates more oxygenation of blood, all of the organs, including the brain and the tissues of the body, come to a greater state of physical awakening. We feel healthier and sharper. After this deep in breath, we simply exhale slowly, but naturally, through the nose, following the same path of entrance.

The second stage of breathing adds to the in breath what is called the "turning of the Tai Chi turbine," or "wheel," in the area just below the tan t'ien so that the energy goes to the lower upper body, and then back up the spine, all the way to the crown of the head. Though this sounds complicated in writing, after several weeks of practice in the first stage, a practitioner will notice that this turning of the Tai Chi turbine and the ascent of the chi up the spine to the top of the head begins to occur almost naturally. It is sensed by a certain tingling or vibration in the various parts of the body as the chi moves into that area, particularly at the crown of the head. The out breath simply goes from the top of the head down the front of the face, and out the nostrils. This creates a completely circular path, from the nose, down to the tan t'ien, around the Tai Chi turbine, up the spine to the crown of the head, and then back down and out through the nostrils.

The third stage is the most advanced, and is the goal of normal Tai Chi breathing. This is the same as the second stage. However, when the breath reaches the Tai Chi turbine and begins to turn and go back up the spine, the turning of the turbine also pulls chi from the heels of each foot, up the back of the legs, meeting with the other flow of air and line of chi at the base of the spine, and ascending to the crown of the head. The out breath conversely goes from the top of the head, back down the entire front of the body, down the front of the legs, and out through the soles of the feet, back into the earth. Simultaneously, there is an outflow that goes through the arms and out the hands and, as in the second stage, out the nostrils, down the front of the face. This creates a complete flow of chi, both from the atmosphere and from the earth, and going back into the atmosphere and into the earth. The Taoists call this, "breathing from the soles of one's feet." It accomplishes a balance and harmonization of the whole human being with the whole of the created cosmos, in its balanced and harmonious state.

MICROCOSMIC AND MACROCOSMIC ORBITS EXERCISES

After learning to sink the chi with the breath into the tan t'ien, or the place halfway between the navel and the pubic bone, you can also learn to direct chi in a circular motion through the body. This restores the free flow of energy throughout the body, and cleanses, harmonizes, and opens the door for refining energy into spirit through breath.

Microcosmic, or Small Orbit

1. Stand in the (see page 223) Horse posture, or sit in your meditation place, and breathe deeply into the tan t'ien. Unite the breath with the Spirit of God at work in the original essence and energy of creation.

2. As you breathe deeply in this way for several weeks or months, you will notice a turning sensation in the area around the tan t'ien and the base of the spine. This is sometimes called "turning the Tai Chi ball," or "Tai Chi turbine."

3. As you turn this Tai Chi ball, visualize, and sense that the breath turns around and up the spine, through the neck, and to the top of the head. Visualize the breath as a thin line. Also visualize chi entering the body at the base of the spine from the earth and ascending the spine to the top of the head. Here the yin chi from earth meets with the yang chi from heaven.

4. When the energy reaches the top of the head, breathe out through the nose, and direct the chi back down the front of your body to the perineum at the base of your torso, back to the base of the spine. Begin again and repeat several times.

Macrocosmic, or Heavenly Orbit

After several months of the above, you may begin to sense a greater flow of chi occurring throughout the body. This may indicate that you are ready to try the macrocosmic orbit in circulating chi with the breath. But do *not* try the macrocosmic orbit until you have mastered the microcosmic.

1. Begin as above in the standing Horse posture, or seated in your meditation place, and breathe deeply into the tan t'ien.

2. This time, as you inhale through your nose, see chi coming from heaven through the top of your head. This is yang chi. Also visualize it coming up from the earth through the soles of your feet. This is yin chi. Direct the chi down from your nose and head, and up from the soles of your feet up the back of your legs, to meet in the Tai Chi turbine at the base of the spine. Here, the yang and the yin chi balance each other.

3. As they meet in the Tai Chi turbine, chi is catapulted, or blown with the deepening breath, up the back of the spine, the neck, and to the head.

4. Here, you will also have strong sensation of the "bellows." This is using the lower abdomen as a bellows to fan the intensity of the chi as it circulates. You will literally get a sensation of a bellows fanning the intensity of the chi circulation from the Tai Chi turbine throughout the rest of the body.

5. Exhale as the chi reaches the head, and consciously direct it down the front of your face and body. Breathe out through the nose, direct chi down the arms and out through the hands and fingers, and down the front of the legs, through the feet, and out through the balls of your feet into the ground. This exhale and the directing of chi out through these various areas happens simultaneously. This creates a complete circuit of both the yang chi, and yin chi, from the heavens and the earth, through the body, and back to the source. It cleanses, harmonizes, and grounds the body, and opens the way for a releasing of energy into spirit, which facilitates rebirth.

As you complete the above chi, small and heavenly orbits united with your breathing, you will feel invigorated, balanced, and peaceful. This type of breathing will become second nature, and will become a way to be in harmony with the Spirit of God, and the original essence of creation through the reconciliation of Christ at all times, wherever you walk, and whenever you breathe.

It is important for the Christian to remember at this point that we see all of these exercises as created realities, operating in and through the person of Jesus Christ, who reconciles all of creation back to the fullness of the Godhead. We are aware that in the fallen order of the world, without Christ, these same exercises and visualizations might open us up both to natural forces that are beyond the wisdom of the human being without God's revelation, and to fallen supernatural forces, which could lead us into illusion and delusion, and to their deceptions, when they appear to be angels of light, and are, in fact, angels of darkness. Without Christ, they may be good, neutral, or bad, but we lack the wisdom of Revelation needed to discern them fully. (Though many Taoist masters, are, indeed, advanced.)

In Tai Chi movement, we try to harmonize the movement of the body with these breathing stages. We begin by focusing just on the bodily movements, and with a minimal awareness of breathing. As we advance, we become more aware of the breathing, and the movement of chi through the body. We culminate with a normative use of the third stage of breathing, whereby with each movement a flow of chi is coming in both from the atmosphere and from the earth upon which we stand, and is flowing through us and then back out into the atmosphere and back into the earth. The whole movement thus becomes a fact and a symbol of the overall harmony of our life with the created order as it was originally intended to be.

Chi can also be transferred into "jing," or physical force, for the use of either self-defense, or healing. This is done through the visualization of condensing chi into jing. In this visualization, you see chi condensing into the very bone and the marrow of the body, and then vibrating down the skeletal system to the point of departure, such as the hands or the feet. I am not, nor do I really desire to be, a martial artist. However, I have heard that in the martial arts, the power of one's jing can be felt even without physical impact, thus indicating the fullness of the flow of each participant's chi. Even in the area of healing, Taoist healers learn to translate chi into jing in order to bring healing to the body of either one's self or to another.

DISSOLVING WATER METHOD EXERCISE

It has been said that the Taoist Water Method is like seeing pure water in a clear glass. If dirt is put into the water and stirred up, the water becomes cloudy. This is like the impurities in our life. If the water becomes still, then the dirt settles to the bottom, and both the clear water and the dirt are plainly visible. But this is not the end. It is really just a new beginning. The impurities represented by the dirt at the bottom still need to be dissolved before the glass of water returns fully to its original state.

Related to the organ and body cleansing methods is the Water Method of dissolving energy blockages in the physical, emotional, and thought pattern levels. This means seeing the blockage as ice, allowing it to turn to water, and then sending it outside of your body as air through your breathing.

1. Begin in either the standing Horse or sitting posture in your meditation space. I have found the standing posture to be better for beginners. It can also be done lying down on the floor, or in bed if you do not fall asleep. Breathe deeply as usual. Invite the Spirit of God and the name and person of Jesus to come with each breath.
2. Lift your hands above your head as before, turn the palms inward, and find your outer energy.
3. Begin slowly moving your hands down your body. As you sense or feel a blockage, stiffness, or pain, visualize it as hard and cold ice. Allow it to turn from stiff ice to fluid water as the cleansing line touches it. Then allow the water to vaporize and lift out of your body and out of your outer energy. With your exhale, send it far away from your being. What you are doing is allowing the area to totally relax and let go until it is gone.
4. Continue down your body, doing this wherever you feel blockage or pain.

5. Conclude by thanking God for these natural powers, and his supernatural assistance in using them.

Emotions and Thoughts

Having completed this practice on the physical level, we now need to go to the deeper causes of our physical ailments. Except in the case of injury and accidents caused by gross external means, these usually exist on the level of the emotions and the thoughts.

1. Begin as above.
2. Scan down the body. As soon as we sense blockage or pain, we wait for a negative or destructive emotion or thought to emerge. Visualize that negative emotion or thought as inflexible ice. Most negative emotions and thoughts, like anger, hatred, or judgment, are indeed most inflexible in forgiving or seeing the other person's side or the situation from another perspective. Simply let go of it, and allow it to turn to fluid water. Continue to let go, and allow the water to vaporize and float out of the body and soul.
3. Give thanks to God for this power of detachment and forgiveness in Christ, and conclude.

These negative emotions and thoughts can also be dealt with most effectively through the cross meditation mentioned at the beginning of this book.

Taoists are also concerned with the development of shen, or spirit. This is the highest and the deepest point of development and brings the ultimate balance and harmony to both the chi and the jing. The development of the spirit is done through a seated or standing meditation, through the practice of what is called "shooing." Shooing simply means to do non-ado and to relax. It is similar to both Hindu and Buddhist seated meditation without the strong emphasis on the lotus posture per se. It does emphasize a solid, straight, and comfortable cross-legged position on the floor, yet without causing undo strain to the legs. As with all of Tai Chi movement, the practitioner is encouraged to visualize a string, hanging from the crown of the head, down through the tan t'ien, to the perineum, at the base of the upper body, between the genitals. The eyes are partly opened but looking into infinity, without focusing on any one particular object. The breath is deep, easy, and natural. The mind is focused on the breath and on the intuition of infinity. This brings ultimate relaxation to the body and to the mind and cultivates the reality of shin. When one is unable to properly enter into this state in moving meditation, we are encouraged to spend some time in this seated meditation.

Chi Kung (Pronounced Chee Gung)

After the moving meditations, I sit down in a straight chair, with my feet flat on the floor, and enter into some Chi Kung practices in order to cleanse the channels of breath, the bone marrow, and the organs. Chi Kung, considered a predecessor of Tai Chi by some, is practiced throughout China alongside of traditional modern medicine, and is currently becoming very popular in Western culture. The breath cleansing begins by closing the right hand into a comfortable and unclenched fist, extending the thumb and the little finger. [Using the thumb and clenching the right nostril, you breathe in through the left nostril, visualize the breath going to the base in through the nose, down the side of the spine on the left, or through the center of the body, slightly to the left, to the base of the spine, up the spine, and to the crown of the head.] Then letting go of the right nostril with the thumb, you clench the left nostril with your little finger, and breathe out, visualizing the breath going down the spine, to the base of the spine, from the crown of the head, and then back up to the right of the spine, to the center of the body, and out the right nostril. Then you repeat the practice going in the opposite direction, creating one full cycle of breath cleansing. Each in and out breath is done approximately to a count of ten, slowly. If the breathing is deep and from the lower abdomen, the individual should sense the breath channels of the body being cleansed of any stagnant chi.

STANDING POSTURE: TAI CHI STANCE, THE HORSE EXERCISE

Postures in Taoist meditation are done in three ways: standing, moving, and sitting. The standing and moving are for the preparatory stages for deeper meditation.

1. Stand with feet about a shoulder's width apart, with your weight evenly distributed.
2. Tuck your tailbone toward the ground, as contrasted to turning it out toward the back.
3. Drop your shoulders toward the ground, relaxing them, as contrasted to pulling them back.
4. Visualize a string holding up your head, and running through your body. This will pull your head up and back, tucking the chin inward, as contrasted to jutting your head and chin out.
5. Let your arms fall to the side naturally, with the palms of your hands turned toward the back comfortably.
6. Breathe deeply to the tan t'ien.
7. Conclude by rocking your weight slightly from side to side, and front to back. Take a deep cleansing breath, and disengage.

Next, I move into the bone-marrow cleansing. It may be done seated or standing. Modern science is showing that many diseases of organs and tissues are related to the health of the bone marrow. Cleansing the bone marrow adds to the health of the body. This is done by closing the eyes, placing the fingertips of each hand together, putting it above the crown of the head without touching the body, until you feel a point of contact with the energy field of the body. For those beginning to practice, this may be very close to the physical body, and for those more advanced, it may be further away, since they have learned how to sense this, and the energy field itself has grown stronger. Then, beginning at the crown of the head, you simply move down the body, in a seated position, across the face, down through the shoulders, then down the spine, with the bone being cleansed of any impure chi. It is pushed downward, down through the pelvic area, then down the legs, the knees, the shins, and then finally down to the feet, where it will be pushed out into the ground, from the soles of one's feet, and also out of the hands, into the atmosphere, and into the ground.

There are a multitude of Chi Kung exercises. The same is true of Tai Chi forms and practices. It can seem that for every teacher, there is a new exercise, method, or practice! But there is a certain consistency seen throughout the various particular expressions of the teachers and methods. This is what we can learn from as Christians. Furthermore, it is good to find a teacher with a clear authentication of their being a real master of the art from a genuine lineage or school.

CHI KUNG BONE-MARROW AND BODY CLEANSING EXERCISE

1. Stand in the Horse standing posture and breathe deeply.
2. Extend your arms from your sides until they are over your head, palms facing down. Feel the energy above and outside of your head, and rest your hands there, palms facing inward.
3. Visualize the Spirit of God giving us the power of healing and cleansing, and coming through our hands. Also realize that from the Taoist point of view, these powers are not really supernatural but are simply part of our unused human energies. Either way, they are all traced back to God, or the Tao.

4. Then slowly begin moving your palms down your face, then your neck, and shoulders. Visualize that a line extends from your hands across your body, and you are cleansing the bone marrow of any stagnant chi and pushing it downwards as the line descends. Continue down your body, your upper chest, and arms, abdomen, lower abdomen, and pelvic region. Notice especially the spine. Continue all the way down your legs to your feet. Then visualize that you are pushing all of the negative stagnant energy out of your body through the balls of your feet, and releasing it into the ground.

5. At first, you will do this pretty much by faith that such a thing is possible. But after a short while, you will begin to actually sense the line moving through your body and releasing stagnant and negative energy. Soon you will not need to use your hands but can scan the body simply by using your mind to direct the cleansing energy.

6. Conclude by thanking God for this power and his assistance in using it.

Body Cleansing

1. Start as above.

2. This time, instead of cleansing the bone marrow only, let the line remove any negative chi from anywhere the line moves across—the bones, muscles, tendons, blood vessels and blood, or the organs. As above, push the negative chi downwards through and out of the body through the balls of the feet into the ground.

3. Conclude by thanking God for this power, and his assistance in using it.

It may be rightly asked whether these visualizations have any basis in scientific fact. The answer is yes and no. On one level, people who do these visualizations seem to be healthier in the areas visualized, such as bone marrow, or particular organs, etc., and they experience greater health in general. However, there is no evidence as of yet from science to indicate that the particulars of these visualizations, as used in these actual methods, follow scientific fact. Visualizations are viewed by Taoists as simple tools that help in the mental process of meditation. They do not try to push the point that the breath, for instance, follows these actual currents in the body. We know that the breath, in fact, goes into the lungs, and back out from the lungs. However, when incorporating the breath with these visualizations on the currents of chi, the chi is made stronger, and body, soul, and spirit are made healthier, so it is both scientific and non-scientific, or perhaps beyond the sciences at this particular point in history.

Next comes the cleansing of the organs. This practice is based on the fundamentals of Chinese medicine. If we compare Chinese medicine to Western medicine, we could say that Western medicine is like a car mechanic. Chinese medicine is more like a gardener. Western medicine sees the car, or the body, in a very utilitarian sense. Chinese medicine sees the body as more of an integral part of an overall whole, of which it is a part. Most people who study these things are finding that an incorporation of both is actually the healthiest way to go, since there are aspects of the body that are, in fact, rather mechanical. There are other aspects that are more living and part of an overall whole of body, soul, and spirit. So we need aspects of the car mechanic and we also need aspects of the gardener.

In the Chinese Taoism approach, there are five major phases. Two are yang, or positive, two are yin, or negative, and one is intermediate, between the two. All are connected between a major organ and a set of minor, related organs, and an external element in creation. These are all interrelated, with a whole network of powers, climates, seasons, directions, times, stages, colors, odors, flavors, and sounds within the macrocosm of creation, and faculties, motives, qualities, activities, expressions, conditions, voices, organs, tissues, substances, and essences within the microcosm of the human being.

The five major categories are wood, fire, earth, metal, and water. These are related to the major organ networks of liver, heart, spleen, lung, and kidney. Each organ also displays a particular emotion when it is in balance in union to the rest. For instance, the emotion associated with the liver network is anger, joy, with the heart, rumination and evenness, with the spleen, sorrow, with the lungs, and fear, with the kidneys. The liver and the heart are yang, the lung and the kidney are yin, and the spleen is balanced in between. If one of these emotions is troubling you, or is lacking, then we try to balance the chi within each respective organ.

However, each organ is related to the other and each organ is related to a particular external category, for instance, wood is burned by fire, which creates earth in which metal is made, which can be liquefied, and become, as it were, water. Likewise, each can control another in a different interdependent pattern. Wood controls earth. Earth controls water. Water controls fire. Fire controls metal. Metal controls wood. The former sequence is called "the supporting sequence," and the latter is called "the restraining sequence."

We begin this organ-cleansing exercise by inhaling the wood element, symbolized by the color green, into the liver. The green color flows in with the in breath, breathing in deeply, and filling the liver with a green coloration completely. Then we exhale through the mouth, with the mouth just slightly open, visualizing the color black, symbolizing the negative chi that may be stored up in the liver. We repeat this two or three times, careful to keep our breath deep, but natural and even, so as not to hyperventilate. Next comes fire and heart. We inhale fire, symbolized by the color red, filling up the heart as we did with wood and the liver. Then we exhale out through the mouth the color black, symbolizing any negative chi that has built up in the heart. Likewise, with the earth element, we inhale the color yellow ocher into the spleen, exhaling the color black, symbolizing any negative chi built up within the spleen. With metal and the lungs, we inhale the color silver-white, filling up the lungs, and exhaling black, symbolizing negative chi. Lastly, we inhale water, symbolized by the color deep purple or blue, into the kidneys, exhaling the color black, symbolizing any negative chi built up within them. Each element and organ can be done once or several times. Many find it more comfortable to take a simple relaxation breath between each element and organ. Repeated use of this over weeks and months shows a definite decrease in negative emotions and physical disorders, and an increase in overall emotional and physical health.

CHI KUNG ORGAN-CLEANSING EXERCISE

1. Sit or stand in your meditation place, and breathe deeply.
2. Breathe in. Visualize a green light, representing the wood element and the life of God, flowing into your body from the top of the head, flowing down into your liver, on the right side of your abdomen. The liver is the seat of kindness or anger, on the positive and negative sides. This green color represents the life-giving qualities of the Spirit of God. It also represents kindness and calm.
3. Breathe out and visualize anger leaving the liver, and your entire body and being. See it as a black color that exits through the nostrils. Repeat the above inhale and exhale three times.
4. You may do a few normal meditation breaths at this point if desired. You may do this between each of the organs if helpful.
5. Breathe in a red light, representing the fire element, into the heart, the seat of joy and hatred. Breathe in joy and happiness with the red fire color. It can also represent positive enthusiasm for the good.
6. Breathe out any hatred in your life, especially in the heart of your being. See it as a black color leaving with the exhaled stale breath. Exhale three times.
7. Breathe in the color brownish yellow, or ocher, into your spleen, the seat of the balance of yin and yang, and empathy or anxi-

ety. Breathe in balance, empathy, and a solid flexibility, like the earth from which life springs, or a solid earthen rock.

8. Breathe out all anxiety and imbalance from your life, specifically from the spleen. Exhale three times.

9. Breathe in a silver-white color from the metal element into your lungs, the seat of courage and grief. Breathe in courage and a sharp clarity—like sharpened metal—to cut through any cloudiness in your life.

10. Breathe out all grief and clouded vision from your life, especially from your lungs. Exhale three times.

11. Breathe in the dark blue color of the water element into your kidneys, the seat of calm and fear. Breathe in calm, and the flexibility of water, which always seeks the lowest place but can cut through the hardest element of rock.

12. Breathe out all fear and inflexibility. See it as a black color going out of your body and your kidneys with the exhalation of old air. Exhale three times.

13. Conclude by taking a few normal meditational breaths in either the seated or standing postures.

This particular exercise can be easily Christianized. For myself, breathing in the wood element, I see the color green as the life of vegetated creation, and Jesus as the author of life. For fire and heart, I see the fire of the spirit, and of purgation, cleansing my heart and the very center of my being. For earth and spleen, I see Jesus as the rock, the author of all that is solid, stable, like the earth, and yet flexible enough to bring forth life. With metal and the lungs, I see Jesus as the ax that is laid to the root of any unhealthy tree in my life, and also as the purifier of metal. Lastly, with water and kidneys, I see the water of the Spirit, coming into my life, making me flexible and fluid, humble and filled with peace. In particular, the Taoists believe that water is the great sign of the person who follows the Tao. Water is the most humble of all the elements, said St. Francis of Assisi, and it always seeks the lowest place. However, though it is soft and fluid, in repetition, it alone can cut through rock.

The following table may be helpful.

Element	Wood	Fire	Earth	Metal	Water
Organ	Liver	Heart	Spleen	Lungs	Kidney
Color	Green	Red	Yellow/ Brown	White	Dark Blue
Emotion	Anger/ Kindness	Hate/Joy	Anxiety/ Empathy	Grief/ Courage	Fear/Calm
Christian Aspect	Life	Spirit/ Enthusiasm	Solid/ Living (Rock) + Earth	Clear/Sharp (Refined, Iron Sharpens Iron)	Living Water of Spirit Lowly/ Flexible

This whole Taoist system is easily integrated into Christianity as a tool that helps to bring the full balancing and harmonization of all creation in and through Christ to the whole human being, body, soul, and spirit, and to all creation as well. While Western philosophy and medicine has easily been Christianized and incorporated into our overall Christian ethics and spirituality, so likewise, this older and more holistic Eastern approach is also used in a similar way. However, in many ways, this system is more compatible with the Christian ethic and worldview, since we believe that Jesus has reconciled not just human beings but all of creation back to the fullness of the Godhead. This entire system can be a tool to help actualize this theological and mystical reconciliation of Christ, in and through the entire world.

For many, this Taoist system of both seated and moving meditation is sufficient. It is a system unto itself, and stands on its own, in perfect balance. When incorporated into the Christian experience, it is easily seen as a tool of Christ, leading to Christ. The moving meditation incorporates the continuing redemption of our bodies in Christ. The visualizations on breath, chi, the elements, and particular organs keep the mind minimally occupied. Both the standing and the seated meditations with the experience of simple shooing, or deep relaxation, allow us to pass over into the deeper realms of shen, or of the spirit, in a way completely compatible with the Christian theology of body, soul, and spirit, in and through the work of Christ.

Buddhist Meditations

I personally also incorporate some Buddhist meditations into my own Christian meditation experience in a way that I find comfortable and compatible with my own experience and theology of Jesus Christ, and consistent with a conservative and orthodox position. I rely most heavily on the Christianized version of the Four Establishments of Mindfulness as described in other parts of this book.

Of course, the Buddhist tradition is famous for its many lists. This is because Buddhism itself is a reform of Hinduism, also famous for its many lists of different yogas and the various steps therein. At first, these lists seem daunting and confusing, primarily because they come from a tradition other than ours. Some fundamentalist Christians criticize these lists as too works oriented. However, if we are honest, we can also see that we Christians also have our own lists— ten commandments, eight beatitudes, a trinity of divine persons, three human faculties, seven vices or eight demons, four cardinal virtues, three theological virtues, seven gifts of the Spirit, nine or twelve fruits of the Spirit, and so forth.

Because these lists all represent the effort of the practitioners of each religion to exemplify, explain, and live a system that is complete unto itself, most respective practitioners and devotees spend a lifetime within their own religious system, finding health, happiness, and fulfillment. However, because the lists are complete and rather lengthy, we also find in our own lives, ways, as it were, to encapsulate all of our own system within just a few basic practices and devotions. For instance, for Christians, meditation on the paschal mystery intuitively completes and includes all the other meditations upon the incarnation and life of Christ, and all that goes before it in the Old Testament.

Cautions

As we move into these various meditations of Taoism, especially in the ancient yet newly adapted discipline of Chi Kung, Christians need to be somewhat cautious in the invocation of various spirits, gods, and deities. This is true not only with Taoist practice but also with the later developments of Buddhism and Hinduism, which by their nature incorporated the various folk and local spirits, deities, gods, and goddesses of a local area into the greater scope of their religious synthesis. For the Christian, we may recognize the good intent in such practices, and even the philosophical or moral good symbolized and exemplified in them. However, all of our visualizations and meditations are centered on the life of Christ, the reality of our one yet trinitarian God, and our life within the Church. For Catholics, who incorporate a veneration and invocation of the saints and the angels, all of these retain a clear and undisputed focus on Jesus, as the Alpha and the Omega and the complete center of our faith.

There are other Chi Kung practices, such as meditation on the Milky Way, and visualizing light coming from the Milky Way through the top of one's head and into one's whole being. I would not recommend this in an unqualified way for Christian practice. I would, though, strongly recommend a meditation on the power of the Spirit of God, visualized in a dove, or a flame, and seeing, as it were, light descending from the dove or the flame into our very body and, as it were, filling us up from top to bottom. This is an example of a healthy, Christian adaptation and completion of a Taoist Chi

Kung meditation, without inadvertently falling into some of the spiritual dangers and impurities of a religion and a practice that, though inspirited, is not part of direct divine Revelation.

TAN T'IEN DEEP BREATHING EXERCISE

1. Sit in your mediation place. Breathe deeply through your nose.
2. Visualize a line to represent your breath. As you inhale, count to ten. Allow the line to enter through the nose, and descend all the way to the lower tan t'ien, halfway between your navel and your pubic bone.
3. As you exhale, count to seven or eight. Allow the line to retrace itself back up through the nose, and out of the body. This is one way to "follow your breath." Repeat once.
4. Now do the same as above, but with a more natural pace of deep breathing.
5. Conclude as usual.

COUNTING THE BREATH EXERCISE

Many people have trouble focusing their mind. It jumps easily from one thing to another. Counting the breath gives the mind something to do, but something so minimal that it trains it for deeper mediation. The following exercise is based on classical practice in some Zen teachings.

1. Sit in a proper posture in your meditation place. Breathe deeply and gently through your nose. Allow your belly to expand on the inhale, and flatten out with the exhale. You may test this by

gently placing your hands on your navel for the first breath
or two.

2. Begin by counting the breath with your mind. First five, then
ten, then twenty, fifty, and up to one hundred breaths. Every
time you get distracted, start again. Do not give up until you
reach one hundred. It will take you several weeks of meditation
periods to reach one hundred comfortably. Do not be discour-
aged if it takes many weeks to reach the full count.

3. After twenty minutes or so, no matter how far you have gone
in counting, conclude in the traditional way. Be grateful for the
growing stillness of your mind, and of your awareness of your
lack of focus, through this exercise. It all serves to help you
practice more earnestly.

BAMBOO BREATHING EXERCISE

Sometimes people get nervous as they try to breathe correctly. This
exercise helps to bring us back to deeper breathing throughout the
normal breathing practice. It is called "Bamboo" breathing because
of the cross-grain pattern and sections on the bamboo stalk.

1. Sit in your meditation place and breathe deeply.

2. Begin by a deep preparatory breath as in former exercises, with
your palms over your navel, and inhaling to a count of ten, and
exhaling to a count of eight or so. Do *not* strain at holding your
breath too long. This can cause hyperventilation. Do this several
times.

3. Now place your hands back into a restful position on your lap,
and breathe normally, yet deeply. Do this for five breaths.

4. Now breathe deeply to the count of ten once more, and exhale
to the count of eight or so. Go back to the deeper, more normal, breathing.

5. Repeat this practice for ten minutes or so. Then move on to another exercise. You may wish to spend the entire twenty minutes on this one exercise.
6. Conclude as usual.

Seated Meditation

The Taoists also practice seated, as well as moving, meditation, and the equivalent of what the Christian West calls contemplative prayer. Ancestor Lu, who lived during the Tang Dynasty (618–905 A.D.), writes extensively, in a way similar to *The Cloud of Unknowing,* on sitting and forgetting. He says, " I know without knowing, see without seeing; I have no ears, no eyes, no mind, no thought, no cognition. Thus having nothing, then reaching absence of even nothingness, after that the mind cannot be disturbed by anything. Being unperturbable it is called sitting, forgetting.

"To learn the Way, we must first kill off the chief hoodlum. What is the chief hoodlum? It is emotions. We need to wipe out that den of thieves to see once again the clear, calm, wide-open original essence of mind. What is this all about? It is about quelling the mind. One removes emotions to quell the mind, then purifies the mind to nurture it.

"To restore the mind to its unfragmented origin, sit quietly and meditate. First count the breaths, then tune the breath until it is imperceptible. [Since the body is like the undifferentiated absolute,] you won't hear anything. Those who can regain their composure after a mountain crumbles before them are second-best; not even being startled is expertise.

"As long as there is any thought left unterminated, one's essence is not whole. As long as the breath is even slightly unsettled, one's life is not secure. It is necessary to reach the point where mind and breath rest on each other, and thoughts are forgotten in the midst of thought. In essence, it requires relaxation and patience. The secret is put this way: 'No need to stay by the furnace and watch the firing, just settle spirit and breath, and trust nature. When the exhalation and inhalation stop and the body is as though dead, you will realize meditation is just a temporary device.'

"As for states of experience of the exercise through quiescence, first there is dullness, oblivion, and random thought. Then there is lightness and freshness. The latter is like being inside curtains of gold mesh. Finally it is like returning to life from death, a clear breeze under the bright moon, coming and going, the scenery unobstructed.

"As for the exercise of sitting until one does not hear, at the extreme of quiet stillness, the mind is not drawn into movement by the ears. One hears only sound, not tone. This is not hearing.

"Walk slowly, at a relaxed pace, and you won't stumble. Sleep soundly, and you won't fret through the night. Practitioners first of all need serenity and patience. Second, they need dispassion, not to think about the past or be concerned about the future. If you think about your past, your former self will not die. If you think about the future, the road seems long and hard to traverse. It is better to be serene and relaxed, not thinking of past or future but just paying attention to the present, acting normally. Each accomplishment is an achievement, and this will build up. If you are eager for completion and vow to do so many deeds or practices, this is still personal interest, calculating merit and striving for gain. Then the mind cannot be pure. This is the root of inconsistency."

The Four
Establishments
of Mindfulness

BUDDHIST

I N BUDDHISM, THE MEDITATION UPON
the Four Establishments of Mindfulness really encapsulate all of the rest of the Buddhist teachings. This meditation
upon the Four Establishments of Mindfulness are part of the seventh
step of the Holy Eightfold Path called "right attentiveness," or
"mindfulness" and is itself included under the fourth of the Four Noble Truths of the Buddha. He taught these Four Noble Truths in order to recognize the reality of suffering and to overcome it in this life.

For myself, after the moving meditations of Hinduism and Taoism, and the breath, bone-marrow, and organ-cleansing of Taoism, I
move into a Buddhist seated meditation, including the Four Establishments of Mindfulness. I do all of this from my own Christian
perspective of seeing all completed and fulfilled in and through the
person of Jesus, therefore opposed to nothing good, true, and beautiful in any other religious tradition.

Traditionally, this includes a contemplation of the body, the feelings, the thoughts of the mind, and the phenomenon. All is preceded

by an ethical and moral system that purifies the body and the ethics and morality of the practitioner. The practice of seated meditation and the following of the breath follow this. This seated meditation and following of the breath is also included in each of the Four Establishments of Mindfulness.

You begin by going to a solitary and silent place, either alone, or with a group of practitioners, and sitting down, in a cross-legged position, with straight back and attentiveness. Then with attentive mind, the breath is followed, first, a long inhalation and exhalation, and then a short inhalation and exhalation.

Notice that in the very beginning, place, posture, and breath are important. The place should be solitary and silent. It should be relatively spacious, airy, and clean. The Buddha describes this as "the forest, at the foot of the tree, a solitary place." The silence is both audible silence and visual silence.

The posture should be stable. As with the Taoist tradition, the back should be straight, the legs crossed, but not so as to cramp or fall asleep, and Westerners may simply prefer sitting in a straight-backed chair. The point of the posture is not physical contortion or athletic accomplishment, but to be as free of the posture as possible once the meditation ensues. We should not have to think about cramped legs, aching backs, sagging shoulders, and the like.

The eyes should be open so as to keep from falling asleep. However, with the exception of one-pointedness meditation, where they are focused on an object, they should not be particularly focused on anything, lest they become distracted by this, that, or the other that they see. The tongue is placed on the roof of the mouth, right behind the front, upper teeth. This is to keep one from having to worry about swallowing, or coughing, and such. Simple placement of the tongue on the roof of the mouth gives the mouth and the throat something to do that is minimal and almost unconscious. Likewise, the hands are placed in the lap, palms up, with the right hand over the open left hand, with the thumbs touching. This is not in order to call on some special spirit, or anything like that, as is the case with some of the hand motions of tantric Hinduism and Buddhism. It is simply to rest the hands comfortably in the lap, again giving them something to do without giving them enough to do to distract one from meditation once we begin.

The breath is deep, but not forced. Generally, you may test this by placing your hands, first the left and then the right, over the naval, [you can tell whether or not you are breathing correctly.] If with an inhalation, your lower stomach is distending outward, and with the exhalation is falling back into toward the spine, then you are breathing correctly. The point of the breath is both to relax the body and to focus the mind on something minimal enough to keep it occupied from distracting thoughts, but not so complex as to become a distracting thought itself.

Christian Perspective

From the Christian perspective, focusing on the breath is done for several reasons. First, the word "spirit" in Hebrew is "ruach," and simply means breath or wind. It was this breath and wind that blew across the face of the waters at creation, and was blown into humankind so that man became a living being. Likewise, Jesus says that the Spirit is like the wind that blows where it wills. Second, it is an expression of our poverty. The last thing that a person does before they die is breathe. It is also the first thing we do when we are born. It is the minimal physical action required in order to stay alive. If we find breathing sufficient, in order to do the greatest spiritual work possible, in and through meditation, then we have come into contact with both the greatest poverty, and the greatest wealth of God in this one action of meditative breathing. And third, we breathe because of the physiological reasons mentioned above, believing that Jesus is interested not only in soul and spirit but in the right ordering of our body as well.

So when I sit for seated meditation, I first sit in a place specifically set aside in my hermitage for meditation, in the right posture, and then begin to focus on slowing deepening my breathing. This happens quite naturally. With the in breath, I breathe in the Spirit of God, and the name of Jesus. With the out breath, I let go of anything that is not in God, and in Christ. With the in breath, I breathe in the poverty of Christ that leads to the greatest riches of the kingdom of God, and with the out breath, I breathe out anything that I may be possessing that is not of God.

Next, I focus on my body. With the first in and out breath, I simply recognize its existence, as a creation of God, and as a gift of God to me. I also see its interdependence with all creation as a mystery and wonder from the Creator. Next, I recognize its impermanence, that it will pass away. With the third in and out breath, I simply let it go. In this process, I may recognize that I have certain physical strengths, weaknesses, health, or sickness this particular day. I recognize it, realize its impermanence, and then let it all go. In this process, my body is calmed, and it finds its rightful and appropriate place in the scope of eternal reality.

This process can also be practiced during the day, while looking, hearing, tasting, touching, or smelling, or during any other bodily function such as walking, standing, sitting, lying down, or simply being conscious of what the body is doing, and finding its rightful and appropriate place in the eternal scope of reality. This practice is called "Stopping and Realizing," and is considered most foundational for those practicing dhyana, or concentration and mental control, at the beginning stages of insight.

The Buddhist meditation on the body is quite methodical and complete. It recommends seeing the human body as a "sack of flesh" with all of the various organs, muscles, ligaments, tissues, and bones within. We are to view it in the same way that a butcher would view the carcass before him. In other words, with dispassion and detachment, recognizing that our eternal life goes beyond the flesh alone.

We are also encouraged to meditate upon the ultimate end of the body in a ten step meditation on death, ranging from first seeing the body dead, then bloated and worm eaten, then with the flesh falling off the bones, then with the bones without flesh but still stained with blood, then with the bones without blood stain, then white-bleached from the sun, then the bones falling one from the other, then seeing the bones deteriorating, finally turning into dust and being blown away by the wind. This meditation is to aid in a true sense of the impermanence of the body.

In Christianity, we also say, as scripture says, that "all flesh is like grass." However, we also believe in the resurrection of the body (1Cor. 15). Granted, the body will be changed and turned into something similar to but beyond what the body is now, but it will nonetheless be a glorified body, not unlike that in which Jesus was resurrected. In this, we both agree with and disagree with a Buddhist theology regarding the body. However, we would agree that the body in its present form, at least, is impermanent at best.

After one has firmly established this meditation on the body, Buddhists say we may expect ten blessings. This is freedom from: 1) delight and discontent; 2) fear and anxiety; 3) physical blessing and cure, such as hunger and thirst; 4) the four trances; 5) magical powers; 6) heavenly hearing; 7) insight into hearing of other beings; 8) remembrance of our previous lives; 9) the heavenly eye, and 10) the complete cessation of the passions and desires, which lead to suffering. Of course, as a Christian "magic" and "previous lives" are not taken literally. Simple belief in the power of God and awareness of the whole interdependent reality of our life is sufficient.

For myself, all of these stages are experienced in the simple breathing in and out, and recognizing the reality of my body in the created order, and then breathing in and out and letting go of all in my body, both the good and the bad, in light of its impermanence in its present state, relative to the state it will take on in eternity.

Following the meditation on the body comes meditation upon feelings and emotions. As with the body, with the first inhale and exhale, you simply greet and recognize the reality of your emotions, whatever they may be that day—joy or sorrow, peace or anxiety, contentment or anger, any emotion whatever. Simply greet it and recognize that it is a reality in your life on this particular day. With the second inhale and exhale, you simply let go of any emotion, similarly as we did with the body, in light of the emotions' impermanence. They come and go. They are directed by the thoughts, but they are also dependent even upon the chemical balance of the body on this particular day. We are not guided by them, for they are fickle—up one day, down the next. So we let go of our emotions, gently and peacefully, in light of their impermanence.

Next, we do the same thing with our thoughts. With the first inhale and exhale, we recognize our thoughts as a reality of this day. Our thoughts may be focused or unfocused, single pointed or scattered. It really makes no difference. We simply recognize the reality of our thoughts at this point in time. With the second inhale and exhale, we simply let go of our thoughts as impermanent. External, objective thought will ultimately give way to the simple experience of truth and reality on a much deeper level, beyond being either objective or subjective. The truth will simply *be*. Our mind will become the mind of Christ, and through Christ, the mind of God. So at this point, we let go of all thoughts, all conceptual images, or forms. We let the mind be at peace.

For the Christian, this does not mean that we do away with any sense of objective truth or doctrine. These objective truths are most important foundations for both faith and morality and the overcoming of vice with virtue, which build toward the more meditative and contemplative experience. They also prove to be most important discernment tools between either good or evil spirits, which may aid or attack us during times of meditation and prayer, and throughout one's life.

FOUR ESTABLISHMENTS OF MINDFULNESS EXERCISE

The Four Establishments of Mindfulness, as found in the sutra of the Full Awareness of Breathing, are considered the core teaching of many Zen masters. It is part of the core of my practice in a Christianized form, and can be found in that form in the breath exercise on the cross and resurrection, or in body, soul, and spirit. The Four Establishments in classical Buddhist teaching are body, feeling, mind, and the objects of the mind, and are covered in sixteen in and out breaths. They are as follows:

1. Be aware of taking a long breath. 2. Be aware of taking a short breath. 3. With an in and out breath, be aware of the body. 4. Be aware of the body being calm and at peace. 5. Be aware of feeling joyful. 6. Be aware of feeling happy 7. Be aware of the mental functions. 8. Be aware of the mind being calm and at peace. 9. Be aware of the mind. 10. Be aware of the mind being happy and at peace. 11. Be aware of concentrating the mind. 12. Be aware of liberating the mind. 13. Be aware of the impermanence of all dharmas. 14. Be aware of the fading of all dharmas. 15. Be aware of liberation. 16. Be aware of letting go. These are divided into three domains of body, feeling, and mind.

I teach it as follows for those more accustomed to the Western anthropology of sense of the body, emotions of the body and soul, and thoughts of the soul or mind:

1. Sit comfortably in your meditation place, and breathe deeply. Take a few deep cleansing breaths, and a few normal deep breaths.
2. Breathe in. Be aware of your body. How is it today? Is it weak or strong, healthy or sick, aware or sleepy? Is it addicted or free, attached to negative sensual habits, or is it detached and free? Simply acknowledge the state of your body today. Be aware of the interdependence of your body with all of creation. Especially be aware of your interdependence with your parents and relatives, who helped bring you into existence in this life.

Thank God "for the wonder of your being," as the Psalmist says. Be aware of the impermanence of your body. It will grow old, sick, and will die. It will decompose in the grave and turn back to compost and dust for the earth. Breathe out. Let your body go. Release all that it is. This simple act of surrender and release will heal it of most of its disordered habits and addictions.

3. Breathe in. Be aware of your feelings today. Are they agitated or calm, enthusiastic or still, negative or positive? Be aware that when the senses of our body are negative, attached, and disordered, our feelings usually become negative, attached, and disordered as well. But do not judge them now. Simply acknowledge them. But feelings come and go with the changing of the conditions of our life. They are therefore external to our deepest being. They are impermanent. So we can just let them go. Breathe out. Let all your emotions go. As you do this, you experience great peace, and the tensions and stresses of body and emotion fall away like a bad set of clothes that do not really fit.

4. Breathe in. Be aware of your thoughts. If emotions are agitated and negative, then thoughts tend to become that way, too. How are they today? Are they clear or confused, focused or cloudy, positive and calm, or negative and in constant unrest? Simply acknowledge them. Do not judge or scold. These thoughts are conditioned by our emotions and senses, and by external stimuli that come and go. We have these thoughts, but we *are not* these thoughts in our deepest being of existence. They are impermanent. So we can let all of our thoughts go. Breathe out, and let go of every thought. As you do so, you can feel the tension and stress fall away from your head and your brain. You experience deep peace and calm, which, in turn, allow you to focus your mind on the positive things, without the attachment of desire, clinging, and craving, as it was originally created to do.

5. Lastly, breathe in. We can now break free to the place of simple and pure spirit. With each in and out breath, simply *be* in this

place of pure *being* with the one who *is*. Stay here until the end
of the meditation period.

6. Conclude as is traditional.

Christian and Buddhist Worldview

There is a difference between Buddhists and Christians regarding
their worldview and their metaphysical realities. For the Buddhist,
all begins in a state of nirvana, or complete stillness and cessation, yet
without extinction of life, and opens into a world that includes objective thought, subjective feelings, bodily forms, and the like. Once
these have been overcome, then we go back to nirvana, or a simple,
peaceful existence of life beyond thoughts, emotions, or bodily forms
in any way.

For the Christian, life was originally more expanded, and beyond what we presently experience in terms of spirit, soul, and body.
Through the fall, these faculties have been disordered, imbalanced,
deharmonized, and greatly minimized from what God originally intended. Through rebirth and enlightenment in Christ, these faculties
are reordered, balanced, harmonized, and brought back to their maximum fulfillment. Heaven will be a cessation of disorder, imbalance
and discord, and a resuming of a maximized use of every human faculty within all of creation, which will have been brought back into
order, balance, harmony, and therefore brought to its maximum potential in and through God.

The illustration on page 246 might be helpful.

It is also true that in the Christian contemplative and mystical
tradition there is a stage of relationship whereby all thought, conceptual images, or forms are given up in our simple union with God. At
this point, we can simply "be" with Christ. We simply "are" with the
"I AM." This is beyond emotion, thought, or bodily form. At this
point, the great Christian mystics have told us that the reintroduction of thought, conceptual image, or form in our thinking is actu-

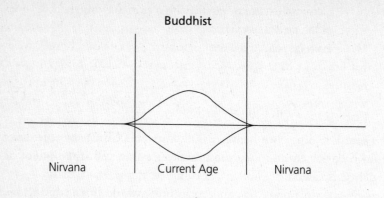

Buddhist

Nirvana   Current Age   Nirvana

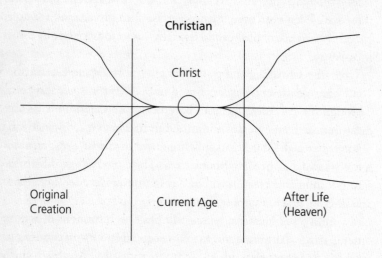

Christian

Christ

Original   Current Age   After Life
Creation   (Heaven)

While the world view is different in both, the line throughout is a
common mystical experience and convergence point.

ally detrimental and even called demonic. At this stage, the Christian
contemplative experience and the Buddhist meditation find common ground, if not in a total union of metaphysical views, at least in
our own human and psychological experience of a greater spiritual
reality, which we Christians call divinity and God.

246

The Buddhist reality begins with a simple living flat line, opens through the present age into an oval, and goes back to that flat line. We Christians would see the beginning as more of a funnel, with a flat line going through it, going into a very small, minimized tube of existing in today's reality, leading back to a funnel opening outward, which would be heaven. Both we and the Buddhists can share this line, which goes through both metaphysical views, and in this we find common ground, though we might objectively differ as to which way the funnels open in the beginning and at the end of human existence.

It is also good to mention that Buddhists do emphasize the need for objective truth. This is especially true regarding the morality and teachings of faith that prepare one for the greater meditation and contemplative experiences of samadhi and enlightenment. For the Buddhist, these objective realities are true, but they are not eternal. They are true insofar as they exist in the realm of functionality in the current world order, and therefore, the Buddhist does not try to simply ignore them and fall into complete relativity. Like Christians, they would adhere to definite teachings regarding faith and morality, which are considered extremely important for them in preparation for the more existential experiences of later meditation, which leads to samadhi, and enlightenment. Again, on this level, Christians and Buddhists share much in common.

The Four Establishments of Mindfulness is meditation and contemplation of the phenomena. This stage in some way digresses and circles all the way back around in summation of all that has come before. It would include "the Five Hindrances" of lust, anger, torpor and drowsiness, restlessness and mental worry, and doubt. It would also include meditation on the Five Aggregates of Existence, namely, bodily form, feeling, perception, mental formations, and consciousness. Likewise, there would be a meditation upon the Six Objective Sense Factors of eye, ear, nose, tongue, touch, mind, and the fetters that arise from overdependence on them. Likewise, there are the Seven Elements of Enlightenment, namely: attentiveness, investigation of the law, enthusiasm, joy, tranquility, concentration, and final equanimity. This would also include a review and continuation in the Four Noble Truths, the fourth of which includes the Holy Eightfold Path, in which these Four Establishments of Mindfulness are found. And the Four Establishments of Mindfulness itself includes a meditation on the phenomena of the Four Establishments of Mindfulness of concentration on breathing, which leads to a meditation on the body, on the feelings, on the mind, and finally, on the impermanence of all phenomenon, which lead to detachment, the cessation of desire, the extinction of desire, and complete renunciation, which lead to liberation and full enlightenment in samadhi and the experience of nirvana on earth.

Personal Experience

For myself, I have found that a simple experience of the above, with breath, body, feelings, and thoughts of the Four classical Establishments of Mindfulness being intuitive throughout, works best for me. It is simple, mentally uncluttered, yet focused enough to keep me active through the meditation. As a Catholic Christian, the theological principles that I intuit are based upon a classical Catholic Christian worldview and ancient and time-tested ascetical practices concerning the senses and feelings of the body and the thoughts of the soul. This is not a mental gymnastic for me, but a simple intuition in and through my relationship with Jesus Christ.

I begin by sitting in either a half-lotus or a full-lotus position. For many people, a simple cross-legged posture or sitting in a straight-backed chair is more comfortable and realistic, since most of us have not been culturally conditioned for either the half-lotus or full-lotus seated position. Again, the point of this posture is not physical gymnastic accomplishment, or ascetical feat, but to provide a simple, comfortable, and stable posture that will enable us to get beyond being drawn back into concerns about posture once the meditation begins.

I then begin a simple and comfortable deep breathing, from my lower abdomen. Since I have some experience now in Taoist meditation, I have found that either the cyclic visualization of the breath, or full body breathing, works best for me. With each breath, in union with the Jesus Prayer tradition of the Christian East, I intuit both the name of Jesus and the Holy Spirit. I first do this mentally but let it pass quickly to simple intuition. Likewise, I am aware of the blessings of poverty, as this basic function of human life brings me such a feeling of liberation, joy, and breakthrough to enlightenment, with God and all creation.

Then I am aware of my body. Some days it is healthy. Some days it is sick. Some days it is awake and clear. Other days it is sluggish. I accept it as it is, interdependent with other days, other people, and all creation, yet impermanent and passing away before its final transformation and resurrection. Then I just let it go. I feel all tension or sickness just flow out from every limb and organ. I am calm and at peace. I am healed and whole. By letting it go, it finds its own place in God's order. It simply is.

I next concentrate on my feelings. I accept the feelings that I have on a particular day, aware that they may change from day to day. Then I simply let them go. For me, I let them go at the foot of the cross of Jesus. I am also aware that my feelings are not to rule my life but are to be guided by my life in Christ, redirected and channeled in a healthy way. This latter point is more of an intuition in the meditation than an actual thought. If it becomes too much of a conscious thought, the thought itself will distract me from the simple meditation.

Next comes the awareness of my thoughts, and then the letting go of them. As with feelings, I simply let them go in Christ. I intuit that there are objective truths, doctrines, and dogmas of the faith that are given by God to guide me to this point, and I am grateful for them. However, at this point of breaking through to contemplation, I simply let them go. I can trust entirely in God and the Church to guide me, but at this point I need no longer have worry, or anxiety, or even theological investigation regarding these same truths. Because of my trust, I can simply let all thought go, in and through the person of Christ. Here, I commune with Christ at the absolute deepest level of essence, spirit to Spirit, beyond soul or body. Again, all of this is intuited and not conscious thinking.

After going through these four stages—breath, body, feeling, and thought—I experience a calm in my body, my feelings, and my thoughts that is really beyond description. It is both ordinary and extraordinary. It tunes me into God, and all of creation in God, through Christ, in a way that is beyond theological speculation or mental concentration. It simply "is." This tuning and harmonization prepares me for the whole rest of my day.

Stopping and
Realizing

THE PRESENT

MOMENT

IN THE CHRISTIAN WEST WE OFTEN speak of "the sacrament of the present moment." Buddhism speaks of mindfulness, and of being mindful of the present moment. The following exercise of "Stopping and Realizing" from Buddhist sources is a helpful tool in realizing this mutually shared concept.

In addition to the formal practice of the "Four Establishments of Mindfulness," the practice of Stopping and Realizing is very helpful throughout the normal activities of the day. With each use of the eye, ear, nose, mouth, touch, emotion, action, or word of the body, or with each thought of the soul, we stop and realize how we are using each faculty. Is it being used with the mindful awareness of eternal realities, or are we getting sidetracked into using the impermanent things of this world as if they were permanent, in and of themselves? Likewise, whether we are sitting, standing, walking, running, resting, working, or any such activity throughout the day, stopping and realizing these realities brings every action, word, emotion, or thought into an eternal use and realization. Each one of these things becomes an activity that allows us to break through to an enlightenment of eternity in the here and the now.

In the classic *Dhyana For Beginners,* we hear, "In the practice of Dhyana there are two aspects to be considered. The first relates to the sitting, the other relates to the circumstances and conditions." This work spends considerable time in establishing the right environment, personal ascetical lifestyle, posture, and breath, etc., to prepare for the right practice of dhyana, or concentration. The ten primary headings for the work are: 1) external conditions; 2) control of sense desires; 3) abolishing inner hindrances; 4) regulation and adjustment; 5) expedient activities of the mind; 6) right practices; 7) the development and manifestation of good qualities; 8) evil influences; 9) cure of disease, and 10) realization of supreme perfect enlightenment. The following appears in the right practices section.

"First is the right practice of sitting. Dhyana can be practiced as one is walking, standing, sitting or reclining, but the position of sitting being the best for the practice, that is considered first . . . It may be considered in its relation to the many and confused thoughts that fill the mind at the beginning of the practice. First we should practice stopping thoughts in order to bring these many thoughts to a standstill and break off thinking altogether. If we have difficulty in doing this, we should next practice the examination of thoughts . . . We must practice stopping and examining . . . (a) As to 'stopping.' There are three ways of doing this . . . recalling the wandering attention to some part of the body as the tip of the nose or the navel, by so doing, the many and wandering thoughts drop out of attention and disappear . . . by bringing attention to only one thought. . . . Again it can be done by recalling the true nature of all objects of thought.

"When we began to practice meditation, at first our thoughts continue and ramble about without any cessation. We try to realize their true nature and to employ different means for stopping them. . . . We should reflect upon the history of the thought that has arisen. . . . We try to realize the true nature of consciousness. . . . This is the ultimate principal tranquility and peacefulness.

b) "Second, as to 'stopping and examining.' . . . Control vagrant thoughts by examining, or observing, or making insight. . . . One way is by opposing a bad state of mind by its corresponding good state, as for instance, thoughts of purity as opposing licentious thoughts and desires, thoughts of kindness as opposing hatred, thoughts of the five grasping aggregates that make up personality as opposing egoism. . . . Another way is to oppose definite things or thoughts with consideration of the causes and conditions that make them what they are, namely, empty, transitory and egoless. . . . 'All phenomenon are impermanent.'

1) Acting. When engaged in any activity we should ask this question: For what reason am I engaged in this activity? If we are conscious that we are acting from some unworthy motive . . . we should cease the action. . . . This is what is meant by practicing stopping the condition of action.

2) Standing. If we're standing because we're vexed or disturbed or are seeking some selfish thing, then we should cease standing. But if we're standing for some good purpose, we should remain standing with tranquil mind.

3) Sitting. Briefly . . . if we are sitting because of vexation and a disturbed mind, we should not do it. But if it is for some good, unselfish purpose, then we should take our seat with a concentrated and tranquil mind.

4) Reclining. We should keep in mind the question as to why we are lying down. If it is because we're lazy and sleepy, we ought not do it, but if it is the regular time for sleep, or because we truly need rest, then we should do so with tranquil mind.

5) Doing things. When we are prompted to do things, we should ask ourselves, Why should we do them? If it is an instinctive act, or an evil, selfish act, we should not do it. If it is a good act for the welfare of others, then we should do it. During the act, various vexations and disturbing thoughts will rise both good and bad. To get rid of these thoughts, we should practice stopping by means of realizing the emptiness and vanity of all thoughts, by reason of which practice the deluding thoughts will disappear.

6) Speaking. While we're speaking, we should keep in mind the reason for our speaking. If it is mere arguing, or vexatious discussion, or wild words prompted by instinctive moods, then we should keep silent, but if it is for some good unselfish purpose, then we may speak.

7) We are to practice stopping whenever our eyes notice sights. This means that whenever our eyes catch sight of any object, we're to recall that the apparent object has no more reality than the moonlight in the pond. So if it is a pleasing sight, we're not to let desire for it arrive in the mind, and if it is a repulsive sight, we're not to let a feeling of aversion arise, and if it is an indifferent sight, we're not to let ignorance of its meaning disturb our mind.

8) We are to practice stopping and examining at the time of hearing sounds by our ears. . . . Think of it as having no more value than an echo. If it is a pleasing sound, we are not to let it awaken any craving desire, and if it is discordant sound, we are not to let it give rise to any fear or hatred, or if it is an indifferent sound, we are not to be curious or disturbed.

9) We are to practice stopping and examining at the time of smelling. . . . Whenever a scent is noticed, think of it immediately as a make-believe bonfire. If it is a pleasant fragrance,

we're not to give away to a craving desire for it, and if it is a disagreeable smell, we are not to let a feeling of aversion or dislike spring up, and if it is an indifferent odor, [any feeling of disturbance.]

10) We are to practice stopping at the time of tasting. This means that whenever we taste something, we should immediately think of it as having no more substantiality than a dream experience. If it is a pleasing taste we should not crave it, and if it is a repulsive taste, we should not be troubled by it, and, if it is an indifferent taste, we should ignore it.

11) We are to practice stopping and examining at the time of touching things. No matter what the hands or body touch, we should think right away that it is unreal and visionary. If we receive pleasing sensations from what we touch, we are not to become fond of it, and if the sensations are disagreeable and painful, we're not to cherish dislike or hatred for it, and if the sensations are indifferent, we are not to try to make distinctions or carry them in memory.

12) We are to practice stopping and examining at all times when the mind is engaged in thinking . . . whether he be acting, standing, sitting, reclining, looking, listening, feeling, or consciousness, he may know that he is practicing . . . truly.

This stopping and examining is simply to ask why and how am I using the various faculties of [my human being,] and of my being human. Why do I use my faculties of sense and intellect, as we call them in the West? How do I use them? Why and how do I use my hearing, sight, smell, taste, and touch? What about my bodily functions and various daily actions of walking, speaking, sleeping, and so on? How and why do I feel emotions, or think thoughts? Stopping and examining on this level is simply to ask some basic questions about these things, and to cease doing the negative, and to start doing the positive things of daily life.

But there is more to it than simply this. There is a deeper stopping and examining that is Buddhism's strong point, and its most frequently criticized tenant. That is the belief that all things are ultimately empty and without what we call a Self. All things knowable are ultimately impermanent and will pass away as they are absorbed into reality, or nirvana. But this does not mean that all things do not ultimately exist, or that ultimate existence is meaningless and empty. The emptiness of which Buddhists speak is only a word to describe the indescribable at best. Supreme Reality is beyond existence and nonexistence, being or nonbeing. It simply *is*, yet is not, since any of our concepts of existence are merely ideas and words that are bound to fall radically short of the reality of Reality itself.

This Reality is to be examined and realized in the full experience of stopping and realizing. It means going through all things of this life to the Reality beyond all we can possibly understand or know, and then coming back to the here-and-now to find both this awesome Reality in the daily functions and events of life, and to find the proper harmony and peace of function of those same mundane realities. It is bringing the perfect peace, or nirvana, of the Beyond to the here-and-now as fully as is possible in the now. It is learning to find the Eternal in the now, and to pass through the now to experience the Eternal. This happens all at the same time in one intuitive flash, yet in a way so ordinary concerning the daily events of life that no one can possibly know it is happening at all except the person him or herself, and one fully trained in the unfolding of such things.

Such stopping and realizing is also a basic and essential part of Christian asceticism. Classical ascetical manuals such as Tankery's *The Spiritual Life,* or Jordan Aumann's updated version of the same for today's environment, *Spiritual Theology,* ask the same questions from a Christian theological, anthropological, and ascetical perspective. These deal primarily with the first level of such stopping and examining.

But the more advanced level is not at all absent from the Christian mystics. It is just stated in different theological and anthropological ways and terms. St. John Eudes says that our breath must become the breath of Jesus, the beating of our heart, the heart of Jesus, the conceptual images and thoughts of our mind, the thoughts of Jesus, our words, the word of Jesus, and our actions, the merciful actions of Jesus. In this way, all of our life becomes a holistic meditation upon and prayer in and through Jesus, beyond just seated or even walking meditation. Our whole way of life becomes a meditation on, in, and through Christ. In this, we fulfill what St. Francis said eight hundred years ago, namely, that he seeks not so much to pray but to become a prayer.

In Buddhism, there is considerable emphasis put on mindful liturgy and walking meditation. These practices are to help make one's whole life an experience of awakening and mindfulness, whether in seated meditation, or zazen, in liturgical practice, like bowing, etc., or in the daily activities of life.

In Christian meditation as well, if our public liturgies and private meditations are done well, they have a most profound effect on the rest of our life. All becomes one in he who IS one. Every action of life becomes part of one's practice of awakening and rebirth in the breakthrough beyond separation and duality in the paradox of Christ. Every step, every movement, every work and relationship becomes a prayer walk and liturgical dance and gesture, and the means to sacred communion in and through Christ. All becomes an extension of the One we receive in liturgy and sacrament, and in our private times of meditation and prayer. There is no longer any separation at all, and so there is no longer any intrusion on the peace we seek through our formal acts of meditation and prayer. It, he, is with us always, wherever we go, and whatever we do, not as something or someone external and extrinsic to our being but as an integral part of who we are in the very depths of our spirit and soul.

The next time you see the activities of life as an intrusion on prayer and meditation, turn that very act into a means of prayer and meditation. Not just, " Oh, Lord, get me out of here" or worse, "Get them out of here," but a real meditation on the presence of reality right in the very midst of "here" and "now." As Christians, we also "stop and examine" all in our life as it is happening so that all in our life might be a means to greater awakening and rebirth to the eternal and the infinite in Christ as it is happening in the here-and-now. It is entering fully into the "sacrament of the present moment."

Prayer
Walking

WALKING MEDITATION, OR PRAYER, HAS become very popular. Thich Nhat Hanh, the Vietnamese Buddhist monk who now resides in Plum Village Buddhist community in France, has written and traveled the world, popularizing the concept of walking meditation. Likewise, in the Christian tradition, there are many books and retreats given on prayer walking. I have also tried to spread this concept within and from Christian circles, with our Prayer Walks, in major cities throughout the United States. In 1997, we were in five major cities, and we continue to receive invitations where feasible.

In our Prayer Walks, we teach our brothers and sisters that, as they place their foot upon the ground, they breathe in, as it were, through the soles of their feet, and receive the blessing of all those who have walked on this ground before us. It may be simply people of good will and integrity; it may be from those who have followed the natural religions of inspiration, all the way from primitive animistic religions, to the more developed expressions of partial or full monotheism. We also receive the blessings of those who have received the Revelation of God in the Old Testament, and all our Christian brothers and sisters who have received the full Revelation of God in and through the person of Jesus. As we place our foot on the ground and breathe in, we receive all these blessings.

We also breathe blessings out, right down through the soles of our feet, onto the ground. We realize that none of us is perfect. Whatever our religious or philosophical tradition may be, all of us have fallen short of the ideal of perfection, and we need help from God. We need his blessing, his holiness, his redemption, and his salvation. As we walk on this ground, we breathe the blessing of God back onto the very ground where we walk, and to every man, woman, and child who has ever walked here before us.

Through this walking and breathing, this receiving and giving, a wonderful meditation and prayer rhythm develops in the walking itself. The pace is neither too fast nor too slow. We are not trying to do an athletic foot race, nor are we to walk so slow that we would become an obstruction in the various cities where we walk. We set a comfortable pace, one that is both natural and prayerful.

With each in breath, we take three or four steps, and with each exhale, another three or four steps. If our breathing is meditative breathing, as in seated meditation, we soon begin to experience a great enlightenment and breakthrough, even as we walk through the hustle and the bustle of American cities. We bring holiness right in the midst of the areas where prostitutes and pimps work the street corners and drugs are sold in the back alleys. We bring peace, even on the very streets where the violence of gangs is rampant. We do not try to walk in places that are overtly unsafe for the participants, but these things are evident even on the most seemingly safe streets of our American cities. This is true especially true if you are walking in meditation, for in walking meditation, you really see, you really hear, you really come into contact with the neighborhoods and the people in the neighborhoods through which you walk.

PRAYER WALKING EXERCISE

We teach this for Prayer Walks all across the troubled cities of America. It brings a great faith and peace to Catholic Christians, ecumenical Christians, people of all faiths, and people of good will who join us. It is a most powerful tool for meditation and prayer.

1. Stand with feet a shoulder-width apart. Point the tailbone toward the ground, and let the shoulders relax and drop.
2. Breathe deeply from the diaphragm. For those who have mastered the microcosmic or macrocosmic orbits, you may breathe in this way.
3. Breathe in. Take a step. As you place your foot on the ground, breathe up from the ground the blessings of the faith of those who have walked before us. Take several slow steps with the in breath.
4. Breathe out. As you do so, breathe the blessings of your own faith back into the ground where you step, making it holy ground for all who follow you. Take several slow steps as you breathe out.
5. Walk at a slow but natural pace, breathing in and out as you go. Breathe in the blessings of those who have walked in faith before us, and breathe out the blessings of your own faith for those who follow us. Do this step by step.
6. Soon all the steps of your life will become a Prayer Walk. You will always be receiving the blessings of those who have come before, and giving the blessings of your own life to those who follow.
7. Stop along the way and be seated. Process what you are experiencing through dialogue with others, or in seated meditation if you are by yourself.
8. Conclude in the standing or seated posture in your meditation place, or another holy place. Thank God for graces, do some final deep breathing, and conclude. If standing, do one last in and out breath of receiving and giving the blessing of God through the very ground we walk upon in daily life.

At Little Portion Hermitage

But I do not practice walking meditation only during these Prayer
Walks. I practice it every day of my life, especially in the place where
I live, the Little Portion Hermitage, the monastic motherhouse of
the Brothers and Sisters of Charity. Every morning, after I do the
moving meditation and seated meditation I described above, I prayer
walk for a short time between the time I leave my hermitage and the
time I enter into the Chapel of Charity, the monastic church where
the Brothers and Sisters of Charity gather daily to pray. Our first
prayer service to greet the day as a community is at 6:45 A.M. There's
a bell at 6:40, and an earlier one at 6:30 to call us into prayer, and
meditation together. At around that first bell, sometimes a little earlier, I begin the short walk up the hill from my hermitage, to the
Charity Chapel, where the community will gather to greet the Lord
as a gathered people at the beginning of the day.

In this short morning prayer walk, every sense and every faculty
is used and awakened. I am almost always refreshed by the coolness
of the morning air on my skin, which enters through my nose into
my lungs as soon as I walk out the door. This is true even on the
hottest days of summer. That morning freshness is always a beautiful
way to start a day that may end in scorching sun, humidity, and heat.

As I round the corner of my hermitage wall to turn toward our
prayer grove, and the area of our community church, prayer garden,
and common buildings, I am immediately struck by the sight of the
sun rising, filling the sky with the colorful hues of dawn. In the
spring and the autumn, there is frequently a slight mist or fog, and in
the winter, a frost or a snow. Each season is different, and each is
wonderful to behold. I also hear the sounds. There are birds singing
in every season. Squirrels running and bickering or playing, and the
distant sounds of our chickens and domestic animals, and even the
small insects buzzing about, beginning their day, to do quite naturally what God has ordained for them.

Of course, there is also the sound of the prayer bell. This sound, after almost twenty years, has become almost embedded into my psyche, ringing at various times throughout every day of my life in the monastery. We are not a wealthy community, so we could not afford a big and glorious bell. It's only an old school bell, used in an early settlement, somewhere in the Ozarks. It's beautiful, but it is not big and sonorous. It's a simple bell, with a simple sound, yet not just an old clangy metallic sound. This sound calls us to pray. It is a musical note that is both sharp and clear and mellowing into the depths of one's soul. It, as it were, awakens creation to greet the dawn, of which we are a part. Many times when the bell rings, the ducks or the geese will begin to squawk and quack. It calls not only the people of the monastery but all the creatures, at least in some way, to praise the Lord. Neighbors have told us that they can hear the bell over a mile away, even through the hills. When we ask them if it is a disturbance, they tell us, on the contrary, that it is a comfort and a call to them as well, calling them to pray, and comforting them in knowing that there are people not too far away praying for everyone in the local area and throughout the world.

As I continue my walk up the hill, I make my way into the prayer garden. It is both silent and a proclamation of God, a solitary place, yet a place of communion, a place of silence, yet of great activity all at once. I see the new flowers opening to greet the new day after having been closed through the night. The insects are already bustling and busy, pollinating these wonderful praises of God through color. The statuary of the prayer garden keeps silent watch, through both the day and the night, in a slow and steady vigil, as God, the angels, and the saints do themselves over the whole world. The stained glass illuminates as the sun rises and streams light through their colorful and deep hues. A myriad of flowers, plants, and native grasses create nooks and crannies throughout our little prayer garden, which evoke solitude and community, sight, sound, and smell to praise God at the beginning of this new day.

Usually before walking on up the few remaining steps to the chapel, I stop by our ponds. They, too, are an ecosystem unto themselves, bespeaking both the Creator and the entire cosmos of creation, in their own way. St. Francis says that water is lowly, and pure, and we are to be like her. The Taoists say that water always seeks the lowest place and is the most fluid of all the elements, but can cut through the hardest and highest of all rock. The ponds always call me to this mystery. Likewise, they bespeak that each soul is like a pond. It can either be muddy or clear. And that the pond of our soul is to be still so that it too can settle and clarify. Thus, maybe for the first time, we can see what really lies within, and then do the appropriate work to make the pond of our soul both clean and a balanced and harmonious eco system within itself, reflecting the harmony and the balance of God.

From here, I walk on up, through our covered walks, past the seated Teaching Jesus, reminding me of the beauty of the Sermon on the Mount, on past the part of our garden dedicated to the gifts of the Spirit, calling me to a life of a true Christlike character and attitude, and then on into the monastic church, our Chapel of Charity. Here, I will enter into all of the liturgical gestures, postures, listening, responses and, finally, the great receiving of Jesus in the sacrament, which are normative within a monastic community and within the Church. It is all one great walking and seated meditation on Christ, which calls and empowers me to be a Christian, "like Christ," throughout all the normal things of the rest of my day.

LITURGY PRACTICE EXERCISE

There is much talk of liturgy practice among the Buddhists nowadays. It has been a part of Christian worship since the beginning. I will use my Catholic experience in the following exercise.

1. Go to a Catholic liturgy. But do not just go as usual. Go as an experience of meditation, prayer, and worship. You may want

to spend time in your private meditation space before you go in order to prepare.

2. Notice the obvious and subtle aids in worship involving the senses of the body in liturgy. We meet in one place. As we enter, we dip our hands into holy water, make the sign of the cross, and sit together in chairs or pews, yet no one can sit in that place but you. Look around you and see the sacred art of the worship space. Enter into the gestures of worship in the liturgy. It is a simple and dignified sacred dance of worship of God. It is all an attempt to involve the senses in worship.

3. Now allow the emotions to get involved. First, the sacred art is supposed to stir your heart beyond mere ideas and words. Second, as the liturgy begins, the opening songs are meant to stir your feelings in a positive way. Next, the Penitential Rite is meant to stir the emotions toward contrition for any time that we have not followed Jesus as disciples well.

4. Next, we move into the Liturgy of the Word. Allow the thoughts of our spiritual mind, our soul, to be directed to the things of God through the readings and the homily, or sermon. Use these as sacred readings, as in *lectio divina,* to stir your meditation and emotions in a positive way.

5. Through the Liturgy of the Eucharist, or the Mystery, allow yourself to pass through and beyond the senses and emotions of the body, and the cognitions and thoughts of the soul, to the total contemplation of the spirit in God's Spirit. As you experience this Mystery through and beyond all that has come before, all else is empowered and transformed by this experience as well. Now every gesture, every emotion, and every word are transformed into an action of awakening and rebirth in Christ. Infinity and eternity are fully present in every particular action and experience of liturgy.

6. Conclude the liturgy as usual. Go back to the normal things of life with a totally transformed understanding and experience of them. They have not changed. You have changed. Now you can make a real difference in changing all things in our world for the better.

Christian Zen
and the Koan

Recently, Buddhism has become very popular again in America. In a way reminiscent of the 1960s, secular bookstores fill their religion sections with titles from gurus and masters from Eastern religions. This is especially true of Buddhism. Perhaps this is because of the widely publicized plight of the exiled people of Tibet, and the role of the Dalai Lama in their religious and political life. It is also due to the efforts of those who first brought Buddhism to America in the twentieth century, such as the avid advocate of Zen, Daisetz Suzuki. The late Cistercian monk, Thomas Merton, did much to popularize Zen among Catholics and Christians. In addition, having rejected what they perceive to be as the dead Judeo-Christian religion of their own culture in favor of the self-indulgent mysticism of the New Age movement, people are now disheartened by the shallowness of the same New Age movement and are looking for religious roots and sacred tradition that is time-tested and true. Hinduism/Buddhism and Taoism/Confucianism fill that need, without simply reverting back to the typical Judeo-Christian faith they have come to culturally reject. Only one of the schools of Buddhism, Zen, has become especially popular in America.

Roman Catholic Christianity rejects nothing of what is good, wholesome, and true in any other major world religion but sees Jesus as the complement and fulfillment of all. These religions constitute the natural religious impetus of humanity to reach out to God and the things of the divine. They find much, and God reaches back through the natural things of creation and the supernatural things of the Spirit. In formal Revelation, God reached back to humanity in an extraordinary way. We would see formal Revelation as beginning in the Old Testament of the Jewish people, and the fullness of revelation as happening beyond ideas and words in the incarnation of Jesus. [The Buddha described himself as only a finger pointing to the moon, but Jesus is the Light who illumines the moon. In his humanity, he would share that humble statement with Siddhartha Gautama, the Buddha (which means the Enlightened One), but in his fullness he is with and beyond him.] In this understanding, a Catholic Christian is a completed Buddhist, Hindu, Taoist, or Confucian. We love and respect each tradition. We read and study their writings and ponder them in meditation. We see Jesus as complementing and confirming much of each faith's teaching and practice. But we also see Jesus as the perfect completion of each, without doing violence to any. This is not a triumphalistic, or religiously militaristic statement. It is said with deep love and humble respect for all, without compromising any.

[As said earlier, Jesus was probably a whole lot more like a Buddha or Buddhist Bodhisattva, or a Hindu sannyasin, or Taoist sage, than he was like the typical televangelist or radio preacher or megachurch pastor, though there is nothing wrong with teaching spirituality through the media, or pastoring a large church.] But the Jesus of the gospels is more in this Eastern tradition than he is like those we often see representing him to our culture.

For many years, Zen has been integrated with the Christian contemplative experience. In particular, the monastics of the various traditions have come together for dialogue for many years with gratifying results that do not jeopardize the integrity of any participant's faith. Much of Zen and other Eastern religions is a simple natural confirmation of what we already have in our own tradition, though expressed in a somewhat different way. Sometimes it teaches us about the gifts we possess in theory in Christ but have not used well, or even at all, in our own contemplative heritage. Most informed Zen teachers have little or no trouble with Christians incorporating Zen into their own contemplative experience within a Christian religious backdrop. It has been argued that this is what Zen is to Buddhism in the first place, as was the Buddhism of Siddhartha Gautama itself to Hinduism. But that is a whole other chapter and book!

"Zen" simply means "meditate." It is Japanese for the Chinese word "chan," or the Sanskrit word "dhyana." All of these simply mean a meditative state that moves beyond all dualistic concepts of "I and you," subject and object, into pure intuitive union, or oneness with reality. The stages of this journey may occur suddenly or gradually, which constitute the difference in the Soto, or Rinzai schools, but all involve entering into "samadhi," or deep meditative absorption, followed by an initial awakening called "kensho," or "satori," culminating in a final awakening called "complete enlightenment."

This is done through "zazen," or "seated meditation." During zazen, certain bodily and mental disciplines are used to aid the practitioner in moving beyond dualistic reality into pure union with reality. But it is important to remember that Zen is a method beyond the notion of method. Zazen simply *is* Zen.

Zazen usually involves a seated posture, which creates physical stability so that one will not have to think about their body during the prolonged period of meditation. In the East, this has traditionally been the lotus posture, or sitting cross-legged on the floor. There are various versions of the lotus posture, ranging from the full lotus, to the half-lotus, to a simple cross-legged position. In Western society, where sitting on the floor is not part of our culture, it is often better to sit in a straight-back chair in a straight, yet comfortable, posture. The point is not the posture but to move beyond preoccupation with the body in prolonged periods of meditation.

These disciplines also involve calming and deepening the breath. This involves "breathing from the naval," or the belly and diaphragm, instead of from the chest, as is usually done by adults in the hectic and fast-paced societies of the West. This calming and deepening also helps to calm the body, the emotions, and the mind so that a true awakening can more easily take place on the deepest levels of the human being. At first, there is a simple awareness of the breath. Then we might be asked to count the breaths and work on deepening them, and then to unite the breath to certain meditations. Ultimately, we go back to simply breathing, simple being in order to find reality as *is*.

Mental disciplines are involved. Ironically, the mind is used to take us beyond the mind. Thought is used to take us beyond thought into pure intuition, or awakening. This ranges from positive meditations on simple Buddhist truths to thinking of not thinking. This is usually accomplished by filling the mind with something, since the mind must think of something in order to be, but something minimal so as to move closer to the paradox that is nothing and all. This is done through thinking of not thinking at all. This is paradox, and involves using something to move beyond anything in order to find everything. It sounds almost like gibberish, but it is the deepest truth that can be known. Ironically, it is only known through what the Christian mystics call "unknowing."

This is very similar to the contemplative tradition of Christianity. After having meditated on the positive truths of the faith, one moves beyond words and ideas, or even positive images about God, Jesus, or the saints, into pure intuitive oneness with reality. Here, we use words to move beyond words in order to find the divine Word. We use ideas to move beyond ideas to find the Idea, and images to move beyond any image and find the ultimate Image beyond all image. Here, we use meditation on Jesus to move beyond concepts of

Jesus in order to truly find Jesus, or God to move beyond concepts of God, in order to truly be in union with God.

Zen is a special school of Buddhism emphasizing the truth beyond words, which is transmitted outside of the orthodox teachings of the sutras, or scriptures, of Buddhism. This transmission takes place person-to-person, life-to-life, through the special relationship between teacher and student. Following the example of the universal student guru relationship as found throughout the East, the student receives the very spirit of the master in order to surpass the master in his or her own lifetime. This is called "standing on the shoulders of the teacher," and is the special privilege and duty for having received the Teaching, or dharma, from the teacher.

Great emphasis is laid on "sanzen," or the private conference between teacher and student. It is here that the real stuff of the teaching is handed on. But this is not just an ordinary lesson or conversation, as we would have with a professor in Western schools. This is a sacred event. The student is expected to reverence the teacher through ritual bowing and humble questioning. The teacher gives responses that are not normal answers. He answers with paradoxical words or actions, which sometimes seem to defy the logic of the student. Sometimes they can even be quite shocking. This is done to help the student come to a whole new way of thinking and perceiving. Often the teacher will give the student a "koan," a paradoxical story or case from the teaching of the great masters of the past. The content of the sanzen is often the student's work and progress on a particular koan given to them by the teacher.

One of the unique characteristics of Rinzai, and even Soto, Zen Buddhism is the use of the koan. A koan is simply a "case," or "story" from the lives of past masters and students, designed to take the listener beyond objective and dualistic truths to complete union with reality through the use of paradox. A paradox is an apparent contradiction that speaks a deeper truth. A koan is a case study that defies logic yet speaks reality to the depths of the human being through pure intuition. This leads to enlightenment.

For the Christian, Jesus is the ultimate koan. The gospel is the ultimate story, and the incarnation and the cross and resurrection is the ultimate paradox. This is true on many levels. It is true of the entire gospel, which is a case study in Jesus' fulfilling the objective and subjective law and the prophets through complete paradox. It is also true of the particular aspects of the life of Christ, especially as seen in his incarnation and his passion. In the incarnation, divinity is manifested in humanity, the great in the small, the full through self-emptying. The divine takes on the human in order to bring the human back to the divine. Divinity is found in and *as* humanity. Here the divine Word simply *is* through the human being of Jesus. This self-emptying reaches its climax in the ultimate paradox of the cross and resurrection of Jesus, where life is seen in death, light in darkness, union and communion in loneliness and desolation, the greatest word in silence, and the greatest glory in humiliation. All of these realities build on the objective truths of the life of Christ, yet go beyond them into the realm of perfect paradox. At first, they may appear to be duality, but in the end they move into perfect oneness through simply Being.

These are all koans from the ultimate koan in the story of Jesus Christ. Of course, his particular teachings are also koans. His wisdom tradition use of the paradox to take his disciple to a deeper level of truth is a koan. This happens again and again whenever he speaks of wealth in poverty, glory in humiliation, greatness through smallness, and especially life in death, and his special presence through his seeming absence. His parables also would qualify as koans. They teach a deeper truth through a simple story. They tell hidden mysteries through the normal things of his listeners' lives. This is like the Zen koan.

But the Christian koan does not stop with the teaching of Jesus. It continues to his apostles and the saints. Both the Fathers of the Church, and the mystical doctors and greats, give us the teaching that becomes the Christian counterpart of the case study of the traditional koans. Book upon book of mystical interpretation and classical approaches to meditation and contemplation are the Christian version of the koan study. Even as the dharma transmission takes place from teacher to student in Zen, so does a succession of apostolic empowerment takes place from bishop to bishop. A succession of saints is also seen in Christianity that is similar to this transmission of the dharma, or teaching. Within the monastic heritage, this transmission takes place in the relationship between the spiritual father and mother and the sons and daughters of their own monastery and spiritual family. The "revelation of thoughts," which is so much a part of early Christian monasticism, is a Christian sanzen if ever there was one! The teachings of both the Church and the monastic saints are also often a Christian koan.

The Christian koan would also include the primary source material from early monasticism, such as the sayings and lives of the Desert Fathers, or the early Franciscan sources about the life and teachings of St. Francis of Assisi, or his actual writings. The Admonitions of St. Francis hold a special place for this purpose, as would the more overtly spiritual parts of the Rule of St. Benedict. All of these are Christian counterparts to Zen koans, though we have never used that terminology to describe them. But the simple fact remains, regardless of external names. As they say, "A rose by any other name, is still a rose!" So it goes with the koan as well.

The koans of Zen are collected in books such as *The Transmission of the Light,* and *The Blue Cliff Record.* These collections include the original koan, plus traditional explanations of them, to help the student break through beyond them. There is a code within them that one must understand in order to fully use them. Without understanding some of the particulars of Far Eastern language and culture, these koans are virtually impossible for the average Westerner to understand. Furthermore, there are references to older koans within koans that require a working knowledge of them, which was simply assumed with the average Buddhist monk or lay practitioner. The same could be said as to having a basic understanding of Buddhism. The average Westerner simply does not automatically possess this knowledge. Therefore, it is ironic that so much study is necessary in order to break through to the real meaning of these koans that were designed to take us beyond logic and dualistic knowledge to the simple and direct experience of reality.

Christian koans also require some explanation, but not nearly as much as their Far Eastern counterparts, since we come from a culture where so much of who we are as a people was formed from these Judeo-Christian stories. Therefore, whether consciously or intuitively, we already "know" some of these Christian koans. Conversely, we live in a culture where the basic spiritual and moral underpinnings have either been grossly misunderstood, or lost entirely, so some explanation will be helpful even with the Christian koan.

A short list of Christian koans would be such beloved scriptures as the Magnificat, the Sermon on the Mount, the various parables of Jesus, the institution of the Eucharist, the death and the resurrection accounts, the preaching of St. Paul on baptism, and the wonderful teaching on kenosis as found in St. Paul's Letter to the Philippians in chapter 2. All of these scriptures, and many more, can be used as "cases," or "koans," from the New Testament of Jesus Christ. Certainly, there are also Old Testament passages that qualify. This is especially true of the "wisdom books," like Wisdom, Sirach, Proverbs, and Ecclesiastes. All of these contain the paradoxes that take us beyond the energies of faith known through objective and subjective knowledge to the things of pure spiritual intuition and essence beyond all knowledge.

Space and time do not permit a detailed study of these particular Christian koans here. Suffice it to say that, when conducted properly, the study of these koans, under an experienced contemplative or monastic teacher in the Christian tradition, serves the same, or similar, purpose as does sanzen within the Zen tradition. I encourage those who are inspired to this end to find a good teacher and begin.

THE CHRISTIAN KOAN EXERCISE

1. Sit in your meditation space, and breathe deeply. Let go of the senses and emotions of the body, and the thoughts of the mind. Let your spirit emerge with each breath.

2. Choose a Christian koan like the Magnificat, the Beatitudes, the Paradoxes, or the paschal mystery. Begin to turn it in your mind, emotions, and senses with each breath.

3. Allow the mind and the emotions to be frustrated with the koan so that you will exhaust their ability to be in control of the process. Realize that there is no sensual, emotional, or logical understanding or solution to the paradoxes of this koan.

4. Allow the koan to drop from the mind, or the emotions, to the spirit, or to the heart. Allow yourself to break through, to be reborn, or to be "saved," by this breakthrough from senses and emotions of the body, and the thoughts of the mind, to pure experience in the spirit, which includes and surpasses all that comes before. This is pure contemplation.

5. Allow yourself to *be* in this place for as long as is helpful or possible.

6. Conclude as normal for seated meditation.

Conclusion

THIS CONCLUDES OUR LOOK AT MEDITA-
tion in the Christian East and West, as well as in
non-Christian Far Eastern sources, and how I have personally integrated them from a Catholic Christian, integrated monastic base. As
we can see, each tradition has its own unique gift to offer; yet there
are common elements in all.

All begin with the foundations of basic teachings regarding faith
and morality, and move on into mysticism through the use of paradox. For the Christian, this takes on a unique aspect through the paradox of the actual incarnation and paschal mystery of Jesus Christ.
All involve some form of asceticism and mortification of the old
habits of the senses, emotions, and thoughts in overcoming vice and
establishing virtue. All use meditational steps and mystical stages
that begin with the objective and perceptible things of sense, emotion, and the mind, and move into the things of pure spiritual intuition beyond objective or subject knowledge and perception.

I have presented this in anthropological terms of moving from
body to soul, and from soul to spirit. The body would include senses
and emotion. The soul is mind, or thought. Spirit is pure spiritual
essence. The body and soul are the energies of the human being.
Spirit is the deepest essence of the human being. Body and soul are
conditioned, interdependent, and impermanent. Spirit is pure being,
and is both infinite and eternal in pure union with the infinity and
eternity of God.

In Christianity, "the fall" is the reversal of the original intention of God for this anthropological trinity in humanity. Instead of functioning in its original priority of spirit, soul, and body, we now function in body and soul, with the spirit being substantially forgotten, or overlooked, in our daily experience of reality. Originally, the pure intuition of the spiritual essence of reality was the first priority of any human experience of creation, humanity, or the Creator. Thought, emotion, and sensual perception all served and facilitated this primary orientation. Consequently, thought, emotion, and sensual perception were in perfect harmony, order, and peace.

After the fall, this orientation was reversed. Humanity now perceived reality primarily through the senses, such as, "I'm hungry, I'm thirsty, or I'm sleepy, etc." These stirred and inflamed the emotions, which clouded and confused the thoughts of the mind. All became separated and lost. We were like beings that had lost their way. The spirit was consequently covered over and substantially forgotten, leaving our perception of reality, and our human experience, fractured and incomplete. The division and violence evidenced in all of creation is the result of this human disorder and its effect throughout the created world.

In Christianity, we speak of the consistent imagery of becoming a child again in order to rediscover this original human orientation. Specifically, we speak of the necessity of becoming a child again, or of being "born-again," or of "rebirth," in order to become a real disciple of Jesus, in order to enter into the kingdom of God. This can only happen when the old self of disorder, delusion, and division totally dies so that a new self, with a new image and order in perfect harmony and peace, can be born. Only when we really let go of the old self of disordered senses, emotions, and thoughts can we really enter in to the selfless love and purity that we all essentially seek. This is the only way that the beautiful teachings of Jesus in the Sermon on the Mount, as well as the beautiful teachings of brotherly and sisterly love in the early Church, can be realized as an actual experience today. This is Christian resurrection. It is a new self being born according to God's original intention for us. This happens quite naturally once we really let go of the old man or woman. In Christianity, this happens, most unquestionably, through the work and example of Jesus.

The Christian West would make the journey from body and soul to spirit as part of our rebirth in Christ. The Christian monastic West first described it in terms of sacred reading, meditation, and contemplation. Later it would be described as the purgative, illuminative, and unitive ways. Sacred reading and meditation would involve the redirecting of thought, emotion, and the senses, preparing the way to break through to pure contemplation beyond any of these. Purgation and Illumination, similarly, would involve the redirecting of senses, emotions, and thoughts, leading on to pure union. Contemplation and union break through to the rebirth of the spirit, building on, yet going beyond, body and soul.

The Christian East similarly uses the trinitarian anthropology of the incensive, rational, and intellective human faculties that coincide with body, soul, and spirit. Specifically, it is in the Christian East that the incensive and rational powers constitute the energies of the human being, and the place where we can know the energies of God. These energies are the things of God and humanity that can be objectively, or subjectivity, known and perceived. It is here that we hear about the battle with the eight demons, or vices, through the traditional use of classical Christian asceticism and meditation. The Spirit of God and humanity constitute the essence of reality, both in creation and the Creator, that can only be known through pure intuition, building upon the knowable energies but going beyond into a knowledge that is found only in what the mystics call "unknowing." As stated above, the incensive and rational powers, of body and soul, function in space and time. Intellection, or the realm of the Spirit, operates in infinity and eternity, even while housed in the vehicle of the body and the soul. Consequently, through rebirth in Christ, a person is present on earth in space and time, *and* in heavenly realities of infinity and eternity, beyond space and time. This reality is known beyond knowledge through pure spiritual intuition, communing in essence with all of creation in the Creator, resulting in the harmony and peace of all of the energies as well.

This threefold anthropology can also be found in Eastern religions. The Taoist, in particular, speaks of the essence, energy, and vitality. These loosely correspond to spirit, soul, and body, or body, mind, and spirit as it is popularly presented. Hinduism and Buddhism speak very differently of these realities, disagreeing with each other on the surface, but many believe they say much the same thing in different terms. The more conservative of each, however, would radically disagree with this assessment. I tend to see more common ground while recognizing that real differences remain on the objective level.

The integration of the non-Christian mystics and masters of the Far East into the Christian meditational and contemplative experience is both possible and helpful in many circumstances. This is most especially true today because of the pluralistic nature of Western civilization, and the Christian's need to be respectfully conversant with those of other faith traditions. It is also true because the majority of the population of the world lives in eastern Asia, and has never heard Christianity explained in a way that they can relate to. If we are to truly appropriately share the gospel of Jesus Christ with all the world, as Jesus has commanded, then we must learn to share his good news with those of non-Christian faith traditions in a way that they can culturally, philosophically, and religiously relate to. This has rarely been done in Asia in Christian history.

It is also good to enter into these integrations because of the effectiveness of many meditational techniques in orthodox non-Christian Eastern religions. Theologically, we believe that Catholic Christianity contains the fullness of truth. Pastorally, however, we acknowledge that those outside of Catholic Christianity often use a particular gift in a more effective way than we do. This is true in many cases in our encounter with non-Christian Eastern meditation techniques. Often, they have more seriously investigated the methods and techniques, as well as the psychological ramifications, of prolonged meditation and contemplation. Likewise, on a spiritual level, beyond the common practice of faith and morality by the world's major religions, the spiritual masters of each faith all advocate a jump into the mystical, beyond objective and subjective reality, through the use, and experience of paradox.

For the Christian, Jesus not only teaches this way of paradox but actually *is* this paradox! In this, he stands with, and complements, the spiritual masters of the other faiths, but he also goes before and completes them. This puts us in a delicate and precious position of great respect for the spiritual masters of the other great faith traditions of the world. But it also gives us something additional to share. Since the sharing is the paradox itself, it can never be done out of self-righteousness or spiritual triumphalism. It is always shared with great love and respect to counterbalance humble confidence. It is an action of divine love.

I have tried to share some of my own experiences of how to integrate the meditation and contemplation methods and techniques from other faiths with an orthodox Catholic Christianity. Some theory is necessary, but I have tried to avoid the theological and philosophical realm that is best left to others more qualified than myself. Primarily, I have tried to integrate authentic methods and techniques with an unquestioned focus, beginning and end, on the person and power of Jesus Christ. I hope you find these Christianized versions of Hindu, Taoist, and Buddhist meditation helpful.

Personally, I believe that the greatest challenge to Christianity in the future will come from the non-Christian religions of the Far East. As the classical Fathers of the early Church learned to use the language of the Greek philosophers in order to reach a largely Greek-formed and oriented Western world, so must we now learn to bring the traditional and orthodox gospel of Jesus Christ to a globalized world that is increasingly influenced by the philosophy, culture, and religion of the Far East. The Catholic bishops of the Far East have asked for it. Even the conservative theologians of the West have predicted it. The magisterium of the Church has given careful guidance for it. All that remains for us now is to simply do it, and to do it properly, in and through Jesus Christ our Lord.

It is my hope and prayer that this little book has, in some way, inspired some of us to do so for the greater glory of God, the peace of the entire human race, and the ultimate reconciliation of all of creation.

FOR FURTHER
READING

PART ONE
THE CHRISTIAN WEST

Light From Light
  Dupre' and Wiseman, OSB
  Paulist Press

Fire of God
The Lover and the Beloved
  John Michael Talbot

Troubador for the Lord
  Dan O'Neill
  Crossroad

Bonaventure, volumes I–V
  St Anthony Guild Press (out of
  Print)

*The Golden Epistle: William of St.
  Thierry*
  Cistercian Fathers 12, Cistercian
  Publications

*The Ladder of Monks and Twelve
  Meditations*
  Guigo II
  Image Books

The Collected Works of John of the Cross
  Institute of Carmelite Studies

*The Collected Works of St. Theresa of
  Avila*
  Institute of Carmdrte Studies

*The Could of Unknowing and the Book
  of Privy Counseling*
  Image Books

Mysticism
  Underhill
  Image Books

Spiritual Theology
  Aumann, OP
  Stagebooks

*The Mystical Evolution in the
  Development and Vitality of the
  Church,* volumes I and II
  Arintero, OP
  Tan Books

*The Spiritual Life: A Treatise on
  Ascetical and Mystical Theology*
  Tanquerey
  Deslee and Co. (out of print)

For Further Reading

*A Bridge to Buddhist-Christian
    Dialogue*
    Yagi and Swidler
    Paulist Press

*Mystical Theology: The Science of Love
Arise My Love: Mysticism for a New Age*
    Johnston
    Orbis Books

*The Buddha and the Christ
Revelation, the Religions, and Violence
LeFebure*
Orbis Books

*Going Home: Jesus and Buddha as
    Brothers
Living Buddha, Living Christ*
    Thich Nhat Hanh
    Riverhead Books

Jesus and Buddha
    Borg
    Ulysses Press

Christ the Eternal Tao
    Damascene
    St. Herman of Alaska Brotherhood

God as Nature Sees God
    Mabry
    Element Press

Jesus and Lao Tzu
    Aronsen
    Seastone Press

*The Golden String
The Marriage of East and West
The New Creation in Christ
Return to the Center*
    Griffiths
    Templegate Publishers

*Hindu-Christian Meeting Point
Saccidananda: A Christian Approach to
    Advaitic Experience
The Further Shore
The Mountain of the Lord: Pilgrimage
    to Gangotri
Guru and Disciple: An Encounter with
    Sri Gnanananda*
    Abhishiktananda (Le Saux)
    Available through Medio Media

A Sourcebook of Indian Philosophy
    Radhakrishnan and Moore
    Princeton Press

A Sourcebook of Chinese Philosophy
    Chan
    Princeton Press

The World's Religions
    Smith
    Harpercollins

Religions of Asia 3rd edition
    St. Martin's Press

Catholics and the New Age
    Pacwa, S.J.
    Charis Books

HINDU/YOGA
THE BHAGAVAD GITA

The Complete Yoga Book
    Hewitt
    Schocken Books

*The Shambhala Encyclopedia of Yoga
The Shambhala Guide to Yoga*
    Shambhala Publications

Tibetan Yoga
    Evans and Wentz
    Oxford University Press

For Further Reading

TAOIST

Tao Te Ching
  Lao-Tzu
  Shambhala Publications

*The Complete Book of Chinese Healing
  and Health*
Traditional Chinese Medicine
  Reid
  Shambhala Publications

*The Yellow Emperor's Classic of
  Medicine*
  Shambhala Publications

Tai Chi Classics
  Liao
  Shambhala Publications

The Way of Qigong
  Cohen
  Ballintine/Wellspring Books

Awakening the Tao
The Book of Balance and Harmony
Essence of the Tao
Inner Teaching of Taoism
Practical Taoism
Taoist Meditation
Vitality, Energy, Spirit
Wen-Tzu: Understanding the Mysteries
  Cleary
  Shambhala Publications

The Teachings of the Tao
  Wong
  Shambhala Publications

Dictionary of Taoism
  Shambhala Publications

*Relaxing into Your Being: The Water
  Method of Taoist Mediation*
  Frantzis
  Clarity Press

BUDDHISM

Dhammapada
  Shambhala Publications

*The Awakened One: A Life of the
  Buddha*
  Kohn
  Shambhala Publications

*Old Path, White Clouds: Walking in the
  Footsteps of the Buddha*
  Thich Nhat Hanh
  Parallax Press

*Entering the Stream: An Introduction to
  The Buddha and His Teachings*
  Bercholz and Kohn
  Shambhala Publications

The Way of the Bodhisattva
  Shantideva
  Shambhala Publications

A Buddhist Bible
  Goddard
  Beacon

ZEN

The Zen Teaching of Bodhidharma
  Pine
  North Point Press

Breathe! You Are Alive
  Thich Nhat Hanh
  Parallax

The Five Houses of Zen
Kensho: The Heart of Zen
Minding Mind: A Course on
   Meditation
   Cleary
   Shambhala Publications

Zen Training
   Sekida
   Weatherhill

Dogen's Manual to Zen Meditation
   Bielefeldt
   University of California Press

Shobogenzo, volumes 1–4
   Dogen
   Windbell Press

Original Teachings of Ch'an Buddhism
   Chung-Yuan
   North Point Press

Complete Enlightenment: Zen
   Comments on the Sutra of Complete
   Enlightenment
   Sheng-Yen
   Shambhala Publications

KOANS

The Gateless Barrier
   Shibayama
   Shambhala Publications

The Gateless Barrier
   Aitken
   North Point Press

The Blue Cliff Record
The Book of Serenity
Transmission of Light
Unlocking the Zen Koan
   Cleary
   Shambhala Publications

Cave of Tigers
Two Arrows Meeting in Mid Air: The
   Zen Koan
   Loori
   Tuttle

The Discourse on the Inexhaustible
   Lamp in the Zen School
   Enji
   Tuttle

TIBETAN

A Flash of Lightening in the Dark Night
   Dalai Lama
   Shambhala Publications

The Path to Enlightenment
   Dalai Lama
   Snow Lion

The Great Treatise on the Stages of the
   Path to Enlightenment
   The Lam Rim
   Snow Lion